I0887670

A NOBLE AND INDEPENDENT COURSE

Forrester A. Lee and James S. Pringle

A NOBLE AND INDEPENDENT COURSE

THE LIFE OF THE Reverend Edward Mitchell

Dartmouth College Press Hanover, New Hampshire

Dartmouth College Press
An imprint of University Press of New England
www.upne.com

Manufactured in the United States of America
Designed by Mindy Basinger Hill
Typeset in Adobe Jenson Pro

Library of Congress Cataloging-in-Publication Data available upon request

Paperback ISBN: 978-1-5126-0284-5
Ebook ISBN: 978-1-5126-0285-2

5 4 3 2 1

CONTENTS

A NOBLE AND INDEPENDENT COURSE

INTRODUCTION

Edward Mitchell, an immigrant from the French slave colony of Martinique, graduated from Dartmouth College in 1828, the first student of African descent to graduate from any school now in the Ivy League and the third self-identified man of color to graduate from an American college.[1] Emigrating to Canada in 1833 as a Baptist minister, he became the first Canadian resident of African descent to hold a college or university degree and the first ordained minister of color in the country to serve predominantly white congregations.[2] But to chronicle Mitchell's life as a series of "firsts" misses the larger context of a man of color who traveled a path of transnational migration across the slave-bound Atlantic World of the early nineteenth century, a turbulent time of revolution and religious revival. To earn the joys of freedom, Mitchell would make strategic choices and forge partnerships across social, racial, and linguistic boundaries.

Founded in 1769, Dartmouth College now approaches its 250th anniversary. Mitchell has become the subject of renewed interest as Dartmouth considers a legacy of diversity that traces directly to Mitchell's 1828 graduation.[3] Dartmouth historians consistently pronounce his controversial admission as a decisive event in opening Dartmouth's doors to twenty students of color during the antebellum years. But despite Mitchell's significant place in the historical annals, Dartmouth archives hold only a thin file outlining a few basic facts of his life.[4] When Robert Bruce Slater published a 1994 study of early African American students at American colleges and universities, he found that "there is very little information of the first black graduate of Dartmouth."[5]

In the late 1990s, inquiry into Mitchell's life started anew with the discovery of the Mitchell Family Fonds at the McCord Museum of Canadian History.[6] Found in this well-preserved but unopened archive were essays, life accounts, and religious sermons authored in the hand of Edward Mitchell.

McCord's archivists had not spotted the potential significance of the manuscripts, since not one document in the entire file can be interpreted or implicated as having been written in the hand of a man of African descent. Thus, Mitchell's papers rested in a Montreal museum archive—cataloged, well preserved, but unknown to Dartmouth librarians and scholars. It would take a local Canadian historian deeply interested in the New England early settlers of Lower Canada and two Dartmouth graduates to connect the dots scattered across a continental border.

In American literature and archive depositories, there are few handwritten, personally authored accounts from college-educated men or women of African descent from the early nineteenth century. Mitchell's writings are likely among the earliest. From them, we hoped to learn more about Mitchell's origins, his strivings, and his reactions to his initial rejection by Dartmouth's trustees. How did he gain the unified support of fellow students, who rallied in support of his admission? Did his early life in a French slave colony shape his actions in the face of American racism? What were his motivations in leaving the young American republic to pursue a Baptist ministry and missionary journey into a sparsely settled Canadian frontier? And why did he leave first the Caribbean and then the United States?

The McCord archive yielded some answers. Among Mitchell's essays, sermons, and religious notes, one manuscript stood out. In 1829, twenty years after arriving in the United States, Mitchell disclosed details of his life, offered as a religious confession and testimony. He entitled his short oration to Baptist colleagues "Outlines of the religious experience of Edward Mitchell." In this book, we refer to this manuscript as the "Outlines."[7] Written as an address to an assembly of religious congregants in rural New Hampshire, his words reference prominent religious men and personal experiences of spiritual awakening and conversion. In this testimony and all other manuscripts in the McCord archive, Mitchell never mentions issues of race or African slavery. His silence seemed puzzling given the overt acts of racial antagonism and resistance he faced. But what thoughts and opinions he chose to share in his writings becomes more understandable as we consider and explore his journey as a relatively isolated man of color in a precarious world riven by racial and political conflict among people and nations.

During our research, we were able to examine eighteenth-century Catholic parish registers of Martinique and locate Mitchell's baptismal record. It was a critical juncture in our work, leading to over two hundred additional primary sources in Martinique and in French and British archives pertinent to Mitchell's life before his emigration to the United States. From these records, we gained a deeper appreciation of the French slave society of his birth and the family influences important to his journey across the Atlantic World. We now know that Mitchell left Martinique to pursue a mariner's life. Within a few years, he abandoned the sea, migrated to Philadelphia, and found low-wage work as a porter in the employ of a socially prominent businessman. He established tentative roots in the world of Philadelphia's black community life of religious uplift and counted among his colleagues Philadelphia's most prominent white and black clergymen. A series of tragedies followed, including the loss of his first wife and two children. Set adrift, he came to Hanover, New Hampshire, where he established affiliations that supported his preparation for successful admission to Dartmouth.

After leaving Philadelphia for New England, Mitchell had no further contact with the men and women of African descent in the United States engaged in the early expressions of social cohesion and group identity as African Americans. After graduating from Dartmouth with no family roots in the United States, Mitchell chose to remain in the near-monoethnic world of northern New England and Lower Canada, where he found family, community, and social affiliations. He became known as "smart preacher," an "indefatigable" Baptist missionary, and a "profound theologian." He found the comforts of family and community as a settled pastor in Lower Canada far removed from the embittered battleground of racial discord in the United States.

Mitchell safely guarded his thoughts and opinions as he walked through the Atlantic World. But modern research and scholarship has opened connections to the past and enabled us to achieve a more satisfying understanding of the subject of our interest. We write to examine and report what has been recorded in the historical record that silently accompanied the life of Edward Mitchell. He must have foreseen the publication of this book. He left papers penned in his hand to guide our inquiry. We write in response to his call.

Part I

A MAN OF COLOR IN THE ATLANTIC WORLD

ONE

Birth and Baptism

On January 30, 1792, in an era of extraordinary global human conflict, the infant Édouard Michel entered the war-weary, embattled world of Saint-Pierre, Martinique.[1] Baptism followed a month later, on February 25, 1792. In the sacred Roman Catholic chapel of slave-owning Dominican friars, the month-old newborn submitted to sacred baptismal rites that blessed and socially branded his place in Martinique slave society. The ceremony took place in the impressive neoclassical-style Roman Catholic Church of Notre Dame du Bon Port erected in 1636 in the shape of the Christian cross at the edge of Saint-Pierre's harbor. Gradually improved and enlarged over the many decades, the church's dimly lit interior offered a good measure of solemnity to ceremonies consecrated at its altar and baptismal font. Polished marble fixtures added refinement to the rude enclosing walls, while the surrounding manicured gardens further embellished an almost perfected setting. Not far beyond this consecrated space lay fertile plantation fields of sugarcane and cocoa. It might not have been obvious to a casual visitor that this beautiful setting owed its existence to the impossibly harsh toil of African slaves who planted, harvested, and processed sugarcane for the benefit of wealthy plantation owners, a small privileged elite comprising less than 5 percent of the island's population.[2]

Martinique in the Age of Revolution

Martinique, the "Island of Flowers," lies in the Windward chain of small islands forming the Lesser Antilles of the Caribbean Sea. Sighted by Columbus during a 1502 voyage to the Americas, the island was not settled by Europeans until 1635, when Pierre Bélain d'Esnambuc, bearing the authority of Cardinal Richelieu and the French Crown, brought settlers from nearby Saint Christopher, now Saint Kitts, to the bay of today's Saint-Pierre. Over time, the uninvited colonists transformed the lush tropical island of dense forests and fertile volcanic soil into a profitable French sugar colony. Guadeloupe, Saint-Domingue (today, Haiti and the Dominican Republic), and other small Caribbean possessions later entered France's colonial realm to form the French Antilles (Îles du Vent). The early colonists exterminated or deported the resisting native Caribs, who previously had displaced the migrating Arawaks of South America. The labors of indentured whites recruited from French villages and cities proved insufficient to profitably farm the land at scale. The colonists established an African slave labor–based plantation economic system that exported profitable cash crops of sugar, molasses, coffee, and cocoa to Europe and America. To meet labor demands in its Caribbean colonies, France invested heavily in the slave trade and became the third-largest exporter of human cargoes from African shores.[3]

As European nations with visions of global dominion maneuvered politically and militarily to expand territorial possessions in the Americas, long-standing, unresolved rivalries converged in the first truly global conflict, the French and Indian War, or Anglo-French Rivalry, in North America and the Seven Years' War in Europe. Among its several military setbacks, France lost Martinique to Britain in 1762. At the war's conclusion, the terms of the 1763 Treaty of Paris reordered national boundaries across Europe and the Atlantic World. France ceded several colonial territories to the British, including all of Canada (then "New France"), but recovered Martinique and maintained possession of its other profitable Caribbean sugar colonies, including Saint-Domingue and Guadeloupe. Great Britain would again secure control of Martinique for several periods during later conflicts, in the late eighteenth and early nineteenth century.[4]

Édouard Michel's early years spanned this turbulent period of cyclical warfare among rival European colonial powers. In France, political and economic strains galvanized a radicalized French populace, newly aligned across political and class lines, to ignite the French Revolution of 1789 and end the rule of French Bourbon monarchs. Events in the French Metropol had its Caribbean corollary, the Haitian Revolution (1791–1804), when Toussaint L'Ouverture rallied enslaved Africans to overthrow white colonists and defeat Napoleon's armies to establish the world's first black republic. The idealism of France's "Declaration of the Rights of Man and of the Citizen" inspired the National Constituent Assembly in Paris to issue the decree of February 4, 1794, that abolished slavery in the French colonies. The news reached Martinique too late. Already the British had dispatched naval and army forces to Martinique, an attack encouraged and supported by Martinique's wealthiest planters, who feared the end of slavery. After a sturdy but brief defense, the outnumbered French forces commanded by General Comte de Rochambeau raised the white flag at Fort Royal on March 24, 1794. The installed British administrators reinstituted the Ancien Régime (lifted briefly during the heady days of the French Revolution), thus preserving the legal apparatus, policies, and social customs of Martinique's slave society. Martinique planters and the British Crown expected generous profits. For British military commanders, Martinique's strategic location in the Windward Islands offered advantages in prosecuting their West Indies naval and land campaigns.[5]

Britain's 1794 invasion of Martinique had come during the first years of renewed hostilities initiated by the French Revolutionary Army against a coalition of European monarchies resisting the diffusion of French revolutionary ideals. In 1802 the Treaty of Amiens temporarily halted fighting and Martinique reverted to French control. When war resumed, British dominance of the Atlantic and Caribbean waters led to yet another capitulation of French forces in Martinique and the return of British administrators in 1809. Another Treaty of Paris in 1815 returned the colony to French authorities. Slave importation continued until 1831. France abolished slavery in 1848.

This background of French-British hostilities and British occupation dominated Édouard Michel's formative years, exposing him episodically to French and English social and cultural influences. Nonetheless, the island retained a distinctly French character. Nearly two hundred years of French colonization had created French-Creole sociocultural expressions and traditions, readily discernible in the island's distinctive patois, the Parisian character of its cities and commercial life, the joyous rhythms of its music and festivals, and the striking beauty of the island's natural and humanly created forms. These influences, however deeply imprinted in the young Édouard Michel, would not be recognized or understood by his later contemporaries in North America, who wouldn't know the details of his birthright.

Edward Mitchell's Birthright

In 1810, at age eighteen, Édouard Michel departed Martinique with an optimistic gaze fixed to northern horizons. Soon he would be known as Edward Mitchell, as if only the future, and not the past, would be relevant in the world that awaited him. But he would not fully escape the imprint of his birthright. He had been born into a rigidly stratified slave society of three principal classes—whites, black slaves, and *gens de couleur*, the latter constituting the mixed-race descendants of black-white liaisons. As Cormack explains, the "*gens de couleur* were an intermediate group within colonial society who stood between the mass of black slaves and the white minority."[6] Many of the *gens de couleur* were free, although not all had proof, and only an exceptional few had heritable access to the wealth of their privileged white blood. While liaisons between Frenchmen and women of color, forced and consensual, were common in Martinique, there was no legal status for interracial marriage or concubinage under either French or British rule of Martinique in the eighteenth century. Among the whites, the planter-elite (*Békés* or *grand blancs*) confidently claimed the top rung of the social ladder. Socially inferior whites—called, oddly, *petit blancs*—were a middle-class stratum whose political and economic interests often ran contrary to those of the wealthy planters. Those born on the island, white or black, were called Creoles to distinguish them from immigrants. African slaves, the involuntary immigrants, vastly outnumbered the voluntary immigrants, mostly from Europe, but also from the Asian and American continents. African blacks introduced bloodlines into the populace from a broad sample of tribes in West and Central Africa, especially the territories of the Kingdom of Dahomey, today's Benin. By the time of Mitchell's birth in 1792, an estimated 132,805 captured African slaves had disembarked in Martinique ports, beginning in 1653.[7]

Once in America, Edward Mitchell confirmed to inquirers what was already apparent from the reflected hues of his skin and the French lilt of his speech: he was the mixed-race son of a white "Frenchman" and a "native of the island," as he put it when asked. Mitchell retained throughout his life "a trace of a French accent" as evidence of his French-Caribbean heritage and, quite likely, as an expedient foil against negative presentiments.[8] Beyond that he remained silent, nearly erasing the remarkable legacy of his years on the vibrant Antillean island of his birth. As an early nineteenth-century

French-Caribbean immigrant to North America with an obscure past, he left some to guess. Was he a former slave? Or was he the son of a wealthy Creole slave owner who sent sons to European and American capitals for education? Ignorance of Mitchell's birthright and family origins survived over two hundred years, but the discovery of his baptismal record revealed crucial and intimate details. Now we can examine more carefully the circumstances that enabled a man of humble origins to cross the Atlantic World and surpass even his own expectations.

BAPTISM OF ÉDOUARD MICHEL

Édouard Michel was born an illegitimate child with a portion of African blood, quantified and detailed in the codified language of the colonial French parish records of Catholicity. In the Mouillage district of Saint-Pierre, we learn from the 1792 parish register of the Church of Notre Dame du Bon Port,

> Le vingt cinq février avais baptisé Edouard Michel métis illégitime né le trente du mois dernier d'Olive mulâtresse libre, comme il compte par son acte en règle du dix-sept juillet 1789. Le parrain a été Michel métis libre la marraine Magdalaine mulâtresse libre en foi de quoi avais signé avec le parrain, la marraine ne sçechant.
> *M. Cazabon, J. Maunier fr. curé*
>
> The twenty-fifth of February I baptized Édouard Michel, illegitimate métis, born the thirtieth of last month to Olive, a free mulatto woman as indicated by her duly certified act [of emancipation] of the seventeenth of July 1789. The godfather was Michel, free métis, the godmother Magdalaine, free mulatto, in attestation of which I signed with the godfather, the godmother being unable to sign.
> *M[ichel] Cazabon, Father J. Maunier, parish priest*

Édouard was baptized a *métis*, the illegitimate son of Olive, a free *mulâtresse*. His appointed spiritual guardians were *gens de couleur*, godparents Michel Cazabon, a free *métis*, and Magdalaine, a free *mulâtresse*.[9] These vital details with enduring consequences were recorded precisely and purposefully by Father Joseph-Jean Maunier, the forty-one-year-old Dominican parish priest of the Church of Notre Dame du Bon Port. Father Maunier had defined the newborn's civil status in conformity with the Code Noire, the complex legal structure that regulated nonwhite personhood and mobility in French colonial slave societies. By stating the illegitimacy of Édouard's birth, the priest confirmed that the parents were not married. In classifying the newborn a *métis*, he specified that the unnamed father was white since by the strict classification scheme of French colonial eugenics, the child of a *mulâtresse* mother and a white father was a *métis*. Confusingly, racial classification nomenclature was not consistent across the French colonies. In Martinique, a *mulâtre* was the offspring of black and white parents, while a *métis* had further-diluted African ancestry as the offspring of a *mulâtre* and a white. Thus, three of four grandparents of the *métis* child were white. In Saint-Domingue, the same child would have been labeled a *carterone*, and in other settings, a *quadroon*.

FATHER MAUNIER'S ERROR

Father Joseph-Jean Maunier was twenty-seven when first appointed parish priest of Saint-Pierre's Mouillage parish, in 1778.[10] He had come to Martinique in the spirit of colonial missionary outreach from the Dominican convent of Saint-Maximin in Provence, France. Among the several Catholic religious orders sent to Martinique, the Dominicans were the most numerous and wealthiest, profiting from active participation in the slave economy. Father Maunier's parish claimed over six hundred slaves.[11] Parish priests were bound by a civic responsibility to record and preserve in parish registers all "acts" of birth, marriage, and death, a role vital to maintaining the embedded racial hierarchy of the slave society. In the spirit of civic obligation and religious authority, Father Maunier had performed Édouard Michel's baptismal sacrament. But priests were fallible, and Maunier's entry for Édouard's baptism contained a significant error.

The godparent recorded as "Michel," who signed his name "M. Cazabon," was not a *métis*. He was Michel Cazabon, a white Creole, the fourteen-year-old son of Dominique Cazabon, a prominent Creole of Saint-Pierre. The one-month-old *métis* son of Olive had thus inherited the goodwill and varied fortunes of the Cazabon family of Martinique. At the time of Édouard's birth, the young Cazabon was *d'âge mineur* in the eyes of the Catholic Church but was not specifically prohibited from assuming the important role of the godparent. In Catholic societies, a godparent accepted the significant and lifelong obligation to support and mentor the child. The advantages thus gained by Édouard Michel could potentially surpass any benefits received from the blessings administered by Father Maunier that day in February 1792.

Michel Cazabon's family had significant means and some influence in Saint-Pierre's civic life. His father and mother were white Creoles, Dominique Cazabon (1737–1802) and Elisabeth Charlotte Fort Beauchêne (1756–81). The son of a French settler, an *habitant*, Dominique was a former slave owner and *huissier au Conseil supérieur* (bailiff of the Superior Counsel), where he administered the "Communal Purse."[12] A month earlier in Father Maunier's parish church, the Cazabon family had celebrated the marriage of Jeanne Rose Cazabon to Louis Mourot, a leading baker of Saint-Pierre. Michel Cazabon, brother of the betrothed and soon to be a godfather, had added his signature to the parish registry page detailing the marriage sacraments blessed that day. Plainly scripted in the unadorned style of a young, well-educated man, Michel had deferentially inscribed his name below those of his parents and assembled witnesses. It was the first of six signatures he would add to the parish registers of Saint-Pierre.

For a priest to racially misclassify a white Creole as harboring any degree of African blood can only be understood as an act contradicting the carefully constructed and managed tenets of the race-obsessed Martinique society. On observing firsthand how importantly race mattered in colonial Martinique, one British visitor wrote, "The separation formed by colour is of immense magnitude with respect to the general practice of slavery. Its influence is beyond all calculation: construed into a sign of physical inferiority, it describes, at once, the line of demarcation; and fixes the stigma of bondage in a more precise and forcible manner than could have been effected by the most rigorous law of human invention."[13]

That Father Maunier had erred in racially classifying the young Cazabon a *métis* is confirmed by consulting the parish registers documenting his birth and family ancestry. Moreover, there would have been no plausible reason for Michel Cazabon to lower his privileged social standing by including himself among those of African descent. Most likely, Father Maunier had made an assumption based on physical appearance—an unusual error for a Catholic colonial priest, who anchored the front line in monitoring and defending the racial hierarchy. Rather than press the fourteen-year-old with delicate questions about his racial heritage, Father Maunier was a victim of the oft-remarked fact that racial classification of mixed-race individuals relying on physical features without knowledge of the family pedigree can be impossible. This wisdom was especially relevant to colonial Saint-Pierre, where *gens de couleur* were often several generations removed from their source of African ancestry. It was also unusual in Maunier's church for an infant's godparents to be of different racial castes. Michel Cazabon was white and Magdalaine, the godmother, was a *mulâtresse*. Among the 120 births (56 white and 64 black infants) recorded in Father Maunier's parish register of free births for 1792, on all but two occasions, both godparents were either white or *gens de couleur*. Thus, on a day when he baptized Édouard Michel along with three other mixed-race infants, a day the chapel had filled with infants, mothers, and godparents of color, he erred in qualifying Michel Cazabon a *métis*. Of interest to the present context, the unusual instance of a white godfather and mulatto godmother standing together as godparents hints at some interracial cohesion and affinity within the Cazabon family, as we shall see.

Aside from this indiscretion on the day of Édouard Michel's birth, Father Maunier was notably diligent, even enthusiastic, in other pursuits. An outspoken patriot, he had embraced the spirit of the French Revolution, even as his daily priestly acts and oversight of the church's slave population contradicted the French Republican cry for "*liberté, égalité, fraternité*." In casting himself publicly in the mold of a French patriot, some judged the Saint-Pierre parish priest to have improperly mixed ecclesiastical duties with politics. The early French historian of Martinique, Sidney Daney de Marcillac, observed disapprovingly that Maunier "thought he could combine republican politics with ecclesiastical functions without scruple." Father Maunier had been called upon in September 1790 to bless the raising of the tricolor flag of the new French Republic during public ceremonies in Saint-Pierre and the nearby parish of Gros-Morne. Before a formal assembly of "new citizens," military leaders, and government officials, he intoned the *Te Deum*, blessed the French Republic flag, and offered a tribute to the commanders and troops who that month had put down counterrevolutionary conspirators on the island. Father Maunier said it was an act to preserve the now "*broken chains of our fellow citizens*."[14] He was referring not to chains of African slavery, but to those binding the commoners and bourgeoisie of Martinique and France to the oppressive rule of royals and nobles.

Father Maunier served as a member and briefly as president of the Assemblée Representative de la Martinique, the elected body of citizens formed by Governor de Rochambeau in 1793. These pro-Republican acts did not go unnoticed by the British who invaded and overtook the island in early 1794. After securing the Saint-Pierre port, a British frigate transported Father Maunier and Saint-Pierre's mayor, Jean Baptiste Aucune, to Fort Royal, where they were deported with over five hundred other civilians to Brest, France.[15] Within this deported group sat Michel Cazabon's father, Dominique, once a bailiff of Martinique's Superior Council. Unlike Father Maunier, Cazabon would soon negotiate his return to the French Antilles.

OLIVE

As the child of Olive, a free mulâtresse, Édouard Michel was born free, and Father Maunier's baptismal record only needed examination as confirmation.[16] The Code Noire decreed that any children of a free black woman, regardless of the race or status of their father, would be free from birth.[17] During the ceremony, Olive presented evidence that her free status had been verified on July 17, 1789, during a historic month of decisive events propelling the French Revolution. (The birth record says only that her freedom was "*en règle*," in order with regulations, and does not indicate *when* she was freed.)

In these earliest days of life, the gift of freedom had little relevance to Édouard's primal needs—milk, warmth, and caring human contact. Each of these wants would be generously met at his mother's bosom. Other gifts would follow from Olive, although none were ordained at birth. A resourceful woman now entering her middle years, Olive had come to Saint-Pierre from Fort Royal, Martinique's capital city, where she was baptized thirty years earlier, on April 12, 1761. She was the mulatto child of Marguerite, *négresse se disant libre* (black woman saying she is free), certified that same month by the Royal Prosecutor (Le Procureur du Roy). In Fort Royal, Olive would witness the emergence of a growing community of free *gens de couleur* who had secured relatively minor but strategic positions in the city's social, cultural, and commercial life as small merchants, fisherman, carpenters, shoemakers, and other tradesmen who profited from the daily exchange of goods and services. After 1790 she relocated to Saint-Pierre and joined a community of single free women of color who maintained households configured under varied domestic arrangements, some offering strategic benefits. Modern historians have given particular attention to the distinctive role of French-Caribbean women of color who headed families of mixed-race children and white fathers while simultaneously maintaining a significant degree of economic and social independence. Cultural historian Avonelle Remey argues that in colonial cities like Saint-Pierre, women of color had "regained some measure of control over their bodies and were independent sexual agents [able to] seek higher favors and privileges for themselves and their children." In so doing, these women "succeeded in gaining material wealth and social standing from her wealthy white or metis lovers."[18] This construction well suits the life of Olive and her relationship to the Cazabons.

THE CAZABONS

Olive and her sons remained linked to the Cazabons. The family patriarch, Dominique Cazabon, was a native of Saint-Pierre born about 1737.[19] He left his native parish to become a small slave owner in Martinique's southern parishes of small rural villages and large plantations. He was labeled an "*habitant*" to credit him as a member of the land-owning French settlers and their descendants.[20] In the parish of Sainte-Luce, he married Elizabeth Charlotte Fort Beauchêne and acquired the property and homestead of her father. She died young, in 1781, but not before giving birth to four children, three of whom survived to adulthood. Dominique Cazabon was thus widowed and left to raise his daughter and two sons. He relocated to Saint-Pierre and in 1783 was appointed bailiff of the Supreme Council. It was a demanding public office requiring frequent contact with the populace and travel between Fort Royal and Saint-Pierre.[21]

According to art historian Eliane Mackintosh, Dominique Cazabon was "was openly liberal—a characteristic ill-viewed in the then morbidly racialist society he lived in—and naturally, he bore the brunt of it in his career path."[22] Cazabon's life paralleled the upper ranks of Martinique's *petits blancs*, the middle-class clerks, merchants, and entrepreneurs who had significant social and political authority in the cities and frequently opposed the power and privilege of the planter-elite in the countryside. Employed by the governing French administrators and apparently known for revolutionary patriotic views, Cazabon was deported by the British (in the "Exodus of Patriots") after the invasion and takeover in the first months of 1794.[23] He surfaced in Brest, France, in October 1794, attending civil proceedings of fellow expatriates from Martinique.[24] In December 1785, he returned to the Antilles on a

French transport that was seized by the British navy, delaying his homebound journey until the following year.[25] He reestablished his life in Basse-Terre, Guadeloupe, some ninety miles north of Martinique, a colonial outpost still under French administration. He was installed as secretary of the military hospital in Basse-Terre, the busy port on Guadeloupe's southern coast. He died there in 1802, leaving a living legacy of mixed-race family lines.[26]

Two mixed-race "outside families" connect to Dominique Cazabon's through two Martinique women of color, Pétronille and Olive. Their mixed-race children took the name "Cazabon" or "Casabon," the latter orthography representing both a common misspelling in parish records and an intentional minor transformation of the Cazabon family name, possibly to avoid legal conflict with the law prohibiting the transmission of white Creole names to blacks. The known mixed-race children of these women were:

I. Pétronille, *négresse*, born ca. 1740, died 1814, Le Vauclin, Martinique, age 74.[27]
   Hélène Casabon, born 1764, died 1848, Le Vauclin, Martinique, age 84.
   François Cazabon, born 1769, died 1855, Trinidad, age 86.[28]
   Sophie Casabon, born 1778, died Basse-Terre, Guadeloupe, 1841, age 63.
   Modeste, born ca. 1773.
   Charlotte, born ca. 1775.

Pétronille was owned by Dominique Cazabon until 1775.[29] Quite likely, her son François is the François Cazabon who left Martinique after 1789 for Trinidad as part of the Cédula de Población issued by the king of Spain in 1783 to induce families to emigrate from the politically unstable French Antilles to Trinidad, then under Spanish control but swept up in 1797 as a British colonial possession.[30] The "coloured" Cazabons prospered in Trinidad, acquiring a sizeable plantation, owning slaves, and achieving social and political influence. The grandson of Dominique Cazabon, Michel-Jean Cazabon (1818–88), today is recognized as Trinidad's most celebrated artist, having studied and trained in England and France before returning to Trinidad. About 1862, he settled in Saint-Pierre, Martinique. Many of Cazabon's paintings survive, offering a visual survey of nineteenth-century Caribbean peoples, lands, and culture.[31]

II. Olive dite Casabon, free *mulâtresse*, born 1761, Fort-Royal, died 1808, Basse-Terre, Guadeloupe, age 47.[32]

Jean Philippe Casabon, born 1790, Fort Royal, died 1846, Saint-Pierre, age 56.

Édouard Michel, born 1792, Saint-Pierre, died 1872, Georgeville, Quebec, age 80.

Joseph Honoré, born 1802, Basse-Terre, died 1817, Basse-Terre, Guadeloupe, age 15.

Olive and her children established living quarters with or near Dominique Cazabon's family. His three white Creole children lived in Saint-Pierre at a home on rue du Précipice headed by Louis Mourot, the prominent Saint-Pierre baker who had married Jeanne Rose Cazabon, Dominique's daughter. Rue du Précipice angled away from the Saint-Pierre harbor and terminated abruptly after three blocks at the steep escarpments framing Saint-Pierre's port. Two blocks away lay the church and monastery of Notre Dame du Bon Port, Édouard Michel's place of baptism. The residents of rue du Précipice were typical of the city's urban middle class and included *négociants, marchands*, a government clerk, a goldsmith, and a baker. Another resident was the master mariner Captain Denis Lamothe Villegente, the son of a noble family in Périgord, France, who was active in the interisland Caribbean cabotage trade.[33]

Olive lived among the Cazabons of rue du Précipice with her sons, Édouard Michel and Jean Philippe, who was born two years before Édouard. By 1800, Olive had joined Dominique Cazabon in Basse-Terre after his return from France. She may have brought her two sons, Jean Philippe and Édouard Michel, or left them in Saint-Pierre under the care of Cazabon household members. In 1802 she gave birth to a third son, Joseph Honoré. Perhaps indicative of an elevated status in the community, the delivery was attended by Madame Roux-Mingot, a *sage-femme* (midwife) of Basse-Terre.[34] Dominique Cazabon died on July 9, 1802, three months after Joseph Honoré's birth.

The specifics of Olive and Dominique Cazabon's intimacy are uncertain, but that their paths were joined over time is well established. Olive died as Olive *dite* Cazabon (Olive called Cazabon) in Basse-Terre on December 7, 1808, two years before Édouard Michel sailed from Martinique to the United

States. She had adopted the common practice among French whites and blacks to amend and extend a birth name in a manner that distinguished an individual from others. The "*dit* name" was not interpreted as a French surname (*surnom*) but often recorded with the *dit* qualifier in official civil records. Among *gens de couleur* it was common for a *dit* name to reference the mother or, less commonly, a slave owner or father.[35]

Olive's child Édouard Michel and a son of Pétronille, François Cazabon, would emigrate from Martinique's shores—Édouard to the United States and François to Trinidad—each seeking to expand his limited boundary of freedom in the French colonial world.

Édouard and Michel: Name Origins

Édouard Michel received from his godfather the name Michel as the second of two French first names (*prénoms*), not as a last name.[36] As an illegitimate child of African ancestry, he could not inherit or adopt a French Martinique family name under the Code Noire. Priests strictly followed this prohibition at the time of baptism, thereby creating one of several layers of protection shielding the identity of a white father.[37] Though clear from the formatting of the baptismal record that *Michel* is a second *prénom*, some could have interpreted it as a *surnom* since Frenchmen had carried the Michel family name to Martinique beginning in the late seventeenth century. Martinique's parish registers and census records occasionally reference the Michel surname; among those listed are two successive Sieurs de la Reynardière, a Judge Royal Civil and Criminal, and others who were prominent in commerce and the military.[38]

The name Édouard Michel should be understood in the context of French colonial slave society as a compound first name, two French *prénoms*. Also, it would be incorrect to consider the second prénom a middle name, a naming convention not practiced in French societies. Although compound French first names of two or more prénoms often referenced ancestral family names, in this case, *Michel* traces directly in parish birth records to the prénom of his godfather, Michel Cazabon, and from him to his godfather and maternal uncle, Michel Fort. By the time of Édouard Michel's birth, many free blacks and slaves had adopted this French custom of granting children two or more prénoms, for example, *Rose Marguerite* and *Jean Philippe Hippolyte*. Commonly, some, if not all, of the prénoms transmitted to the newborn could be traced to parents, godparents, and relatives.[39]

Édouard Michel is uncommon both as a compound French first name and as a first and last name (as is "Edward Michael" rare in the English-speaking world). Among the hundreds of Martinique parish records and thousands of indexed names examined, we found no other examples of Édouard Michel in Martinique, either as two prénoms or as a prénom and surnom. We did, of course, encounter Michel commonly as a prénom. Had Édouard Michel remained in the French-speaking world, he could have taken Cazabon as a surname or *dit* name, as did his other mixed-race relatives. Ultimately, the compound French first name served him well, as its later anglicization to Edward Mitchell rendered the name in conformity with first-/last-name English conventions.

Less obvious, and unstated in the baptismal record, is the inspiration for the first prénom, Édouard, a variant of the Old English name Edward, prevalent among English royals and passed into many European families. In Vincent Cousseau's in-depth study of patronymic origins and name transmission in the Martinique society of the seventeenth to nineteenth centuries, Édouard was rarely found among whites in the period of Édouard Michel's birth but did occur in the names of slaves and free blacks, though not commonly.[40] In our study of Martinique births of free black and white children between 1785 and 1815 in Saint-Pierre's Mouillage parish, we found only ten instances of Édouard out of approximately three thousand births, all but one clustered between 1789 and 1799. We therefore considered the possibility that Édouard referred to a locally or regionally well-known individual, as did the name *Toussaint* in all parts of the French Antilles.

In principle, parents had a strong voice in naming a child (with varying degrees of "guidance" from the priest), and Olive was diligent in exercising this privilege. Her first son, Jean Philippe, gained his first prénom from his godfather, Jean Isaac dit Soubeiran, a mulatto leader during the 1790–93 uprisings among black slaves and allies among the *gens de couleur*. Olive named her third child after Jean Isaac's brother, Joseph Honoré.[41] Her attraction to the name Édouard may have been inspired by another mulatto leader in Saint-Pierre, Édouard Meunier, a native of Saint-Pierre and commander of black and mulatto troops aiding General de Rochambeau's unsuccessful defense of Martinique during the 1794 British invasion.[42] Before that battle and a month after Édouard Michel's birth in 1792, Father Maunier (no relation to Meunier) had baptized Édouard Meunier's goddaughter, Elisabeth Gabrielle. A year later, Father Maunier entered Meunier's full military title and name into the Saint-Pierre parish record: *Lieutenant Colonel Commandant, Le Second bataillon du Chausseurs de la République Édouard Meunier,* the appointed godfather of the infant Rose Elisabeth. Before joining Rochambeau's forces, Édouard Meunier had been a senior member of the black militia of Saint-Pierre. Given these associations and contexts, we surmise that Father Maunier and Olive likely concurred in blessing her newborn child after the locally popular and respected Édouard Meunier. The prénom Édouard would pass to another nine free black infants of Saint-Pierre born in the last decade of the eighteenth century.[43]

After Édouard Michel left Martinique, his name would survive only in its anglicized version, Edward Mitchell. The first handwritten sample of this name can be located in the Philadelphia Baptist Church archives of 1811. That year, Mitchell was living in Philadelphia, a city with many examples of French name transformations among the more than two thousand emigrants who fled the French-Caribbean slave-led rebellions of the 1790s. Some took on English surnames, as an expedient concession or an imposed renaming, or as an expression of the belief that their future rested on American soil. Edward Mitchell's name appears in the minutes of the Sansom Street Baptist Church of Philadelphia from October 16, 1811, in which the spelling of his surname reads as "Mitchelle."[44] The terminal letter of the name is an unmistakable *e*, distinct from the mention of another church member named "Mitchell." At that time, Edward Mitchell may have been using the French surname Michel or some transitional variant with the accent on the second syllable, interpreted as "Mitchelle" by the recording secretary, or because that spelling occurs in Scotland. Almost all other American and Canadian references use the anglicized version and appear as "Edward Mitchell" or, in several cases, "Edward Mitchel."[45]

Early Years in Saint-Pierre

Mitchell came to America with an ability to read and write and the skills of a young mariner aspiring to ascend to a captain's rank. He had likely been exposed to language primers and introduced to basic mathematics in preparation for subsequent training in nautical astronomy and navigation. With public education unavailable, informal schooling would have come from the home. His mother, Olive, may have been instrumental, even if she was not literate (and we do not know). The birth and death parish and civil records referencing her name did not require her signature, and we found no records in which she signed as a witness or godparent. She did have associations with Saint-Pierre's *gens de couleur*, including Jean Isaac and Édouard Meunier, whose mature signatures appear in several records, suggesting some degree of literacy. All the white members of the Cazabon household were literate, and Édouard would have had opportunities to absorb informal or formal educational instruction from them. After leaving Martinique, Mitchell pursued training and educational opportunities with great conviction, surely following habits and passions nurtured earlier in life.

Whatever support and advantages Édouard gained at home, his early motivations were more decisively guided by exposure to the commercial and cultural life of Saint-Pierre, a city that travelers and merchants of the nineteenth century described as the "Paris of the Antilles." This comparison was understood in its relative context, since the narrow streets and modest residential structures of Saint-Pierre could not compare to the boulevards, lavish architecture, and conspicuous iconography of the Parisian streetscape. Other than the large defensive fortifications in the hills overlooking the harbor, Saint-Pierre had no built structures of significant height. But the gaily wrought two- and three-story stone structures housing the city-dwellers and the well-executed architecture of the religious and government buildings created a vital urban character unmatched in the Caribbean world. Fresh water from nearby hillsides and distant mountain slopes continuously washed the streets, rendering the city neighborhoods clean and wholesome. Favorably located on Martinique's northwestern coast, the wide harbor carved a graceful arc at the city's edge, offering deep and generally calm waters to passenger boats, sloops and rigs of local commerce, and foreign ships of any size. Fort Royal, accessible only with difficulty on poorly maintained inland roads, could be reached within an hour by the versatile *canoe*, the taxi of Martinique's waterways. The port city's piers remained open to commercial trade for nine of twelve months each year and received without prejudice merchant ships laden with commodities from all foreign ports and slave cargoes from West Africa.[46]

Saint-Pierre was the island's busiest port and the administrative center for French colonial officials of the Îles de Vent. The constant energy of its commercial trade and the beauty of its brightly adorned streets and surrounding verdant countryside inspired evocative narratives—books, travelogues, and fictional tales. Rising prominently and far beyond the steep escarpments overlooking the city lay Mount Pelée, whose cataclysmic eruption in 1902 killed thirty thousand inhabitants (of forty-two thousand), the worst natural disaster of the twentieth century. One wall and the foundation of the Church of Notre Dame du Bon Port survived the devastation, thereby preserving a physical fragment of Mitchell's baptismal legacy. On this same site, the modern La cocathédrale Notre Dame de l'Assomption was later erected.

During Mitchell's years in Martinique, Saint-Pierre's 7,500 inhabitants witnessed British–French naval battles, occasional slave uprisings, protests by *gens de couleur* to extend their limited civil rights, and the constant grind of contested class privilege and political authority. The *gens de couleur* claimed an increasing proportion of the free population, whose numbers had accelerated beginning in the mid-eighteenth century. By the 1790s, everywhere on the island, and especially in the urban districts, the *gens de couleur* approached or exceeded numerical equality with the white population. In Saint-Pierre in 1807, free *gens de couleur* outnumbered whites 612 to 365, living amidst 6,557 slaves.[47] Political authority and social privilege remained securely in the hands of the white aristocracy. The working- and middle-class whites, *les petit blancs*, rarely found common cause with the planters, except in their mutual interest in self-preservation and profit on the backs of black subjugation. Loyalties and alliances among the planter-elite, *petit blancs*, and *gens de couleur* shifted over time. William S. Cormack concludes that "ultimately free-colored loyalty to different white factions in the *Îles du Vent* was not fixed on the basis of racial solidarity or attachment to revolutionary principle, but was always conditional upon changing assessments of interests."[48]

Édouard Michel's younger years centered in the Cazabon family of Saint-Pierre's port area, his daily concerns distanced from the labors of the enslaved black plantation gangs and their overseers of the countryside. Sheltered from the harshest realities of the slave society and nurtured by the mother of a mixed-race Creole family, the decisive events of Édouard Michel's life would turn in response to events outside the familiar harbor and city of his birth.

TO SEA

In the extended Cazabon family, Édouard Michel could find guiding examples to motivate a restive spirit. It was his godfather, Michel Cazabon, the youngest of the Cazabon brothers, who first took to the sea about 1798, and Édouard would follow seven years later. At age twenty, Cazabon joined the crew of a French privateer based in Guadeloupe. Unlike Martinique, Guadeloupe had withstood the British military onslaught of 1794 and remained under French control. Michel's father, the deported Dominique Cazabon, had returned in 1796 to Basse-Terre. Even as the British governed Martinique (1794 to 1802), Michel Cazabon found his way to Guadeloupe, joining his father and setting the stage for his recruitment by Captain Paul Canaud to the Guadeloupean privateer fleet of lightly armed schooners.[49]

On July 26, 1798, Captain Dolachy and first mate Paul Canaud of *La Démocrate* captured the *Eagle*, an American merchant ship of Captain Jeremiah Goodhue. Sailing from Boston, the *Eagle* had attempted to land cargo at British-controlled Martinique and as such was a valid wartime target. The *Eagle* was "seized in front of Saint-Pierre, island of Martinique, where she was trying to enter when made prize" and was escorted to Basse-Terre and presented to Guadeloupe's prize court.[50] The following year, Canaud returned to sea as captain of *La Démocrate* with Michel Cazabon on board. Despite its speed and maneuverability, the armed schooner failed to elude capture by the *Amphitrite*, a forty-gun frigate of the British Royal Navy. On May 31, 1799, Captain Elkins of HMS *Amphitrite* reported, "Captured, off Martinique, after a very long chase, the French privateer schooner Democrat, 12 guns and 80 men, of Guadaloupe, and carried her to Barbadoes; she is a fast sailer, and had for some time past eluded the vigilance of our cruisers."[51]

Michel Cazabon and fellow crewmembers were delivered as prisoners to Barbados and released two years later in a prisoner exchange on June 3, 1801, at Martinique, still under British control. Cazabon had been released to home six months ahead of Martinique's return to French rule in 1802.[52] He turned to more sedentary pursuits, joining his brother-in-law, the baker Louis Mourot, and acquiring a new professional identity. Mourot was said to possess entrepreneurial talent and profited from Martinique's renewed French colonial status in securing a contract to provide bread for troops stationed in Saint-Pierre.[53]

In this period of Napoleonic French rule in Martinique (1802 to 1809), Édouard Michel entered the formative years of adolescence. Around him in Saint-Pierre, the prevailing spirit on the island was patriotic and celebratory on the return of French-speaking administrators, who exercised some independence from metropolitan authority. But the toll of continuous sea warfare, increasingly dominated by British naval blockades and open-sea commerce raiding, progressively stifled the city's commercial life. Perhaps ignoring these foreboding signs and following the example of his godfather, Édouard Michel joined the French war effort on the high seas. Fresh from victories in Europe and the Middle East, Napoleon sought a wider scope of land conquest. At sea, he hoped to counter British dominance by focusing French naval forces at Great Britain's strategic dependence on sea commerce conducted by a fleet of highly motivated British merchantmen. The small French Navy, initially no match for the heavily invested Royal Navy, counted in its ranks a large fleet of privateers flying the French flag from home and colonial ports. The lightly armed ships pursued what was called a "*guerre du course*," the strategic deployment of small, armed vessels to harass and keep occupied British warships protecting merchant ships and maintaining blockades of foreign ports. "Strike at England's commerce; pour out your cruisers in every sea; let them find shelter in every colonial harbor."[54] Meanwhile, Napoleon hoped to advance his successful land campaigns, threatening the British colonies in the East and the British homeland across the English Channel.[55]

In his adolescent years, Édouard would have had little appreciation of Napoleon's war stratagems, but many in the French world knew the tradition of French corsairs and pirates that had once savaged ships in Atlantic and Mediterranean sea-lanes. He undoubtedly had gained some practical sailing experience in the coastal and interisland merchant trade. He likely turned to the friend, neighbor, and business associate of the Cazabons, Captain Denis Lamothe Villegente, an active participant in the cabotage trade.[56] By 1807, at age fifteen, Édouard was ready for the challenges of deep-sea waters ventures. Aboard Captain François Morisseau's privateer, *L'Hortense*, Édouard would be introduced to the rigors and perils of the mariner's world on the open sea under conditions of armed conflict. Morisseau had gained a reputation as a daring, efficient corsair captain. Martinique's military commander, Capitaine-General Villaret de Joyeuse, once praised Morisseau for capturing three British naval ships en route from England to the West Indies "employing only a 6 pound gun on a pivot." On bringing the prize to Fort Royal's harbor, Villaret de Joyeuse had proclaimed it to be "one of the most beautiful acts of our navy." In subsequent actions, the "accounts of witnesses" celebrated the "heroic struggles" of Guadeloupe's corsair captains and included Morisseau's name in a list of honorees.[57]

In August 1807, Captain François Morisseau and Second Captain Auguste Rostenne sailed from the Saint-Pierre harbor on the schooner *L'Hortense* carrying eight guns and a crew of ninety men, which included the fifteen-year-old "Edward" who had signed on as a "boy."[58] The rank of "boy" exposed a young sailor to many essentials of seamanship, from learning the intricacies of working the rigging and setting sails to fundamentals of day and nighttime sea navigation. This was probably Édouard Michel's first experience on an armed warship, a French corsair, and it would last just under two weeks. After leaving the Saint-Pierre harbor and sailing near Barbados to the south, the schooner was overtaken by HMS *Blond* of the British navy. On August 16, 1807, Captain Volant Vashon Ballard reported with unmuted pride to Admiral Cochrane, commander of the West Indies naval group:

> His Majesty's ship Blonde captured this morning the very fast sailing French privateer schooner L'Hortense, (late Éclair) mounting four nine-pounder carronades, two long twelve pounders, and two eight pounders (the whole of which were thrown overboard in the chase), and ninety men belong to Martinique, after a chase of twenty hours; she is a very fine schooner, well adapted for his Majesty's service; had been out thirteen days, and taken nothing. V. V. Ballard.[59]

Captains Morisseau and Rostenne, along with Édouard and the surviving crew, returned to Martinique four months later in a prisoner exchange, on December 23, 1807. Captain Rostenne remained for a time in Saint-Pierre, as a neighbor of the Cazabons, and would attend the death of Michel Cazabon's brother Jean.[60]

On returning home Édouard experienced a series of unexpected events that fundamentally altered his course. His godfather's only brother, Jean Cazabon, died in April 1808. In the final month of 1808, news of his mother Olive's death reached him. In early 1809, the British attacked and regained control of Martinique. Afterward, we find no further trace of Édouard's godfather and suspect that Michel Cazabon was lost to the events of the British assault.[61] As the decade closed, Édouard Michel would need to recruit new allies and mentors.

Leaving Martinique

Edward Mitchell in his youth had pursued the seafaring life against the darkened backdrop of full-scale sea warfare. His brief apprenticeship aboard *L'Hortense* and other Martinique-based coastal vessels had satisfied youthful yearnings for a life at sea and prepared him to pursue an independent course. Twenty years later, at the time of his first ordination, Mitchell would relate details of his life's journey to coreligionists. He titled the oration "Outlines of the Religious Experience of Edward Mitchell." (In this book, we refer to his handwritten manuscript as the "Outlines.") Although principally concerned in this document with matters of spiritual conversion, Mitchell confessed that his early interests had been drawn to the seaman's life. He omitted any reference to his Martinique years and understandably avoided replaying his experience aboard *L'Hortense*. He could not have told the story of joining the crew of a privately owned armed vessel, whose hostile acts in the service of a sovereign power, although falling within the boundaries of prevailing maritime law, were commonly viewed as actions of French *flibustiers*, or sea pirates. In these latter years of the Age of Sail, the mixed motivations of profit, patriotism, and adventure that had tempted generations of young men were not readily explained or excused in genteel circles. Nonetheless, for Mitchell, these experiences must have clung to his soul, energizing a constant forward motion to seek new opportunities beyond the visible horizons of the Caribbean.

Mitchell's years in Martinique, from January 1792 to May 1810, spanned the island's most turbulent period of social, political, ethnic, and class conflict. He was born in the fervor of the French Revolution, but the spirit of "*liberté, égalité, fraternité*" inspired by the rise of new democratic "*citoyens*" of the French Metropol had precipitated sharply divergent outcomes in the French colonies. Slave-led rebellions in Saint-Domingue had freed its enslaved population and established a black republic. In Martinique, a committee of *gens de couleur*, cognizant of the growing influence of liberal ideologies in Paris, articulated strong prorevolutionary beliefs and coupled notions of universal rights of man with slave emancipation. Jean Isaac, Joseph Honoré, and Édouard Meunier, *gens de couleur* of Édouard Michel's young world, had signed the January 1793 Adresse des citoyens de couleur de la Martinique à l'Assemblée Coloniale, signaling their willingness to fight in the name of revolutionary ideals, rather than continuing to suffer "humiliating demarcation that separate us from the white citizens."[62] A frightened, reactionary ruling white minority responded by reinforcing and more rigorously surveilling the slavery-freedom boundary imposed by the Code Noire. Small-scale slave and mulatto uprisings were defeated in 1790, 1793, and 1800.[63] Dissident revolutionary voices, black and white, were deported to France or otherwise neutralized.

Napoleonic rule of Martinique beginning in 1802 further consolidated the racist social order. White Creoles, congenitally inclined to fear unification of slaves and *gens de couleur*, implemented harsh decrees against free blacks that pruned already-limited civil liberties. French authorities prohibited access to public education, intensified scrutiny of claimed free status with threats of re-enslavement, and legislated new petty prohibitions on public behaviors judged to be inconsistent with servile status.[64] The briefly aroused French antislavery voices of the French Revolution were now muted. Progressively, the ancient chains enforcing racial hierarchy and class privilege tightened. Meanwhile, Martinique, severely strained by a failing economy and internal divisions, again became a vulnerable target of British military ambitions. A long-expected British invasion, directed by Lieutenant-General George Beckwith and Vice-Admiral Alexander Cochrane, struck on January 30, 1809, and concluded with island's capitulation on February 24, 1809, at Fort Royal.

Having already lost his family and now his homeland, Mitchell must have felt that he had lost everything. Looking up from his grief, he would again turn his gaze to the sea. Fate and providence would favor him, but for eighteen years he had prepared to take every advantage of opportunities, however gained. Arrayed before him was a world of uncertainty. National powers sought hegemony in a disorderly world as new republican democracies and dictatorships contested ancient monarchies and dynasties. Slave masters ruled most people of African ancestry in the Atlantic World. Mitchell would leave behind an intransigent slave society to test freedom's limits in the United States, where, as in Martinique, almost 90 percent of blacks were enslaved and free people of color lived on the margins, largely invisible and only beginning to understand the promise of freedom and full citizenship. Having witnessed varying expressions of freedom's call and fully indoctrinated to the seafaring life, Mitchell would find support among new friends, start a family, join a community, and, most urgently, seek a permanent livelihood. In all these efforts, he would succeed, but the fortunes and turns he would encounter and conquer could not possibly have been imagined or foretold.

TWO

Martinique to Maine

I went to sea, with an intention of following the sea-faring life.
—*Edward Mitchell, "Outlines," 1829*

In the Age of Sail, young men of all classes and ambitions were drawn to the sea. Raised in the midst of Martinique's busiest commercial seaport, Edward Mitchell had looked to the sea and envisioned his future as a sea captain. In following his godfather, Michel Cazabon, to sea, Mitchell entered the mariners' ranks as a "boy" at age fifteen. Leaving Martinique three years later, he was prepared for more demanding assignments and responsibilities. He could now be counted among the many black mariners working aboard American ships of the Atlantic sea-lanes. Nearly 20 percent of early nineteenth-century crewmembers on American ships were black. Some were slaves, especially in American coastwise shipping, but in a climate of fear and suspicion arising from slave rebellion across slave plantations of the Atlantic World, black sailors were predominantly free men of color.[1] Although black mariners held varied positions aboard ships, as pilots, mates, and carpenters, Mitchell's expressed design to become a ship's captain (the highest rank) was highly unusual for that time, with few examples or precedents among American men of color.

Martinique's *gens de couleur* served various roles in coastwise sailing commerce. A nineteenth-century French historian noted, "Many colored men also commanded small boats for the use of the coasts, and thus prevented the white sailors from benefiting alone from this industry."[2] A few Martinique *gens de couleur* attained master-mariner ranks and piloted vessels in local cabotage trading, but, as in America, most mariners ranked low in social status. French captains and their fiscal agents, the *commissionaires,* dominated the commercial shipping life of Saint-Pierre. For Mitchell to have contemplated attaining the rank of captain on a ship plying international trade routes was misplaced youthful exuberance, given the closed ranks of upper-echelon mariner positions.[3]

After coming to the United States, Mitchell may have known the example of Paul Cuffee (1759–1817), the mixed-race Massachusetts sea captain, shipowner, and businessman of African and Native American ancestry. Cuffee sailed vessels from New England and mid-Atlantic ports to coastal and international destinations, often with all-black crews. When Mitchell came to the United States, Cuffee was busy planning a sail to Sierra Leone. It is unlikely that the two met.[4] But Mitchell had known and possibly enjoyed the mentorship of master mariners in Saint-Pierre. And we learn of his lofty ambitions only after he had arrived safely in the United States. Once freed from the grasp of Martinique's racial caste, and before feeling the full limitations imposed by American racism, Mitchell's ambitions may have had room to range, even soar. After all, the same idealism had propelled thousands of immigrants onto routes of success after reaching America's shores. Mitchell's decision to go to sea initiated a chain of events that, with seeming inexorability, led the young sailor from Martinique to the improbable future as a graduate of Dartmouth College—the "ancient college" of New Hampshire—and then as an esteemed Baptist clergyman in Canada. Equipped only with the small advantages of some education and familiarity with French and English languages and customs, Mitchell next encountered a series of remarkable individuals who profoundly shaped the course and character of his life.

Captain Prentiss

When a lad he embarked upon a vessel under the command
of Captain Prentiss, and came to Portland, Maine.
—*from Mitchell's obituary*

The captain's name was not explicitly revealed in the "Outlines," which identified men of influence in Mitchell's religious conversion. But years later, historians of Sutton, New Hampshire, who drew on memories of Mitchell's first years after college graduation, noted the assistance Mitchell had received from "a sea captain." Much later, the obituary published in a Rock Island, Quebec, newspaper at the close of his life mentioned Captain Prentiss by name. Since the author of that obituary in Quebec would have known Mitchell only after he moved to Lower Canada, it is uncertain whether Mitchell acknowledged Prentiss by name earlier.[5]

Captain William Prentiss (1778–1826) was a prominent merchant sea captain of Portland, Maine. His son, Seargent Prentiss, a US Congressman, described his family heritage as belonging to "one of the most distinguished families, and includes in it some of the most prominent men in New England."[6] The captain had spent his youngest years in the countryside of Gorham, Maine, twenty miles inland from the Portland harbor. He went to sea in his teens, perhaps rebelling against family expectations, and rose rapidly from crewmember to captain and shipowner. Learning, in the academic sense, was appreciated in his family. His father had graduated from Harvard and two of his sons would later graduate from Bowdoin College. One of them, the Reverend Dr. George Lewis Prentiss, writing from the recollections of older members of his family, described the captain as "a highly respected and prosperous shipmaster . . . a man of quick intelligence and strong domestic affections," whose returns to his family in Portland were "season[s] redolent of oranges, pineapples, and other products of foreign climes." George Lewis Prentiss wrote of the captain's "hair-breadth escapes [from] storms and hurricanes," an account consistent with Mitchell's recollection of his voyages with Prentiss. Another biographical note calls Prentiss "a man of decision and energy," who "met with equal fearlessness the perils of the sea and the dangers of pirates and British men-of-war."[7]

For New England sea merchants, the Atlantic sea trade promised substantial rewards and exceptional risks in an era of uninterrupted political and military maneuvering among European combatants and countermeasures by the American authorities aiming to preserve American neutrality. Ships and crews along the international sea routes were subject to impositions imposed by US and British trade embargoes, unpredictable foreign port tariffs, and the constant threat of seizure by privateers and the rival French or British navies. Prior to these restrictions and their culmination in the American War of 1812 against the British, American merchantmen had developed a brisk trade with the West Indies. New England sea merchants sailed to Caribbean ports and carried home sugar, molasses (a by-product of sugar refining), and coffee purchased or bartered in exchange for lumber, boxes, shooks for cask-making, salt fish, meat, and other commodities and manufactured goods. These imports were vital to the prosperity of the French-Caribbean slave colonies whose fertile soils served an economic system based on slave labor and exported cash crops.[8] Nineteenth-century American sea trade with the Caribbean islands coexisted alongside the slave trade banned in US waters as of 1794.[9] Other countries continued to transport human cargoes to Martinique and other Caribbean ports. Prentiss indirectly benefited from this system of exploited African slave labor that brought profits to merchant interests in Europe and the Atlantic World in a system of commerce commonly termed the "triangular trade." There is no record or suggestion that Prentiss directly engaged in slave transport.[10]

Prentiss captained at least ten voyages into Caribbean waters, beginning in 1803 and continuing until the outbreak of the War of 1812. His vessels were typical cargo ships of the Age of Sail: the schooners *Clarissa* and *Joseph* and the brigantines *Edward, Triton, Ocean, Tropic,* and *George*.[11] The brigs were versatile two-masted, square-rigged vessels while the more easily navigable fore-and-aft-rigged schooners carried three or four masts and required relatively small crews in proportion to their cargo capacity. Prentiss typically sailed with seven crewmembers, ensuring that anything remarkable about any of them would have come to his attention. Prentiss lost at least three mariners during his voyages: a mate, George Clark, in 1804, and two seamen, William Thomas, "a colored man," and Benjamin Jordan, in 1809.

British and French Interference at Sea

Prentiss made four successful voyages to Martinique between 1804 and 1810, the last with Mitchell aboard on the return leg to Portland. Earlier in 1807, Prentiss had piloted the brig *Triton* to Martinique. On returning he was overtaken by the larger British ship *Alligator* and hauled to Antigua, where the cargo was "condemned" for alleged illegal trading. After formal protest and legal proceedings, Prentiss recovered his Portland-bound cargo of molasses, sugar, and coffee, but new international restrictions on sea trade would severely curtail subsequent voyages.[12]

From 1807 until the War of 1812, a series of crippling impediments to American trade arose as an indirect consequence of entanglements between Britain and France during the Napoleonic Wars.[13] In January 1807 the British issued the orders-in-council prohibiting neutral nations, including the United States, from trading with France unless having first paid a tribute to Britain, a ruling enforced by blockades and direct seizures on open waters. The orders remained in effect until June 1812. France countered by directing its naval forces to confiscate any neutral vessel in a French port that had visited Britain or paid the tribute. As a direct result, US ship cargoes were subjected to seizures and crewmembers to impressments, a violation of the American neutrality. The US response, the Embargo Act of December 1807, succeeded only in further complicating issues. The law prohibited exports by US sea merchants to foreign nations. Aimed at Britain and France and their respective colonies, the intent was to inflict economic hardship on the two warring nations by denying access to American products. But the American attempt to influence armed conflict through commercial warfare had little effect. Controversial and divisive at the time, and deemed a colossal mistake by historians, the 1807 Embargo Act halted the maritime economy of Maine, confining most of its merchantmen to harbor, including Captain Prentiss. The United States' international sea commerce languished for two years, until its repeal in March 1809.

The US Congress enacted a more targeted version of the Embargo Act, the Non-Intercourse Act of 1809, which permitted American commerce with all foreign and neutral countries except Britain, France, and their possessions. The Non-Intercourse Act was largely unenforceable since American ships could easily use the ports of neutral countries for transshipment of goods to and from embargoed countries, in particular, the British ports of the West Indies (including captured French islands), where New England products were still in demand. A narrow window of opportunity for American merchantmen opened between April 19 and August 9, 1809, when America concluded negotiations with British envoys that lifted Non-Intercourse Act restrictions and reopened American trade with British ports.[14] Upon hearing this news, Captain Prentiss, along with hundreds of other US merchant crews, rushed from American ports to the Caribbean Sea in the final weeks of April 1809.

To Portland

It was during this perilous era of conflict among nations engaged in sea commerce that Edward Mitchell, still in his late teens, came to American shores in 1810 with Captain Prentiss. The timing of his arrival at Portland, Maine, can be fixed by correlating the events described in his "Outlines" with the known domestic affairs of Prentiss's life requiring his presence in Maine, the record of Prentiss's voyages into the Caribbean, and the dates of prevailing international trade restrictions. In May 1807, after returning to Portland from Havana, Cuba, Prentiss could not sail again until the US Embargo Act had run its course in 1809. During the interlude, Prentiss bided his time in Portland, tending to family matters and pleasures. In the Caribbean, Britain launched a wide-ranging naval campaign to control the Caribbean seas. A successful two-month British naval and ground assault captured Martinique on February 24, 1809, further expanding British dominance of the Caribbean sea-lanes.

On April 20, 1809, the first day after the restrictions of the US Embargo and Non-Intercourse Acts as applied to Britain were temporarily lifted, Prentiss set sail on the brig *Tropic* 150 tons burden.[15] According to shipping news reports, his destination was the "Spanish Maine," the South American coast bordering the Caribbean Sea and the Gulf of Mexico, ostensibly to a British or neutral port in compliance with prevailing laws.[16] At that time, Prentiss would not have returned to Martinique. The aftershocks of the British capture of the island had not yet settled, and activity in Martinique's commercial ports did not normalize until the summer of 1809. Instead, Prentiss steered to an alternative British port at Paramaribo, Surinam (today, the Republic of Suriname), a Dutch colony on the northeast coast of South America, which had submitted to British sea power and occupation (1804–16). Prentiss reached Surinam on the last day of May 1809 and found the port in full operation. He sold his cargo of New England products and left on July 20 laden with a large cargo of molasses—"Cargo of brig Tropic: 262 hhhds, 36 tierces, 3 bbls first quality Surinam Molasses [18,112 gallons, 112 tons]."[17]

Prentiss laid over in Maine for six weeks before returning to sea in the fall of 1809 for what would be a rendezvous with Edward Mitchell in Martinique. The Non-Intercourse Act restrictions were in effect, the briefly opened trade window to British ports now closed. Accordingly, Prentiss registered his voyage destination as the "Spanish Maine," again masking his actual plan by appearing to visit an unspecified neutral port. In fact, he sailed to Martinique and reached the harbor of Saint-Pierre on January 17, 1810, with a crew of seven mariners and laden with New England commodities much needed on the island. It took Prentiss three months to sell his New England products and procure a return load of Martinique molasses—the largest shipment to leave Saint-Pierre that winter. On his departure from Saint-Pierre on April 17, 1810, his crew had expanded from seven to nine men. One of the two new crewmembers was the young Édouard Michel.[18]

According to Mitchell's testimony in the "Outlines," this was his first voyage as a crewmember on an American vessel. Having survived his brief apprenticeship as a "boy" on a French privateer, he was undoubtedly ready to take on the challenge of a sailor's duties. According to W. Jeffrey Bolster's study of black seamen on American ships in the Age of Sail, "some [black seamen, especially stewards and cooks] made careers of sailing repeatedly with the same captain." Such an arrangement enhanced a captain's status, assured him of reliable and trustworthy service, and freed a black seaman from recurrent competition in an anonymous and often glutted labor market and from concern about signing on with an unknown, possibly abusive captain.[19] Few would have known or cared much about the literacy or the aspirations of a young, newly recruited crewmember. But Mitchell expressed gratitude for the help and encouragement he received from this remarkable captain. He must have informed Prentiss that he could read and write, that he wanted to improve his English and to learn more about many subjects, and that he would be grateful for access to books and charts. Well prepared for the challenges, Mitchell undoubtedly made a good impression on the captain, as he would make on many others throughout his life. His years living aside the busy Saint-Pierre wharves had instilled a deep reverence for the mariner's life, an attitude surely noted by Prentiss. Years later while a college student at Dartmouth, Mitchell reflected admiringly on the veteran sailor:

> View the weather beaten sailor. To him, nothing is so pleasant as the well riged and swift sailing ship, with expanded sails. The height, to which his ambition aspires, is the name of the *able mariner*. In the persuit of this, he encounters waves rolling high as mountains; he exposes himself to danger and hardship; yet he moves to different

> parts of his ship, with as much composure, as the farmer would on his farm. So united is he to his labour, that neither the independent persuit of husbandry, nor the enriching revenue of a profession, can induce him to forsake the boisterous ocean.[20]

Prentiss employed many seamen, black and white, during his maritime career, but perhaps no others impressed him as did Mitchell.

On May 17, 1810, Mitchell returned to Portland with Prentiss (see appendix 3). The shipping news in Boston newspapers reported that Prentiss had sailed from "St. Bart's," or Saint Barthélemy, a small Caribbean island of volcanic rock with a busy seaport but few arable lands of sufficient size to grow sugarcane crops.[21] Its capital city of Gustavia served as a neutral "port of convenience" for transshipments, enabling American merchantmen to skirt restrictions of the Non-Intercourse Acts by concealing the originating port of their cargoes. The hold of the *Tropic* contained a large shipment of molasses—276 hogsheads and 43 barrels (18,743 gallons weighing 115 tons).[22] After the brief stopover in St. Bart's and payment of port fees, Prentiss brought his cargo and young crewman to Boston on May 17, 1810: "Arrived, brig Tropic, Prentiss, 32 days from St. Barts."[23] After unloading the cargo at the Thomas & Edward Motley warehouse on Boston's India Wharf, Prentiss and Mitchell returned to Portland. Mitchell's first appearance on the busy docks of Boston and Portland, however exhilarating to him, probably went largely unnoticed. As a young mariner of color in Prentiss's employ, he would not have invited special notice or scrutiny at the docks.

Prentiss's 1810 rendezvous with Mitchell must have occurred without advance planning. He had made three prior voyages to Martinique, between 1804 and 1806, and the last trip, arriving at Saint-Pierre on January 17, 1810, was foremost a risky commercial venture in a volatile era of full-scale privateering and impressments against American merchantmen by the French and British. Once in Saint-Pierre, Mitchell came aboard the brig *Tropic* as a crewmember at a time when Prentiss needed to replace lost seamen. The *Tropic* moored at the Saint-Pierre port for three months, giving Prentiss plenty of time to observe and even test his prospective new hire. The unifying force motivating their new relationship was a shared desire to leave Martinique. As events unfolded, it would be, for both, the last time.

Rev. Payson and Rev. Beman

About this time I heard two sermons, one on the solemnity of death and judgement, and on the other, the great reparation, which will take place on the day of judgement.
—*Edward Mitchell, "Outlines," 1829*

With Mitchell on board, the *Tropic* reached Portland's harbor on May 18, 1810, where Prentiss received poignant news: his eldest child, four-year-old Caroline, had died on May 6. The captain doubtless wanted to spend some time with his wife and their two young sons. Consequently, although Mitchell expected to return to sea, he could not anticipate doing so immediately. According to the "Outlines," he had already lost interest in religion, presumably the Roman Catholic faith. The perilous seafaring life with its constant temptations to vice and profligacy created self-doubts and uncertainties. Awakened from a self-proclaimed "deep sleep," he confessed, "I was and had been a great sinner against God." Providentially, he heard the message of two extraordinary Portland ministers, Rev. Edward Payson and Rev. Nathan S. S. Beman, who became pivotal agents of his religious conversion. In Mitchell, the two evangelicals would find a receptive supplicant, already prepared to rethink his fundamental ambitions and aspirations.

Mitchell's encounters with the two remarkable religious clerics were undoubtedly encouraged, directly or indirectly, by his relationship with Prentiss. The "Outlines" tell us that Mitchell roomed and boarded in the home of a "gentleman" whose wife was "a woman of great piety." The wife became a religious confidant and "made serious impression" on his still impure thoughts. Probably the "gentleman's wife" was Prentiss's wife, Abigail Lewis Prentiss, daughter of an Orthodox Church deacon. The Prentiss household was ample in size as the family was still small. Others would give generous testimony to Abigail's piety, religious devotion, and capacity to nurture youthful potential. She and the captain were members of Rev. Edward Payson's Second Congregational Church, and she had been converted and baptized by Payson in 1809. Her substantial contribution to her son, Seargent, was chronicled years later and read, in part, "She was 'a mother in Israel,' and to her influence her distinguished son, Seargent Smith Prentiss, the celebrated orator, owed the finishing traits of his character, and largely his success in life."[24] With her encouragement, and presumably the captain's, Mitchell attended services led by Rev. Nathan S. S. Beman,[25] pastor of the Third Parish Congregational Church of Portland, and Rev. Dr. Edward Payson, colleague pastor of the Second Parish Congregational Church.[26]

Beman was new to the ministry when Mitchell heard him preach in Portland, but he would later be called "one of the best known and most controversial clergymen of his time."[27] Beman ardently opposed slavery and thirty years later would become a theological mentor of the black abolitionist Henry Highland Garnet. The second religious divine to enter Mitchell's life was Payson. "The Seraphic Payson," as he became known, was a charismatic revivalist, "eminent for his electric genius," and a prominent figure in the religious movement known as the Second Great Awakening, discussed below. His reputation was already established in 1810 and, although he chose to remain in Portland, churches in Boston and New York had eagerly sought him. Payson's theology has been characterized as "a mild type of the old New England Calvinism," with his "one overmastering passion [being] to win souls for Christ." He was credited with "rare conversational powers," and enthusiastically engaged in many conversations with "inquirers" in Portland. Prentiss and his family were members of his congregation, and Payson became "endeared to [them] not merely as a teacher and friend, but as the father of their religious life." Later, the families were united when the captain's son George Lewis Prentiss married Payson's daughter Elizabeth, the prolific author of religious poems and short stories.[28]

Mitchell's sea voyages left him burdened with confusion and guilt over his sinful ways. Having no prior "reference to the Atonement of Christ," Mitchell received a "solemn impression" from Payson's message on the "reparation which will take place on the day of judgment" and requested a private meeting. Although Payson during these months suffered from periods of severe depression as well as frequent physical illness, he was his usual genial self when Mitchell approached him, and he welcomed Mitchell as a serious "inquirer." Mitchell later described their meeting as a "faithful and pious conversation."[29] Payson's ability to universally reach deep into hearts of men and women of all classes and social standing extended even to the world of the mariner. He once addressed a large gathering of seafaring men (later published worldwide) that invited the comment, "[It was] not an oration for the alumni of a college . . . but an address to seamen . . . and [he] understood their vocabulary, almost as well as themselves—so well, that an experienced sea-captain was able to detect, in the whole address, but a single nautical term, whose application involved a misconception of its use."[30]

Beman and Payson were religious men who modeled the life of a passionately devoted disciple of Christ and the glorious award awaiting those who followed His calling. On the way to becoming a thoroughly committed Christian, Mitchell had much to learn, much to study in the Bible, much upon which to meditate, and much to interpret, but he never departed from his conviction of the Bible's divine inspiration and absolute reliability.

Mitchell's Final Voyage

Nearly at the close of this voyage on my passage home,
it pleased God once more to awaken me.
—*Edward Mitchell, "Outlines," 1829*

Prentiss set sail again on September 27, 1810, with Mitchell aboard the *George* on a bearing for Kingston, Jamaica, where the brig docked on November 1, 1810.[31] This passage was probably Mitchell's "second voyage" described in the "Outlines." Mitchell confessed that he had continued "in [his] wicked course and carelessness about [his] soul," presumably while ashore in Jamaica. On the return voyage three weeks later, a violent storm beset the ship and he "feared going to eternity in an unprepared state. It pleased God to spare me." The brig was forced to return to the US mainland and docked at Wilmington, North Carolina, for repairs. Mitchell had survived, but two of his shipmates did not. A Maine local historian quoted a passage from Captain Prentiss's logbook:

> In a furious storm, a perfect hurricane, one of our ablest sea-men a carpenter was carried overboard. He swam very strong, and it was with the utmost concern that we found ourselves incapable to assist him. Indeed we were the more grieved at his unhappy fate, as we lost sight of him struggling with the waves; and thought from the manner in which he swam, that he might continue to live and struggle for some time longer, without avail.[32]

Once back in Portland, Prentiss gave notice of the lost sailors in the *Portland Gazette and Maine Advertiser*: "William, a colored man" and "Benjamin Jordan, seaman."

Mitchell's and Prentiss's courses diverged at this juncture in December 1810. Mitchell resolved to reconsider his life ambitions and decided to go to Philadelphia.[33] Prentiss went on to complete three additional voyages into Caribbean and Gulf Coast waters right up to the War of 1812. In 1812, Prentiss gave up his seafaring career and returned to the countryside of his boyhood, settling his still-growing family in West Gorham, where he remained until his death in 1826.

In leaving Portland for Philadelphia, the chastened young sailor of Martinique promised to abandon his "wicked ways" and pivoted his life's work to seek a reward in the Kingdom of God. In early 1811, Mitchell arrived in Philadelphia to start the new life path opened by his fateful encounters with Portland's influential Calvinist ministers. Now grounded in a life of religious discovery and devotion, this combination of circumstances and events must have seemed to be the intervention of providence. He had become convinced that the seafaring life was conducive to vice, and that regardless of when he might again have the opportunity to go to sea, he should not do so, even though he believed "my prospect for worldly gain in that was every day brightening." This confidence was unrealistic but consistent with the youthful exuberance and refreshed belief that attended his choosing a life of religious devotion and self-sacrifice. Prentiss had represented the worldly circle of prosperity in maritime life that once had captured Mitchell's imagination. But the captain's world in Portland contrasted sharply to the mariner's lot. Sailors' labors aboard ships and on the docks were physically demanding, compensated by low (albeit livable) wages, and increasingly uncertain as the issues leading to the War of 1812 threatened their livelihood.

In abandoning the sea, Mitchell could now look to the prospects of a life in the ministry. He had witnessed the inspirational evangelism of Beman and Payson and observed the respect accorded them by their parishioners and the public. Impressed by their devoutness and erudition, and having personally discussed spiritual matters with Payson, for Mitchell, the aim of seeking a religious life now seemed worthy of his ambition and essential to restoring comfort and sanctity in his life.

THREE

Philadelphia

I went from Portland to Philadelphia, where I remained from 1811 to 1820.
—*Edward Mitchell, "Outlines," 1829*

Mitchell came to Philadelphia in 1811 and would remain until the spring of 1820. While a resident of the city of Benjamin Franklin and American patriots, he would marry, father two children, and suffer the death of all three. The "Outlines" only hint at these details of his secular life in Philadelphia, a period of ascendancy into manhood and continued religious awakening. He would encounter the rising drumbeat of antislavery voices articulating moral and humanistic arguments to a society unable to honor its founding principles of the "natural rights" of man. This emerging struggle had its strongest signposts in Philadelphia, where the roots of black religious, educational, and social institutions were already firmly planted.

Mitchell had good reasons to come to Philadelphia, which was still the beating heart of America's revolutionary heritage. The Embargo Act of 1807 and Non-Intercourse Act of 1809 had severely impacted the nation's busiest commercial port, but Philadelphia's economy was more diverse than Portland's, and the effects on shipping had been offset somewhat by other opportunities for employment. In the city's social and political realm, a Jeffersonian democratic spirit still burned. Its cosmopolitan character reflected a blend of wealthy upper-class landowners, energetic middle-class merchants, striving immigrant families from Europe, and a discernible strand of French cultural traditions. More than two thousand French-Caribbeans had escaped to the city in the 1790s—wealthy plantation owners and their slaves fleeing the slave rebellion and internal political struggles of Saint-Domingue. Some slaves were freed under Pennsylvania's gradual emancipation law while others were forced into coercive indenture contracts with former masters. Other Caribbean blacks had come from the British West Indies, former slaves of Quaker masters whose coreligionists in Pennsylvania had persuaded them to relinquish slaveholding.[1]

Philadelphia's wharves hosted a constant stream of human migration and commercial intercourse that energized this early nineteenth-century American example of expansion and growing wealth. Black Americans of the city did not participate equally in the city's progress, even though Pennsylvania had been the first state to legislate the abolition of slavery. The Act for the Gradual Abolition of Slavery of 1780 banned the slave trade and included other provisions to eliminate residual elements of slavery in the state. The law offered no protection to fugitives from the South, and even slavery prohibitions could be circumvented through the indenture system, which victimized some Caribbean slaves. Philadelphia blacks had been granted a modicum of civil and legal rights in a society still decades away from the abolition of slavery and relief from the many disabling residues of its entrenchment.

Mitchell would find that Portland's small free black population could not compare to Philadelphia's large and firmly rooted African American populace. Philadelphia's African American population recorded the year prior to Mitchell's arrival numbered 10,522, constituting 9.6 percent of the city's total population. Their numbers would increase to 12,110 free African Americans (and no slaves) counted in 1820, the year of Mitchell's departure.[2] Philadelphia by 1811 had a reputation as "a city of hope for African Americans."[3] The development of black religious, cultural, and self-improvement organizations had progressed from their early beginnings two decades earlier.[4] The Free African Society of Philadelphia, founded in 1787 by Richard Allen and Absalom Jones, harnessed an emerging spirit of black community cohesion and self-sufficiency to the founding of mutual aid societies and independent black churches. Religious leaders like Allen and Jones aligned with a visible and organized cadre of black civic leaders to establish the city as a national center of black organization and influence in the emerging discourse on race.

Despite nearly uniform oppressive discrimination against blacks, work was available to those prepared to lend their backs to the task. Disproportionately relative to whites, black men and women held positions of low pay and rank—as laborers, carters, washerwomen, and porters. A third were employed in domestic service as maids and house servants. Some enterprising blacks had found niches in the seams of the city's steady commerce as barbers, hairdressers, polishers, and mariners. Several emerged as black community leaders and anchored their social position as property holders, real estate investors, and masters in crafts such as sailmaking, painting, and plastering.[5] Additionally, the recurrent epidemics created a need for persons to nurse and otherwise serve the sick, a demand that was supplied mainly by African Americans who, especially if born in Africa or the West Indies, were believed to be more resistant to such diseases. It was not understood at the time that natives of the tropics often contracted yellow fever in childhood, and the survivors thereby acquired permanent immunity. The later generations of blacks were not protected.

Mitchell's attraction to Philadelphia may have been focused on its reputation as a "center of African American religious activity."[6] Philadelphia was home to one of the earliest expressions of African American evangelism. By 1810 the city hosted five African American churches.[7] Mitchell would come to know and break bread with leaders of these congregations, who tended toward conservative politics and religious orthodoxy but served effectively as civic leaders and occasionally collaborated with Philadelphia's well-born white citizens of wealth and influence insofar as mutual interests permitted.[8]

From the Quaker and Mennonite populations came movements that established the city as an early center of abolitionist thought, action, and organization. By the 1780s the Quakers' pro-emancipation activities had spread to the Methodist and Presbyterian churches and, significantly in the present context, to the Philadelphia Baptist Association. Their influences, together with the prevailing idealism of the American Revolution, had led to enactment of Pennsylvania's gradual abolition law of 1780. Many freed and runaway slaves sought the relative protections of Pennsylvania, whose southern border delimited the northeastern limit of American legal slavery. In those early years, freedom seekers escaping from the South often sought out or were directed to the African American churches and black or Quaker abolitionists. These precursors of the Underground Railroad, which later became especially active in Pennsylvania, were only beginning to take form. The major black leaders who organized the South-to-North freedom trails were all born after Mitchell departed Philadelphia in 1820. William Still (1821–1902), for example, came to Philadelphia in 1844, and Harriet Tubman (ca. 1822–1913) in 1849. African American abolitionist leaders such as Frederick Douglass and Robert Purvis, and the brothers Joseph Cassey Bustill and Charles Hicks Bustill of Philadelphia, would not become active until after the 1830s.[9]

From early 1811 to May 1820, Mitchell would live amidst Philadelphia's nascent black institutions and witness signs of an evolving African American collective consciousness. For a young man of color, nowhere but in Philadelphia were opportunities and perils so conspicuously presented and contrasted. He was, after all, a young Caribbean immigrant with no American family or community roots who had cast himself into the chaotic maw of America's most vibrant urbanized city, where black Americans were visible and energetic, but economically depressed and still lacking basic civil rights and protections despite their free status. Mitchell would be molded by his years in Philadelphia. But as he cast his fate to the City of Brotherly Love, his path remained consistently bound by ambitions awakened in Martinique and now wed to a path of spiritual redemption. Going forward, the choices he would make would be circumstantial and, at times, highly improbable.

Rev. Dr. William Staughton

Having been hopefully converted and baptized by Rev. Dr. Staughton, [Mitchell's] attention was at once turned to the Christian ministry.
—*"Mitchell, Rev. Edward," in* Baptist Encyclopaedia, *1881*

Shortly after arriving in Philadelphia in 1811, Mitchell attended Episcopal services for two or three months. The "Outlines" mention "an episcopalian society" without further qualification, but refer to the African Episcopal Church of St. Thomas and its rector, Rev. Absalom Jones, the first person of African descent to have been ordained an Anglican or Episcopal priest. Perhaps impatient for absolution and salvation, Mitchell was unmoved by the church's "live and do" Old Testament religious temperament. He apparently steered clear of Philadelphia's Catholic churches, where, in common with many churches of that time, black and white worshippers were segregated into separate pews and church services.[10] Mitchell's interest shifted to the Baptist Church, as did that of other blacks who found comfort and spiritual uplift in the nonhierarchical organization and evangelical traditions of the Baptists. Mitchell's attraction to the Baptists crystallized in the presence of yet another evangelical who entered his life.

During this time Mitchell heard highly complimentary accounts of the Reverend Dr. William Staughton (1770–1829), the best-known white clergyman of Philadelphia. Staughton was a Calvinist Baptist, renowned for his "fiery eloquence" and evangelical zeal. While pastor of the Philadelphia First Baptist Church, he and a large contingent of the worshippers separated to form a new congregation, many of whose members were prosperous contributors.[11] The new church, an expensively constructed structure capped by a massive cupola, was completed in 1812 and named for its location: the Sansom Street Baptist Church. Mitchell first met Staughton in 1811 when the church members were meeting in temporary quarters.

Staughton's ecumenical reach extended well beyond his own congregation. People throughout Philadelphia gathered in large numbers at sunrise on Sundays to hear his message under a wide-spreading willow near the Philadelphia Navy Yard, along the Delaware River. During the week, smaller gatherings met the evangelist in Philadelphia neighborhoods. He taught theology to students at his home and lectured at several schools, including two female seminaries, on subjects that included botany (in which he was considered an "adept"), chemistry, and sacred and secular history. He authored the lyrics of several hymns, edited religious periodicals, and founded the first Baptist theological school in the United States. Pertinent to his role in Mitchell's preparation for Dartmouth, although not seen as such at the time, Staughton had translated Greek grammar and two editions of the collected (Latin) works of Virgil and authored "botanical, mythological, and historical notes" on Virgil. He was a fervent opponent of slavery at a time when the first antislavery and abolitionist societies in America were galvanizing support for political and financial influence.[12]

Having heard glowing reports, Mitchell attended a funeral service presided over by Staughton. (Funeral sermons were considered a particular forte of Staughton's.) The oration on the occasion, as Mitchell recalled seventeen years later, was on "the holy rest of heaven," with the text from Matthew 11:28: "Come unto Me, all ye that labour and are heavy laden, and I will give you rest." Mitchell attended more church services led by Staughton and became convinced of the necessity of faith for salvation and that one must "look to Jesus alone for righteousness and strength" rather than rely on "works," the modification of one's behavior through daily efforts. Mitchell experienced "no sudden change" but gradually emerged from a period of being "quite low in mind" and came to feel "a calmness in believing in Christ, and a delight in him to which [he, Mitchell] had before been a stranger."[13]

Mitchell had several private conversations with Staughton. A "memoir" of Staughton notes his readiness to discuss spiritual matters privately with individuals—most, like Mitchell, unnamed—and contains many quotations from his correspondence.[14] In his "Outlines," Mitchell wrote only that he greatly valued his conversations with Staunton in Philadelphia and Payson earlier in Maine. In the context of his "religious experience," written nearly seventeen years after his first meeting with Staughton, these two men were the religious guides he considered significant and to whom he wished to acknowledge his debt. He did not write about his feelings when he approached these clergymen, or of their initial reactions. Yet, as with his oblique references to Captain Prentiss in Portland, Mitchell's wording conceals an element of drama. He was a nineteen-year-old former sailor with obvious African ancestry and a French-Creole accent. Although literate, he was probably lacking a formal classical education, and so for Mitchell to have initiated these meetings must have required an extraordinary combination of courage and self-confidence. Approaches to eminent white clergymen by a man of color might have been rebuffed, perhaps callously or even with punitive consequences. But Mitchell was not turned away. Payson's and Staughton's willingness to engage in these conversations was remarkable, too, indicative of attitudes significantly more advanced than those of many of his white contemporaries, even those who opposed slavery. After his private conversations with Staughton and further Bible study and prayer, Mitchell sought membership in Staughton's church.

In taking this step to join Staughton's Sansom Street Baptist congregation, Mitchell would have known that the black Baptists of Philadelphia had separated from the First Baptist Church in 1809, a year before Staughton's split with the church. It may seem unusual that Mitchell would have rejected the black Baptists to follow Staughton. Years later, the black church's historian noted with some pride that in breaking away from the white First Baptist Church, "it is beyond controversy that the relations between the white and colored members of the First Baptist Church were of the most cordial and Christian Character."[15] On this optimistic footing, thirteen black members (including nine women) had formed the First African Baptist Church of Philadelphia on June 19, 1809. The congregation had its origins in a small group of fugitive slaves who had fled the "eastern shore of Virginia to escape the cruel treatment of slave masters." The Southern-born Rev. Henry Cunningham, who was not ordained, served as pastor until 1812 while concurrently pastoring a black Baptist congregation in Savannah, Georgia. After his departure, the church did not have a settled pastor for another six years. That Mitchell chose to follow Staughton rather than a fledgling black congregation of former slaves is not surprising. Mitchell, who had no history of servile bondage, was seeking religious guidance. Thus, he chose the path of mentorship and education opened by Staughton. Mitchell would later have opportunities for direct affiliations with Philadelphia's black Baptists.

Mitchell's acceptance into membership of the Sansom Street Baptist Church is documented in an extant manuscript of "meetings of the Church," which seem to refer, in essence, to regular sessions of what would now be called a church board. The names of the minister and certain prominent members were recorded regularly. Sometimes lists of names were followed by phrases such as "and many others," indicating that at least some of these meetings were open to all members of the congregation. Individuals seeking membership, upon condition of baptism when appropriate, "went before" the church leaders and members to be examined on their "faith and religious experience." (Relating one's "religious experience" was a customary requirement for admission to membership in a Baptist church at that time.) The minutes of the meeting on October 16, 1811, read, "Sarah Witham, Rebecca Frazier & Edward Mitchelle appeared before the church & related their religious experience, which being approved, on Motion, Resolved that they be rec'd into Union with this Church after Baptism to be administered at the usual place on Saturday, next at 3 o'clock."[16] Mitchell was baptized, as scheduled, by Staughton on October 19, 1811, and was received into the church on Sunday, October 20. Full of repentance and hope, Mitchell embraced a new life as a follower of Christ. Soon afterward he tested his ability to "exhort," only to conclude that his notion of being suited for preaching was an illusion derived from pride. He relinquished the idea for several years. "If I had any talent to preach," Mitchell decided, "God would show it to the Church, and they would call me to it."[17]

Eager to learn from Staughton, Mitchell found opportunities to meet with his religious mentor during the next nine years. He quite likely attended not only public worship led by Staughton but also classes and discussions that

Staughton conducted for persons interested in theology, especially potential candidates for the ministry. Whatever the forms that Staughton's mentoring took, the evidence of its significance to Mitchell's life and career is ample. Until Mitchell arrived in Portland, his ambition had been to become a ship's captain. His prior studies would have focused on seamanship. When he arrived in Philadelphia, he was still in his teens, not long away from the sea. His motivation might already have been strong, but aside from what he had picked up from Prentiss, Payson, and Beman in Portland, his knowledge of Christian doctrines and theology would have been limited. He would need new resources beyond the Bible alone for his newly envisioned studies and would need guidance and access on where to find them. He would leave Philadelphia nine years later confidently determined to become a minister.

It was probably through Rev. Staughton that Mitchell gained entry to the elite circle of Philadelphia's black religious and civic leaders who, in 1816, formed the Philadelphia African Bible Society. Staughton had a long-standing relationship with American and international missionary organizations and Bible societies. As cofounder and manager of the Philadelphia Bible Society, founded in 1809, he had advocated "a more general distribution of the bible among their destitute fellow-citizen residing in their neighborhood" through "auxiliaries."[18] As in most important issues of both secular and religious life, Philadelphians organized and voiced their programs and actions in separate spheres, and these auxiliaries were no exception.

Among the several auxiliaries formed with Staughton's encouragement in 1816 was the African Bible Society of Philadelphia, with Edward Mitchell listed among the leaders, a group that included the founding clerics of Philadelphia's black churches and the city's leading black citizens:

AFRICAN BIBLE SOCIETY OF PHILADELPHIA

President
Rev. Absalom Jones, St. Thomas African Episcopal Church

Vice-Presidents
Rev. Richard Allen, Bethel African Methodist Episcopal Church,
Rev. John Gloucester, African Presbyterian Church,
James Forten
James Johnson

Corresponding Secretary
Edward Mitchell

Recording Secretary
Russell Perrot [Parrott]

Treasurer
Robert Douglass[19]

Each of the identified church leaders—Rev. Jones, Rev. Allen, and Rev. Gloucester—is an icon in the history of independent African American churches. James Forten owned a sailmaking enterprise located in the Front Street wharves; he amassed "a fortune" and accumulated substantial political and social capital as the city's wealthiest black citizen. The erudite Russell Parrott, who founded the Philadelphia African Literary Society, was a printer and spokesperson for antislavery and anticolonization causes. Both James Johnson, a painter, and Robert Douglass, a hairdresser, were continuously active in black leadership circles. Mitchell, the youngest member of the group, posted meeting notices and sent reports to parent organizations and newspapers.[20]

The Bible Society movement, which began in England in 1804, grew to a worldwide network of religious leaders who shared the common goal of distributing the Bible broadly, especially to individuals and families who had limited resources and were "destitute of the word of God."[21] In Philadelphia's African Bible Society leadership group, only Mitchell can be identified as a member of a Baptist congregation. Since the other clerical members of the group led black churches, this may suggest that Mitchell had a meaningful connection to the small First African Baptist Church, which continued to meet regularly but without stable pastoral guidance. In relating his Philadelphia experiences in the "Outlines," Mitchell mentions, "A few times in some small circle I would try to exhort, but I found my gift so small here, that I again and again gave up the thoughts of preaching." These words provide a hint of his possible connection to the African Baptist congregation. Mitchell remained in his position with the Bible Society from 1816 to 1818, and possibly until he left Philadelphia. Whatever Mitchell's role and standing with the black Baptists and the new African Bible Society, his involvement necessarily ended once he left for Hanover, New Hampshire, in 1820. Other members of the African Bible Society leadership circle remained central actors in Philadelphia civic and religious matters after his departure. Years later, Mitchell would resume work with Bible societies as a settled pastor of a Canadian Baptist congregation.

Free Blacks, Antislavery, and Colonization

Mitchell's association with Absalom Jones, Richard Allen, and James Forten would have given him opportunities to discuss and hear slavery issues as viewed by American free men of color. The American society had only begun to warm to the coming antislavery and abolition debates. The years from 1800 to 1830 have been called an "often neglected period" in studies of abolitionism and African American history.[22] In comparison to the following three decades, the period was relatively quiescent. As the Dartmouth historian Baxter Perry Smith wrote in 1878, the 1820s were a time "before the great problems which have since controlled [American] history were recognized or appreciated among the people at large."[23] Following the War of Independence, the historian James Oakes notes, antislavery fervor waned among whites in the United States and did not fully revive until the 1830s.[24] Antislavery organizations, almost exclusively white, were still cautious and nonconfrontational, relying on "moral suasion," as their philosophy was called, rather than political action.[25] So too were Philadelphia's black leaders strategically cautious in how to induce often hostile Americans to respect and respond positively to claims for equality and full civil rights.

During Mitchell's years in Philadelphia, antislavery discussion and agitation among blacks centered on the controversial plan of the American Colonization Society to encourage the resettlement of slaves and free blacks on African soil. Some black leaders protested that the colonization proposal was impractical and inherently corrupted by contradictory principles. After a period of airing differing views, black Philadelphia leaders coalesced in opposition to the proposed scheme to repatriate American blacks to ancestral origins. Africa's children, once chained and dragged against their will to American shores, were now full Americans with decades of toil and suffering already sacrificed to the nation's growth and prosperity. Moreover, 2,500

Philadelphia African Americans had constructed defenses to protect the city during the War of 1812.[26] For the city's blacks, home, family, religious, and community life were all firmly rooted in Philadelphia's soil.

The American Colonization Society's chief organizer and proponent, Rev. Robert Finley, a Presbyterian minister of New Jersey, hoped to find allies among Philadelphia's philanthropists and social reformers, like Robert Vaux and Benjamin Rush, and from the several organizations with a long history of antislavery activism, however mild. Finley sought support from Staughton, who had a reputation for sympathy to slavery's abolition and a good relationship with black leaders. Finley hoped to enlist Staughton to gain support from Philadelphia's black leaders. Stirred by these and other influences, Richard Allen, James Forten, and Russell Parrott organized meetings—or rallies, as they came to be called—to debate the colonization plan.

Three thousand men and women of color attended the first rally, the Convention of Color, in January 1817, led by Forten and Allen and held in an ancillary space of the Mother Bethel AME Church. Similar gatherings followed over the next three years. Contrary to Finley's hopes, blacks of Philadelphia expressed overwhelming opposition to the colonization proposals.[27] Forten and Parrott reported the consensus of a community meeting, which rejected the resettlement plan as an insult to free blacks who were united with enslaved blacks in having already purchased a stake in American society: "We view with deep abhorrence the unmerited stigma attempted to be cast upon the reputation of the free people of color, by the promoters of this measure. . . . [W]e never will separate ourselves voluntarily from the slave population in this country; they are our brethren by the ties of consanguinity, of suffering, and of wrong."[28]

Mitchell must have been aware of these rallies, which were led by members of the African Bible Society and held just a few blocks from his residence. At home and everywhere, he could not evade the tortured soul of American slavery.

PRINCE SAUNDERS

In the years of colonization debate, Mitchell would have encountered Prince Saunders, a graduate of Moor's Indian Charity School, founded in 1754 by Dartmouth's first president, Eleazar Wheelock, as a missionary outreach to Native Americans.[29] The Charity School coexisted alongside Dartmouth but progressively strayed from its founding aims, admitting increasing numbers of white students. Saunders was the second black student at Moor's. After completing studies and a brief tenure as head of Boston's Abiel Smith School for African children, Saunders immigrated to Haiti. Rising quickly to a quasi-statesmanlike position, he authored a treatise describing progress in the republic and later, with the approval of Emperor Henri Christophe, returned to the United States to recruit American blacks as colonists to Haiti.

In 1818, Saunders lectured twice in Philadelphia, first to a Bethel AME predominantly black audience in September and then to the American Convention for Promoting the Abolition of Slavery in December. While in Philadelphia, Saunders steered clear of the African colonization debate, instead focusing on Haiti as a rising citadel of black achievement. In speaking to the Pennsylvania Augustine Society for the Education of People of Color (the formal sponsors of the Bethel Church gathering), in language and phrasing that reflected his classical education, Saunders delivered an impassioned plea to American black families to attend to the education of their children: "The hope is encouraged, that you will never be weary in laboring for the promotion of the cause and interest of science and literature among the rising generation of people of colour. For upon their intellectual moral and religious improvements, depend the future elevation of their standing, in the social, civil and ecclesiastical community."[30] We do not know if Mitchell attended Saunders' lecture or if he learned that Saunders had studied at Moor's but was subsequently rejected by Dartmouth College in 1811.[31] His mentorship with Staughton and his association with Philadelphia's black leadership certainly would have prepared him to harken to Saunders's message.

Secular Life in Philadelphia

Although Mitchell's religious strivings and affiliations can be documented from the earliest months of his arrival in Philadelphia, information about his family, employment, and home life is harder to find. Definitive evidence of his domestic affairs is found in an everyday transaction that occurred in 1818, seven years after his arrival in Philadelphia. On an early morning in June, Mitchell walked a short distance from his home on Gaskill Street to the office of George Billington, secretary and treasurer of the Philadelphia Savings Fund Society. Opened only eighteen months earlier, and the first of its kind in the United States, the society pursued a charitable mission to encourage habits of moderation and thrift among poor and working-class wage earners. It would grow to be one of the nation's two largest savings bank. Mitchell deposited twenty-five dollars, to become the bank's 227th subscriber. From Mitchell's entry and signature in the bank ledger, we learn important details. He lists Benjamin Ives Gilman as a reference and 55 Gaskill Street as his home address. Another entry, a year later, names Bicknell & Johnson, a new employer, as a reference. After correlating these data with census returns and city directory data, a more complete picture emerges.[32]

Mitchell's employer in 1818, Benjamin Ives Gilman, had relocated to Philadelphia five years earlier to establish a commission business for goods and supplies transported from the Midwest and Southern states. Gilman was the scion of a notable New England family headed by the Hon. Joseph Gilman, a War of Independence patriot who had served in the New Hampshire legislature as representative and senator. In the late 1780s, he partnered with other investors to form the Ohio Company of Associates and became one of the earliest settlers of the Northwest Territory (today, the Midwest). The young Gilman was raised in the pioneer outpost of Marietta, Ohio, on the Ohio River, with federal troops garrisoned nearby to protect settlers from attacks by resisting Native American tribes. As a young man, Gilman traveled to New England to court and marry Hannah Robbins, the well-educated daughter of the Reverend Chandler Robbins, a prominent Congregational minister who had earned a Doctor of Divinity degree from Dartmouth. Gilman and his wife exchanged frequent letters, which were later assembled and chronicled in *A Family History in Letters and Documents*. One letter included a reference to Mitchell.[33]

Gilman began his commercial ventures as a financier and builder of shipping vessels that carried goods between Ohio and eastern and southern ports via the Ohio River. As with Captain Prentiss in Maine, the economic and commercial disruptions of the War of 1812 forced Gilman to abandon shipbuilding. Having established a network of good business contacts, he moved to Philadelphia in September 1813 to launch a wholesale merchandise business in partnership with Otis Ammidon of Massachusetts, who had connections to American and European merchants. Both Gilman and Ammidon lived on Arch Street, in Philadelphia's "high rent" district; they located the

"Gilman & Ammidon" office and warehouse on High Street (today, Market Street).

Mitchell's employ with Gilman probably began in 1816, when he lived within easy walking distance of the Gilman & Ammidon warehouse. The 1816 and 1817 Philadelphia directories place Mitchell's residential address on Burd's Row, a tightly packed strip of shallow two-and-a-half-story residential structures squeezed between South Tenth and Eleventh Streets.[34] The dwellings lined a passageway leading to a small court and finally an alley that opened to Spruce and Locust Streets. The residents formed a cross section of the city's transient, lower-class workers. Residents must have appreciated the favorable location in Center City near Pennsylvania Hospital, churches, and the commercial establishments lining High Street. The directory reported Mitchell's employment as a porter. He was not denoted a "person of color." The identified men of color on Burd's Row included two bag porters, a carpenter, and a victualer. The white families were headed by a baker, a tayloress, a shoemaker, and a laborer.[35]

By 1818, Mitchell had moved to 55 Gaskill Street at the southeastern edge of Center City, a fifteen-minute walk from the central business district. Gaskill was narrower than was typical of streets of the Philadelphia grid, although not classified an alley. Located in the New Market Ward between South (Cedar) and Lombard Streets, Gaskill ran three blocks between South Second and Fifth Streets. The compact dimension of the street created a demographic slice of Philadelphia that later attracted the attention of researchers studying the shifting social dynamics of the city.[36] In the early and mid-nineteenth century, Gaskill Street consistently housed a demographic mixture of ethnic and social classes. In Mitchell's time, there were a few concentrations of black families one block west of his address. His block between South Third and Fourth Streets comprised an ethnic mix of working-class and middle-income individuals and families. His shared household and immediate neighbors were free persons of color with French and Caribbean surnames, distinct from the white middle-class artisans, small merchants, and professionals on the street. The block of row houses that includes his address—which stands today—is described in an 1839 insurance survey as one of six "three story brick dwelling houses and piazzas situated on the north side of Gaskill Street, 13.6 foot front."

The 1816 and 1817 Philadelphia directories record Mitchell's employment as a "porter." A few years later, in 1820, Hannah Gilman, while relating a detail of Mitchell's work for her husband, wrote that Mitchell had been "Benjamin's porter."[37] The Gilman household of Philadelphia had several black house servants, who were occasionally mentioned in Hannah Gilman's letters describing family comings and goings. Mitchell is never discussed in these contexts, and it appears more likely that his job was related to Benjamin Gilman's commercial business. Mitchell lived apart from the Gilman family. His employment tasks as Gilman's porter concerned the handling and manual transport of goods of Gilman's Market Street warehouse to and from the Philadelphia wharves. Porters and "bag porters" were common occupations among black men, ranking in salary and status with common laborers, carters, draymen, and sweeps, but well below the more-coveted positions held by a few successful blacks (barbers and hairdressers) and distinct from mariners and skilled tradesmen.[38]

A WIFE AND FAMILY IN PHILADELPHIA

Mitchell married while in Philadelphia, and we know that "by the time he went to college" his wife and children had died.[39] In 1816, the twenty-four-year-old Mitchell had a wife and two children, but the Sansom Street Church minutes do not mention their names, gender, or dates of birth or death.[40] Mitchell's wife is recorded in the 1820 US Census as head of household at the 55 Gaskill Street location. The census enumerator identifies her as "Legome Mitchell." An unnamed adult male occupant, undoubtedly Edward Mitchell, and Legome were enumerated in the same age category, "26–45," and both were denoted "free persons of color." Legome is likely the "Lagune Mitchell" living on Elizabeth Street in the 1814 Philadelphia city directory and described as a person of color and a washerwoman. As will be discussed, one of Mitchell's children died in 1816 and the other, a young daughter classified in the census as less than fourteen years old, lived with the family in 1820.[41] It is not known whether Mitchell left Philadelphia as a widowed or married man, but it is unlikely that he would have left behind a wife and young child. Thus, we assume they died just before or within the year after his departure in 1820.

DEATH OF A CHILD

A scene of affliction I was called to pass through in 1816
awakened my mind much to the subject of preaching.
—*Edward Mitchell, "Outlines," 1829*

One of Mitchell's children died in April 1816, and his wife and second child a few years later.[42] They all may have been victims of one of the periodic epidemics that beset Philadelphia, although 1816 was not a year in which any of the most severe occurred.[43] The celebrated Philadelphia water system, which since 1799 had brought water to the city from the Schuylkill River upstream, did not extend uniformly or reliably to all households, and certainly did not protect the populace from all pathogens implicated in epidemics. The year 1816, with abnormally cold temperatures and ice days every month of the year, was known as the "the year without a summer" and as "eighteen hundred and froze to death."[44] The extreme cold caused droughts and widespread food shortages in the northeastern United States. The death of Mitchell's first child is recorded in Baptist records. At a meeting of the Sansom Street Church in April 1816, "a letter was presented by br. Mitchell (of colour) wishing to know whether he may be allowed the privilege of burying his child in our burial gr'd, the answer to the question according to a resolution past (Aug. third 1812) was that no coloured person can be allowed the privilege of a burial in our ground and he is referred to the Deacons."[45]

The minutes do not record in detail the response of the deacons but do indicate that the request was denied.[46] The following month, Mitchell, perhaps with the encouragement of a compassionate member of the congregation, presented the church with a bill for seven dollars for the interment of his child's remains. This amount probably represented the difference between the burial fee he incurred and the three dollars customarily paid by members of the Samson Street congregation. The church officials deemed this request "inexpedient to pay, being contrary to the resolution" of August 3, 1812, and, according to the minutes, "the bill was returned."

Whether Mitchell's request contradicted that resolution is questionable. As recorded in the minutes, with perhaps some editorializing by the secretary, the church had resolved in 1812

> that it is inexpedient to grant the privilege of Burial to our Brethren & Sisters of Colour, in our Burial Ground, on acct. of the smallness of the Ground, the expected numerousness of our Congregation, together with the prejudices obtaining in Society, against such a measure, which the Church regrets, it is not in their power to surmount in respect to renting their pews. The Church, however, engages to pay all the expenses to secure them a burial in the ground of the African Baptist Church of this City.[47]

Although the minutes do not specify where the child's remains had been interred, the denial of any recompense to Mitchell seems inconsistent with the spirit of the latter part of the resolution, which may have been an added comment and not a literal part of the stated church policy. There is no indication that Mitchell pursued the issue further. The church minutes do not mention Mitchell's wife or his other child.

Thirteen years later, in his "Outlines," Mitchell wrote, "A scene of affliction I was called to pass through in 1816, awakened my mind much to the subject of preaching." Mitchell's matter-of-fact wording and the finessed language of the church's recording secretary becloud the decision's impact and the emotions that Mitchell must have felt. Undoubtedly he was deeply saddened by the loss of his child, but in the impassive wording, he conveys a sense of sorrow commingled with anger, however ephemeral it may have been. After the rebuff that followed his first bereavement, he probably considered it pointless to make any further such requests of the church. He determined that he "would search the Scriptures more diligently, and obtain in reading such help as might be useful, and leave the event with Providence."[48]

A Call to the Ministry

The prayerful deliberations in the period of bereavement following his first child's death renewed Mitchell's sense of a call to the ministry. Convinced that his call was genuine, he found occasional opportunities for preaching, enough to establish a reputation as a "smart preacher," as Staughton's Baptists in Philadelphia would later inform Mitchell's church in Hanover. For any aspirant to the ministry, regardless of race or educational background, to have been encouraged by Staughton in this pursuit would have been remarkable.

No other blacks are known to have received the sponsorship of the popular reverend.

A few years before he first met with Mitchell, Staughton had expressed concern that although many persons had a newly engendered or revived desire to preach, few were well suited for the ministry. The four most important qualifications for the Christian ministry listed by Staughton were "godliness," "knowledge," "readiness of communication" (also termed "aptness to teach"), and "a divine call."[49] Here one sees fidelity to Calvin. In the introduction to the later editions of his *Institutes of the Christian Religion*, Calvin had stated that the central purpose of that work, and indeed of all his theological writings and teachings, had been to lead people to "true godliness." Calvin had also emphasized "knowledge" (he considered the neglect of its pursuit to be disrespectful toward God's creation) and accordingly promoted education. Exceptional though it must have been, Staughton evidently perceived ministerial potential in Mitchell. And Mitchell would credit Staughton as his primary inspiration. Mitchell's later admission to Dartmouth and his record as a student indicate that he had acquired a significant background in philosophy, theology, and the classics, likely encouraged by Staughton. Mitchell's aptitude for and dedication to independent study may have been extraordinary, but his conversations with Staughton had importance. Mitchell would later name one of his sons Edward Staughton Mitchell, a living testimonial of his indebtedness to the Philadelphia Baptist divine. Staughton's influence would be publicly acknowledged in Mitchell's short biographical entry in the 1881 *Baptist Encyclopaedia*, which read, in part, "having been hopefully converted and baptized by Rev. Dr. Staughton, [Mitchell's] attention was at once turned to the Christian ministry."[50]

FOUR

To Dartmouth College

In the year 1820 Providence so ordered, I came to Hanover.
—*Edward Mitchell, "Outlines," 1829*

In 1820 Mitchell would meet the Reverend Dr. Francis Brown (1784–1820), president of Dartmouth College, and his wife, née Elizabeth Gilman. Brown, a native of Chester, New Hampshire, graduated from Dartmouth College in 1805 and then spent four years as a tutor, first privately in Williamstown, Vermont, and then at Dartmouth, while concurrently studying divinity. In 1809 he had become pastor of the Congregational Church in North Yarmouth, Maine, where he remained until he assumed the presidency of Dartmouth in 1815. Beginning while in North Yarmouth and continuing in Hanover, Brown had engaged in a debate, in print, with Martin Ruter, the Methodist theologian and historian of Christianity, in which Brown defended Calvin and Calvinist theology.

President Brown and the Dartmouth College Case

Brown's call to the Dartmouth presidency at age thirty-one came during a time of turmoil and peril for the college. Dartmouth, along with Harvard, Yale, and Princeton, was one of nine colonial colleges chartered before the American Revolution.[1] Rev. Eleazar Wheelock, an inspired New Light evangelist, founded Dartmouth in 1769 and dedicated its mission to educating Native Americans, English youth, and "others." For a time, the college prospered in its isolated rural setting along the Connecticut River on the Hanover Plain of New Hampshire.

In 1816 the college's board of trustees dismissed its second president,

John Wheelock, the unpopular, autocratic son of Eleazar Wheelock, and appointed Francis Brown as his successor. Wheelock's ouster came after a series of multifaceted disputes with the college trustees. Competing factions formed as the controversy hardened into a standoff. One faction, led by Wheelock and in defiance of the trustees, encouraged the State of New Hampshire to assume a major role in the college's governance. The original trustees created by Dartmouth's charter and led by President Brown resisted. Wheelock and the new trustees appointed by the state succeeded temporarily in removing Brown from office. For a short time, there were two institutions in Hanover: Dartmouth College, led by President Brown and his trustees, and Dartmouth University, headed Wheelock and a new, legislatively empowered board. Most of the faculty and students were loyal to President Brown's leadership. Brown and his trustees filed a suit contesting the state's attempt to take control. After a preliminary round in state courts, the Dartmouth College case came to the US Supreme Court before Chief Justice John Marshall on March 10, 1818. Daniel Webster (Dartmouth class of 1801), future Massachusetts senator and secretary of state, carried the college's case to the court in defense of his alma mater.[2]

Webster's legal argument, delivered for more than four hours, and "a statement so luminous and a chain of reason so easy to be understood," persuaded the justices that the State of New Hampshire's action in usurping the college from its appointed trustees was "repugnant to the Constitution of the United States." With "quivering" lips and tearful eyes, Webster added, quite famously (in Dartmouth lore), a final rhetorical flourish: "'This, Sir, is my case! It is the case not merely of that humble institution, it is the case of every college in our Land! . . . Sir, you may destroy this little institution. . . . But if you do so . . . you must extinguish, one after another, all those great lights of science . . . over our land! It is, Sir, as I have said, a small college. And yet there are those who love it!"[3] Webster and the Dartmouth trustees won the day by a vote of 5 to 1 by the justices. The ruling for many years afterward was considered a landmark, protecting the rights of chartered private corporations (educational and commercial) from state interference. Dartmouth College survived and the competing Dartmouth University was dissolved.

By one account, when word reached Hanover in early February 1819, loyal Dartmouth faculty and students fired cannons, lit bonfires, rang bells, and engaged in "a thousand other unseemly demonstrations of joy."[4] But the price of victory was severe. The three-year struggle had left President Brown thoroughly exhausted, his health rapidly declining from a pulmonary ailment. He began to cough blood, a sure sign of pulmonary tuberculosis. The death of his infant son in January 1818 had added to his stresses, and a restful pause from his labors in the fall of 1819 did not bring relief. His doctors advised a restorative trip south in the hopes of a cure.

President Brown's Journey South

From October 1819 to June 1820, Francis and Elizabeth Brown traveled south from Hanover to Savannah, Georgia, with the faint hope that by avoiding the harsh northern winter he might recover his health. En route south they traveled by chaise, driven by Elizabeth Gilman Brown, who had sent word ahead to her cousin Benjamin Ives Gilman in Philadelphia. Along the way, she maintained a private diary chronicling her husband's relentless decline. From Hanover they proceeded along a well-traveled route through the lower New England states, New York City, and New Jersey before reaching Philadelphia on October 30, 1819. They rested with Mitchell's former employer Benjamin Gilman and his wife, Hannah, for three days before continuing their journey south on November 2. Afterward, Benjamin Gilman left to attend to his commercial interests in Marietta, Ohio, which had suffered significant setbacks related to the 1819 financial panic. Not expecting to return quickly, he wrote on November 21 to his youngest daughter, Elizabeth, in Philadelphia, "If my dear Cousin, Mrs. Brown should call on her return, present my best regards, and assure her that it would have been a great gratification & pleasure to me, to have seen her at Philadelphia."[5] At this point, it was not apparent that President Brown and his wife would require the services of Gilman's former porter.

In the South, the Browns' longest stays were in Columbia, South Carolina, and in the vicinity of Waynesboro, Georgia. Throughout the journey, the Browns benefited from the hospitality and assistance of many relatives, friends, and fellow clergymen and theologians. Initially, a recent Dartmouth graduate, David Lowell Nichols, who also was traveling south to restore his health, accompanied them. Nichols left the Browns at Salisbury, North Carolina, while they were still southbound, but, contrary to at least one account, Mitchell did not "replace" him at that point.[6] Shortly before they reached

Savannah, the Browns unexpectedly encountered Barnabas Gibson Tenney, a relative of Mrs. Brown and a recent Dartmouth graduate, at an inn. From Savannah, Tenney accompanied them on their return as far as Philadelphia, sometimes on horseback and sometimes driving the chaise while the Browns traveled by ship. In Charleston, South Carolina, the Browns met Rev. Samuel Gilman, a Unitarian minister in that city, who was a third cousin of Mrs. Brown. He and his wife, Caroline, were about to embark on a trip to visit family members in Philadelphia.

The Gilmans and the Browns traveled north separately, but by design, they rejoined each other at intervals en route. Upon reaching Philadelphia, on May 23, 1820, the Browns returned to the Gilman home and were greeted and accommodated by Hannah Gilman and her children. Benjamin Gilman was still detained by business matters in Ohio. The Browns remained in Philadelphia for a week, until May 30. Mrs. Brown recorded that on May 24, their first full day in the city, "many gentlemen called upon Mr. B[rown]," and that many more ladies and gentlemen called during the next few days.[7]

Mitchell Hired

While in Philadelphia, the Browns needed to address their need to replace Tenney, who now departed for Georgetown. Additionally, there was the continuing concern for the president's declining health, which alarmed their host. In a letter to her son Chandler R. Gilman at Harvard, written May 30, Hannah Gilman described a scene of despair: "President Brown and his wife were with us eight or nine days, every hour of which I expected would be his last. . . . They have hired Edward Mitchel [*sic*] who was your father's porter, to live with them, one year."[8] The tragedy of the circumstances deepened in Hannah Gilman's telling as she informed her son, "They left us last monday [*sic*] with a hope to reach home, before his death. They were out of money, and Benjamin let him have the within amount—which was to be paid to you—for your quarter bills—when due. They will probably send you the money soon after they arrive."[9]

The "amount" was a bank draft for one hundred dollars. For her son Chandler, this news must have been distressing but not unexpected as he was well aware of his father's financial strains. Already Benjamin Gilman had written a stern letter admonishing his son to strictly conserve his financial allowances: "I assure you, my dear son, that it is with the utmost difficulty that I can raise money for current wants. You can have no idea of the distress prevailing in the Commercial world."[10] Such ancillary details were unknown to Elizabeth Brown, whose crisp diary entry on May 31, 1820, read, "In Philadelphia . . . we hired a man of color for a year who attends us on horseback, named Edward."[11] Her journal gives no details of Mitchell's introduction to the Browns or their impressions of him. He was by then a *former* employee of Gilman's commercial enterprise. Hannah Gilman, whose letters reveal an intimate knowledge of her husband's business affairs, likely provided the relevant supporting recommendation to the Browns regarding Mitchell's integrity and reliability. Others may have contributed. Her houseguests at the time also included the theologian Samuel Gilman, whose presence would have been of interest to Staughton, especially because Rev. Brown, like himself, was a Calvinist and was likely known to Staughton through, among other possibilities, Brown's published debate with Ruter. Staughton would have known of the care that Mitchell had given his late wife and children during their illnesses, and Staughton may, if asked, have passed on confirmatory recommendations to President Brown and his wife.

Mitchell probably had little time to ponder the Browns' offer, and he may not have needed even that. It was the first week of May 1820, and Mitchell faced uncertain employment prospects in a "time of general distress" for Philadelphians still beset by complications of the 1819 financial crisis.[12] He had quickly made a good impression on the Browns, quieting any lingering concerns from their southbound journey. Mrs. Brown had recorded her apprehension in the presence of two African Americans at "a very miserable inn" in Virginia and had thanked God for preserving her husband and herself through the night. But she expressed no misgivings about hiring Mitchell. Although they could not have afforded to pay him much, the Browns' offer of a year's steady employment was undoubtedly a better prospect than he could have expected in Philadelphia.

By 1820, Philadelphia was no longer the "City of Hope" for its black residents. In the 1830s and 1840s, Philadelphians would witness the naked, pent-up wrath of American racist nativism, in recurrent race riots. The City of Hope nearly died and its companion, the City of Brotherly Love, would require energetic resuscitative efforts in the following decades. Despite its attractions and paths to upward mobility, employment for most of the black population remained limited. Ensuing upon the impact of the Embargo and Non-Intercourse Acts, the city had been hard-hit by the Panic of 1819. African Americans lost jobs to white workers, who closed ranks to subvert competition. Blacks were consistently forced to accept low-paying, often short-term jobs, irrespective of training or experience.

Mitchell's nascent dream of becoming a minister would certainly find a guiding example in his affiliation with the erudite, devout, and staunchly Calvinistic Brown. He may have foreseen (or already experienced) the end of his mentorship with Staughton. In another year, Staughton would be named the founding president of Columbian College (now the George Washington University) in Washington, DC—a position that, after long and troubled consideration, he accepted in 1821 and took up in 1823. If Mitchell was aware of Staughton's impending departure from Philadelphia, his own decision to leave was doubtless made easier.[13] Whatever the interplay of thoughts and motives among those returning to Hanover, Mrs. Brown's journal makes clear that her most compelling concern was the impending death of her husband and the urgent need to rest his soul in Hanover. She had hired Mitchell to aid in bridging the ailing president from near death to a peaceful rest.

African American religious leaders later in the nineteenth century would sometimes encourage blacks to leave the degrading stresses and ever-present temptations of urban life in favor of smaller towns and rural byways.[14] Mitchell's familiarity with northern New England from his earlier years in Maine would have encouraged such a perspective, given the salubrious living conditions of rural New Hampshire. The disappointments of his Philadelphia years would certainly linger alongside the many smaller daily insults endured by men of color and, for Mitchell, painfully etched by his church brethren's affront in denying permission for the interment of his child in the Sansom Street Church's cemetery. Surely he was ready to escape Philadelphia and the insults of its people. In leaving Martinique he must have hoped to encounter relief and freedom from the predictable depredations of a society of fixed racial boundaries but instead found a riven American society seemingly helpless to honor its founding declaration of freedoms and the pretty language of its Constitution. No matter where he turned, racial discord stared back at him.

The newly employed Mitchell, once a sailor, then a porter, and now an attendant to a college president and his wife, returned with the Browns to

Hanover, arriving in June 1820. Mitchell was twenty-eight years old, about nine years after his baptism by Staughton and four years since the loss of his first child. Mitchell's association with President Brown was short. In the South, Brown had become "troubled lest he should leave his bones in a land of slavery." He lived to return to Hanover, but his physical condition continued to deteriorate, and he died a month later, at the age of thirty-six. The despairing words of Mrs. Brown's journal chronicled the president's decline. If Mitchell's uncertain fate troubled her daily ruminations and final thoughts, she did not record them.

The death of President Francis Brown in July 1820 could have concluded the terms of Mitchell's employment, but instead he remained in Hanover to study the next four years in preparation for college studies. Throughout his life's journey, Mitchell always seemed to reach points of no return, and Hanover was certainly yet another. And although he had experienced insults in various guises throughout his life, he was not likely prepared for the setbacks he would bear in the gaze of the hoary trustees of Dartmouth College.

"Brought from the South"

The Dartmouth tradition that Mitchell retained some connection with the Brown family after Francis Brown's death is correct. In the details, however, such accounts misread some facts, including the persistent but incorrect assumption that Mitchell had been brought to Hanover from the South as a young boy. The statement by Dartmouth historian John King Lord in 1913 that, following the death of Francis Brown, Mitchell "remained in [Brown's] family on equal terms with [the Browns' own] children" cannot be factually correct.[15] In 1820, Mitchell was a twenty-eight-year-old widower who had been living on his own for about twelve years, whereas the Browns' surviving son and daughter, Samuel Gilman and Mary Elizabeth Brown, were, respectively, seven and six years old when their father died. After Francis Brown's death, Mitchell could not have remained in the home as a de facto member of the family without the appearance of impropriety. More likely, he continued to reside at the Brown home, clearly identified as an employee or as one of several lodgers, as the social conventions of the time did permit a widow to operate a public boardinghouse. Prior to their southern trip, the Browns had provided room and board for Dartmouth students in their home, as did some of the other faculty members and townspeople. After Francis Brown's death, Mrs. Brown resumed and expanded the operation of a boardinghouse for students, and Mitchell, during his first year as a Dartmouth student, was one of six who boarded there.[16] Because of Mrs. Brown's financial circumstances, and the reduced need for his services, it is unlikely that Mitchell continued in full-time employment with the family, but he may have worked for Mrs. Brown part time or intermittently for his room and board while seeking additional employment elsewhere.

Components of the myth that Mitchell had been brought to Hanover from the South while a young boy have a long history. As early as June 1828, during Mitchell's senior year at Dartmouth, Sarah Parrott, while visiting in Hanover, wrote to her mother that she had seen "a Mr. Mitchell . . . whom President Brown brought with him from one of the southern states."[17] Presumably she had heard such an account from someone in Hanover. Those with whom this myth originated knew that Brown had traveled to the South, as far as South Carolina and Georgia, and presumed simplistically that northern free persons of African descent came from the South.

The use of "brought" was applicable in the sense that the Browns paid Mitchell a modest salary and presumably paid for the horse and other expenses of his journey with them. From that recurrent wording, it appears that writers inferred that the decision had been Browns', with Mitchell having had no realistic opportunity to refuse. Such inferences were probably based on the assumption that Mitchell was a minor child, who would have had no say in the matter, considered in conjunction with the enslaved status of most persons of color in the Southern states. The belief that Mitchell had been a young "boy" (a "colored boy" in another account) when he came to Hanover with the Browns derived in part, albeit inadvertently, from a common, disparaging designation applied to men of non-European ancestry. In Dartmouth historical annals, Native Americans were similarly labeled. Indeed, Dartmouth's founding president, Eleazar Wheelock, while operating a school for Native American youth in Connecticut, referred to his bringing some of the "boys" into his home as residents.

A speculation that Mitchell was "most probably the slave—not the servant as he was typically described—of President Francis Brown" was based on a misconception that Brown had "brought [Mitchell] to Hanover from the Caribbean," and is neither consistent with extant records nor fair to the reputation of Brown, an avowed abolitionist.[18] In Pennsylvania, where Mitchell joined the Browns, the purchase of slaves had been outlawed since 1780. Although the recent discovery of Mitchell's baptismal record clarifies this issue, other considerations should have settled the question of slave origin. The census recorded only three slaves in the greater Philadelphia area in 1810 and none in 1820, the year Mitchell was enumerated as a free person of color. The suggestion that Mitchell was probably Brown's slave is, moreover, at variance with Mrs. Brown's statement that he had been hired for one year. Francis Brown's son Samuel Gilman Brown offered a more accurate account in an address at Dartmouth's centennial in 1869, noting that Mitchell "had accompanied President Brown on his return from the South."[19] Brown would have known the circumstances of Mitchell's arrival in Hanover since Mitchell boarded in the Brown family residence when Brown was a mature youth. It is significant, therefore, that he chose this wording in the active voice, rather than saying that Mitchell had been "brought" to Hanover by Francis Brown. The implication, consistent with that in Mrs. Brown's journal, is that Mitchell had been free to accept or decline the Browns' offer of employment in 1820 and had made his own decision to come to Hanover.[20]

The absence of facts naturally led to assumptions, speculations, and statements that have carried into contemporary accounts. One likely source of these errors is the news items published in an antebellum abolitionist weekly, the *Philanthropist*.[21] The July 28, 1837, issue contained a short sketch about a "little slave boy" and a separate unsourced account of Mitchell's achievement in graduating from Dartmouth College. The Mitchell item, which includes the erroneous and uncredited statement that Mitchell had been "brought from the South by President Francis Brown of Dartmouth College," is attributed to the *Emancipator*, an abolitionist weekly published in New York by the American Anti-Slavery Society and edited by Theodore Dwight Weld. The several inaccuracies of the story indicate that the author had not obtained the information directly from Mitchell. The unrelated "little slave boy" story is attributed to an antislavery discourse delivered at a convention in Boston by the British abolitionist Rev. Charles Stuart.[22] Over eighty years later, the *Philanthropist* news items concerning Mitchell and the slave boy were reprinted in a 1918 issue of the *Journal of Negro History* under the heading "Some undistinguished Negroes" (i.e., not well known but deserving recognition).[23] From the printed layout in the journal text, it is not clear that the "slave boy" paragraph does not refer to Mitchell, and later writers missed the absence of a connection. For example, a 1932 article by historian Bella Gross in the *Journal of Negro History* provides a list of slaves and former slaves who had become literate. Gross erroneously names both Mitchell and Lemuel Haynes, who, although he was for a time an indentured servant, was never a slave.[24] The basis for this listing of Mitchell as a former slave was not cited but likely was from the above-noted material in the same journal. Later references to Mitchell as having been a slave are consistently associated with this misstatement (and sometimes additional errors) and should be considered unreliable.

Hanover Baptists and Religious Explorations

If I had any talents to preach, God would show it to the Church,
and they would call me to it.
—*Edward Mitchell, "Outlines," 1829*

Paralleling his experience in Portland a decade before, Mitchell arrived at this new station in life under the protection and sponsorship of a devout Congregationalist family. But in Hanover, Mitchell's Baptist religious identity, now forged in the passion of spiritual conversion and emotional pain, guided his religious affiliations. In the fall of 1820 he sought out Baptists in the Hanover area, finding the remnant of a Baptist congregation that met for services in Etna, a hamlet within the municipality of Hanover just over four miles east of the Dartmouth campus. In his view, these Baptists were "a feeble body, scattered and few." According to the church's history, the congregation had "gathered" twenty-nine years earlier. Another wrote that the church "suffered from the quarrels, upheavals, and schisms typical of small-town churches of the time." By the time of Mitchell's arrival, the brethren had retired past differences. Within a few years they would welcome a new pastor, Elder Jesse Coburn, "a man like David after God's own heart. . . . His care of the church was like that of a kind parent over his children."[25]

Once again Mitchell was fortunate in the people he met. With determination and self-confidence he made known his intent to become a Baptist minister, and in May 1821 he rose to address the congregation. Following the sermon, according to his "Outlines," "One and another of the brethren began to invite and urge me to a more public exercise of my gift." Earlier, in Philadelphia during a period of self-reflection, Mitchell had concluded that "if I had any talents to preach, God would show it to the Church, and they would call me to it." The Baptists at Etna did respond, instilling hope and answering his prayers. During the autumn and winter of 1821–22, he found further opportunities "to exercise [his] gift with them in prayer and exhortation."[26]

Mitchell remained with the Etna Baptists during his college years and would look back on his eight-year fellowship with Hanover-area Baptists with some satisfaction. His "exhortations" had helped his Baptist friends revive their status as a congregation. Their new minister, Elder Jesse Coburn, according to tradition, "laid every brick" of a church completed in 1827. One later source commented that "among those who preached in the new building was Edward Mitchell, a Dartmouth student and Creole 'mulatto' from Martinique."[27]

Mitchell retired from the Etna Baptist congregation after his graduation in 1828. Coburn died in 1832 but his church survives today.[28] Although recollections of Mitchell were distant when a history of the church at Etna was compiled in 1881,[29] Mitchell's membership and participation in the life of this congregation were regarded as a significant contribution. A church historian recorded that he had come "from one of the churches in Philadelphia" and had been "represented to [the Etna church] as a smart preacher." This assessment, another example of Mitchell's ability to elicit favorable impressions, would have come from the Sansom Street Church in response to a request from the Etna church for confirmation that Mitchell had been baptized by immersion and admitted to membership in a Baptist congregation. Opposition to slavery already prevailed in the Dartmouth community and, through Mitchell's influence, extended to the Etna church, as reported in a later history of the church: "It is believed that this fellowship with Mitchell led the church in 1841 to resolve to 'have no fellowship with slavery' nor permit slave holders to become members of the church."[30]

Mitchell probably recognized while in Philadelphia that a more formal education would be advantageous but unreachable, at least not then. Staughton, who considered "knowledge" an essential qualification for a minister, may have encouraged him to find the means of obtaining a college education, although neither Staughton nor Mitchell could have been sanguine about the prospects. Now that he was in Hanover, a village dominated by a "literary institution," as Dartmouth was then characterized, Mitchell determined specifically that he wanted to earn a college degree. In his teens he had chosen to seek a living as a sea captain, and now, with new possibilities before him, he was again determined to excel on a new plane of achievement.

Although many small-town pastors and itinerant revivalists were self-taught or had studied privately with established ministers, an increasing number of the Protestant clergy were college or university graduates, especially among the Congregationalists, Episcopalians, and Presbyterians. These included most of the more highly regarded ministers and theologians of the time and leaders in the Second Great Awakening. Among them were Beman, Payson, Staughton, and Brown (although their doctorates of divinity were *honoris causa*; PhDs and similar doctorates did not appear in North America until after 1860). Understanding Staughton's conception of the positive relationship between scholarship and the pastoral ministry, Mitchell concluded that if he were to preach, he would do so from an intellectually sound foundation. These early influences and decisions became even more apparent as his life progressed. His academic motivations were anchored more by acquired personal standards and a native love of learning than by a desire for prestige among his peers in the clergy or with parishioners. At the same time, he must have realized that a college degree would go far toward allaying any doubts about the abilities of a man of color harbored by those in a position to approve or obstruct his future ordination or call to a pastorate.

Dartmouth Rejection and Student Intercession

Therefore whilst within the precinct of an Academy or College, "let us live," as though we felt the work of time and the importance of improving it.
—*from Mitchell's college essays*

During Mitchell's first years in Hanover, from 1820 to 1824, although specifics are lacking, he doubtless divided his energies between supporting himself and pursuing independent study in preparation for admission to Dartmouth. Presumably he received encouragement and guidance, as well as loans of books, from students and faculty members at the college and from Hanover clergymen. It would become clear that he was well known among Dartmouth students. Having devoted nearly four years to the effort, in 1824 Mitchell felt ready to apply for admission to Dartmouth. First he had to satisfy a requirement certifying that the applicant "sustains a good moral character." The clerk of the Baptist Church of Hanover/Etna wrote, "The Baptist Church of Christ in Hanover, to any charitable religious education society, whom it may concern certify That brother Edward Mitchel is a member in good standing in this Chh. And is esteemed a person of piety, and promising talents."[31] Having earned this favorable endorsement, Mitchell would have to prove himself in entrance exams before gaining admission—or so it seemed.

In 1824, Mitchell passed the qualifying examination and the Dartmouth faculty approved his admission. The decision would need ratification by the college trustees, usually a formality. Perhaps Mitchell counted on President Bennett Tyler, a former resident of Portland, faculty member, and trustee, to persuade his fellow board members. But the trustees at a meeting in the fall of 1824 refused Mitchell's admission. Rather than acknowledging any personal objections or unwritten policies hostile to a prospective applicant of African descent, they cited a concern that Mitchell's presence would not be well received by the students, and this, they averred, would be a detriment to the college.[32] In later years, college officials at other institutions parroted this same rationale in turning away black student aspirants.

Accounts by two of Mitchell's contemporaries tell of his being on the college premises, apparently having begun attending classes (confirmed by Dartmouth essays written in April and May 1824), when he was ordered to leave and sadly returned to his residence.[33] In what has been called the "first vital test [of] the democracy of Dartmouth,"[34] the students, through a committee comprising one representative from each of the four classes at the college, thereupon petitioned the trustees on September 25, 1824:

> We are happy in being able to say, that there is but one feeling throughout the college . . . a desire for [Mitchell's] return. From what we know of Mr. Mitchell's moral character, and intellectual attainments, we wish him every success, and so far from feeling any disrespect towards him on account of his colour or extraction, we think him entitled to the highest praise, that notwithstanding these, he has persisted in his *noble and independent course* [emphasis added]. And should he be permitted to return, and enjoy, with us, the advantages of our institution, we are decidedly of opinion, that every member

> of his, and of the other classes, will cheerfully receive him as a companion and fellow student, and that the feeling of pleasure upon his return, will be as universal, as that of regret was at his departure.[35]

Charles Dexter Cleveland, one of those who signed the petition and who has been described as "relatively dark for a Caucasian," told the trustees that if skin color was a criterion for admissibility to the college, he might himself be disqualified.[36] Their argument thus exposed as specious, the trustees presented no further obstacles. Mitchell returned to his studies forthwith, and thereafter, Dartmouth would memorialize this episode as the source of its tradition of a liberal and progressive attitude on race.

Sarah Parrott, in her letter cited previously, noted that as a student Mitchell was "very highly respected by the government [of the college, i.e., the faculty] and the students." Mitchell's fellow student Alpheus Crosby, reminiscing years later, wrote that "his character, bearing, and intellect were such that he must have been shameless who could have treated him with disrespect." Mitchell graduated with his class in 1828, "without, so far as [Crosby was] aware, a single insult from a fellow student," a conclusion that would be later paraphrased and then canonized in the college history annals. Never again would the trustees of Dartmouth College deny admission to a student because of his race. Crosby characterized this outcome as "one of the brightest honors of the College, its freedom from distinction on account of color."[37]

In a recent retelling by Ore Koren, this early nineteenth-century example of student intercession, relatively mild and decorous by today's standards, was cited as one of the earliest instances of Dartmouth student dissidence and activism.[38] Koren points out that in the previous month of the same year (August 1824), the sophomore class had unanimously challenged the trustees for improperly leveling a disciplinary action on a fellow student, the error of which was admitted but only reversed in the face of the strongly worded student dissent. This episode may have conditioned the trustees to seriously consider the dissent registered on Mitchell's behalf in the name of the "entire student body." Moreover, as Dartmouth professor Raymond Hall wrote in 1986 in recounting the history of Dartmouth's black students, the "Mitchell affair" was the first time the college or the trustees had faced organized student opposition on a racial matter.

Their petition requesting (not demanding) Mitchell's admission was clear in its support of egalitarian ideals contained in the Constitution; it was unequivocal, well-reasoned, and widely supported. The trustees had never faced the intensity of conviction about a racial issue contained in the students' petition, and certainly not the direct expression of individual and group sentiment in the students' testimonies of support of Mitchell's admission.[39]

Dartmouth moved on and Mitchell resumed his classical education in the calmed embrace of a community that understood and rewarded his proven ability and future potential. In the end, both the college and its new freshman student would profit from the lessons of this singular moment in Dartmouth's history.

Dartmouth in 1824: A Time of Evangelism and Transition

Study at Dartmouth College would have been an attractive prospect in the 1820s for a Calvinist student who aspired to the ministry. The trustees, who still included some of those who had ousted John Wheelock, a layman, had perceived and deplored a growing disrespect for Christian values among the students and envisioned a more evangelical orientation for the college. They found a president much to their liking in the Reverend Dr. Bennet Tyler, a Yale graduate and Congregational clergyman, who assumed the office in 1822.[40] Tyler, president throughout Mitchell's four years, has been described "as a spirited defender of orthodox Calvinism . . . far more interested in theological disputes than [in] heading a college."[41] Others have characterized Tyler with more positive wording, noting that he was "eminently successful" in soliciting financial support for the college. On the subject of his presidency, all agree that he was greatly concerned with "the spiritual nature of his undergraduates" and emphasize his preaching, evangelism, and religious fervor. He took an active role in both the preaching and the teaching of religious courses at the college. Tributes to Tyler note especially a religious revival in both the college and the town, which Rev. Asa Dodge Smith, of the class of 1830, deemed thirty-three years later to have been "one of the most remarkable revivals of religion [Dartmouth had] ever enjoyed." The revival climaxed in 1826 during Mitchell's second year of studies.[42]

Under Tyler's leadership, Dartmouth, like most other US colleges and universities at that time, was unequivocally a Protestant Christian school. According to Dartmouth historian Leon Burr Richardson, "a person whose creed was not thoroughly Calvinistic [would not] have stood much chance of appointment to the teaching force or of election to the board [of trustees]."[43] Each morning at four-thirty a bell could be heard throughout the village of Hanover, rousing students for the mandatory prayers in the chapel at five o'clock (or, in winter, as soon as it was light enough for the president to read the Bible). Other mandatory sessions of prayer were held later each weekday, and four mandatory services of worship and prayer each Sunday. Students conducted Saturday-evening religious meetings for the village.[44] Required course reading included *Evidences of Christianity* and *The Principles of Moral and Political Philosophy*, by William Paley, an English philosopher and educator who popularized notions of "natural theology" in explaining God's existence.[45] The "philosophical theologian" Jonathan Edwards's treatise on the *Freedom of the Will* and Joseph Butler's *The Analogy of Religion, Natural and Revealed* were the subjects of other courses. More than half of Mitchell's contemporaries at Dartmouth became clergymen, although, except for one who changed his denominational affiliation later in life, no others were Baptists.[46]

Shortly after Tyler's election to the Dartmouth presidency, the college raised its requirements for admission. The Dartmouth College catalogue in the 1820s stated, "For admission into the Freshman Class it is required that the candidate be well versed in the grammar of the English, Latin and Greek languages, in Virgil, the Greek Testament, Dalzel's Collecteana Graeca Minora, Latin and Greek prosody, Arithmetick, and Ancient and Modern Geography; and that he be able accurately to translate English into Latin." As noted above in reference to Mitchell's admission, it was further required that each candidate for admission "produce a certificate, to the satisfaction of the Immediate Government, that he sustains a good moral character."[47] College preparatory schools in New England, so-called academies, oriented their curricula toward prepping students to meet such requirements. Mitchell had had no such advantage, and without the means to engage the services of a tutor, admission to the college had presented a formidable challenge, which he nonetheless met.

The Dartmouth faculty, including the president, numbered eight or nine plus one or two tutors during each of Mitchell's student years. The total enrollment in the "Academical Department" (i.e., not including the medical students) ranged from 140 to 174 while he attended. Mitchell's classmates were between fourteen and twenty-five years old when they enrolled as freshmen; at thirty-two, Mitchell was the oldest. There was a single curriculum for all. Classical Latin and Greek literature, both biographical and philosophical, figured prominently, especially during the first year. More modern philosophical literature gradually succeeded the classical in the second year and dominated the philosophical component of the curriculum for juniors and seniors. "Exercises in Reading, Declamation, Translation, and English Composition" and similar subjects were required throughout a student's four years.

Algebra, geometry, and other branches of mathematics also had a prominent place in the curriculum during the first two years. Apparent concessions to the development of more marketable skills, specified in the college catalogues although largely ignored in histories of the college, appeared among the second- through fourth-year courses, with the inclusion of various kinds of mensuration and surveying. Navigation might seem a surprising requirement in view of Dartmouth's inland location, but it was commonly included in American college curricula at that time, probably more because of the mental challenges it presented and the knowledge of the universe to be gained from its study. In that subject Mitchell presumably had a distinct advantage. Astronomy and chemistry were also required. Hebrew was not included, but Dr. Daniel Oliver, a medical faculty who also taught philosophy, was a scholar of that language, and other faculty members may have had a reading knowledge. Nor were modern languages included in the regular curriculum, but instruction could be arranged privately.[48] The format of the courses generally consisted of assigned readings, followed by "recitations" in class. Each student was required to prepare a declamation and a composition every four weeks, and one member of the senior class presented a dissertation following the evening prayers each Tuesday.

Mitchell's Dartmouth Essays

The Mitchell family fonds at the McCord Museum of Canadian History in Montreal, Quebec, contain thirty-six manuscripts in Mitchell's hand composed while he was a Dartmouth student. Some may have been course assignments, but probably most were written for the required presentations of "compositions" and "dissertations." At least two were presented to student literary societies, a regular exercise in their programs. As it is unlikely that many student essays from Dartmouth in the 1820s are extant, this repository provides rare insight into academic life at the college during that period. Allowance must be made for Mitchell's having been in his thirties while the other students at the time were younger, and for his having determined before entering the college that he wanted to be a clergyman. Even so, his essays probably did not differ substantially from those of his fellow students. They indicate that he entered Dartmouth with well-developed abilities in composition and grammar and an excellent English vocabulary. They also suggest that his earlier guidance by Staughton and his extraordinary autodidactic preparation had included studies of theological and philosophical subjects. That his preparation had indeed been largely self-taught is substantiated by his fellow students' reference, quoted above, to "his noble and independent course."

The manuscripts include the following:

First on thy friends, deliberate with thyself
Nothing that is human made is not sometimes reduced
to destruction
Translation of Demosthenes First Philippic
Know thyself
A thousand furlongs of sea for one acre of barren land
Many men, many minds
Religious bigotry
A criticism on Orpheus' visit to hell
Benefits of the Reformation on the human mind
Honour and dignity
Spring
Memoir on Buchanan
The theatre
Disappointment
While we live, let us live
Humility a necessary precursor to great attainments
The disposition to regard the early periods of society, as periods
of virtue and happiness

The brave love mercy, and delight to save
Knowledge of history enlarges the powers of the mind
Strange enjoyment of a bliss unsent
Christian eloquence
Duties of one generation to it successors
Reflection of President Hancock before signing the Declaration of Independence
Ignorance and folly of the Atheist, apparent from study of nature
Cowards are cruel
The obstacles in the way of Christianity in the Turkish Empire
Nature has impressed a various bias on the minds of the multitude
The moral senses
Translation of Latin or Greek text
Homily on John 9:1–41
Practical points on John VIII
Harangue of Antony over the dead body of Caesar
Inferences from Dr. Paley's definition of virtue
Is a vivid and ardent imagination an admirable enhancement?
Is the Age of Pericles or Leo X more glorious?
Memoir of Buchanan for Social Friends

Which essay topics were assigned and which were chosen by Mitchell is not indicated. A few, such as "A criticism on Orpheus' visit to hell," were probably either assigned outright or selected by Mitchell from a limited list of approved topics. Some essays have brief annotations and comments added by faculty members who were quick to point out obvious missteps in reasoning or logic.[49] The faculty margin notes do help verify that the hand-scripted essays are original products of Mitchell's college work.

One essay was on the importance of "Know thyself," with the premise that one who has studied human nature in himself is better prepared to understand human nature in others and in society. (Human nature had been a major topic in Joseph Butler's writings, which had a prominent place in the Dartmouth curriculum.) Mitchell concludes his essay with an eye to the future. "How important then is this [self-]knowledge to our own interest? Let the student then with all his getting, get this noble science. It is this that will buy a foundation for his future greatness." Another essay was on mankind's innate love of society, "First on thy friends, deliberate with thyself," subsequently supplemented by an essay on "The disposition of mankind to regard the early periods of society, as periods of virtue and happiness." Another topic was "Christian eloquence." Philosophical subjects predominate, but a few are on topics that, although related to Christianity, are somewhat more mundane. An essay on "The obstacles in the way of Christianity in the Turkish Empire" was presented at a meeting of the Society of Inquiry Respecting Missions.

Some of the topics indicate the directions that Mitchell's later theology and preaching would take, notably "The moral senses," in which he states, in wording that had been used by many philosophers, Christian and otherwise, that "It is obvious that man was made for action," and that "all men have a moral faculty." Mitchell's emphasis on the "moral senses" suggests that the works of Butler and Edwards may have impressed him, although in this respect he seems to have been somewhat at variance with Paley. (Paley's attitude toward that subject, being perceived as somewhat ambivalent, would soon cause his work to lose favor in the universities. Emphasis on the humankind's "moral faculty," or an innate "sense of right and wrong that made sin truly sinful," in accord with the mid-eighteenth-century writings of Francis Hutcheson, was increasing during Mitchell's student days and early years in the ministry.) This emphasis in Mitchell's essay was probably in harmony with the views of most of the Dartmouth faculty, especially those who had established Butler's and Edwards's works in the curriculum, but perhaps not entirely with the theology of President Tyler, as suggested by the latter's identification with Old School Calvinism.

In an essay on the "Benefits of the Reformation on the human mind," doubtless in accord with the views of some Dartmouth faculty and probably with their encouragement, Mitchell took exception to the theological and moralistic authoritarianism perceived in Roman Catholicism. He wrote that "the human mind, for ages, under the domineering insolence of the Roman See, has been in the most abject state of vassalage. Men were not permitted, nor, while the chain of superstition was held fast, were they disposed to think for themselves."

Moral philosophers of the time, according to historian Daniel Walker Howe, were "valued . . . for their reconciliation of science with religion." The quest for indications of "intelligent design" in nature, sometimes using this wording that has become associated with more recent controversy, was much in vogue among theologians.[50] In his essay on the "Ignorance and folly of the Atheist, apparent from study of nature," with his statement that the development and growth of a new plant shoot provides evidence of "intelligence and design," Mitchell was in harmony with Butler, Edwards, and, in this respect, also with Paley, especially with Paley's widely read and much-reprinted *Natural Theology*. This essay was probably quite typical of student essays in the 1820s.

In his essay on "Religious bigotry," written in his sophomore year, Mitchell deplored the expulsion of Jews and Moors during the reign of Philip III, king of Spain from 1598 to 1621. In another essay, "The theatre," which would not be so well received at Dartmouth now as then, he decried the lack of respect for religion and Christian values that prevailed in theatrical productions. He called for libraries to be searched for copies of the offensive dramas, which he proposed should be burned in a public "auto-da-fé." His professor added a note saying, perhaps dryly, "Your plan has been tried" and cited examples from history, but if he held objections in principle, he did not explicitly state them.[51]

A lot was going on in theology in the United States during Mitchell's years at Dartmouth, much of it in New England and some at Dartmouth itself. These developments, discussed further in chapter 4, undoubtedly impacted what was taught, and how, at Dartmouth, what was available for reading, and what was discussed among the students. Little evidence exists, however, to indicate how much Mitchell or other students, in the relative isolation of Hanover in the 1820s, were aware of these theological currents and their influence on their own learning environment.

Mitchell's emphasis on the "moral sense" philosophy, while at Dartmouth and later, suggests that he may have been impressed not only by Butler and Edwards, as noted above, but perhaps also by such philosophers and theologians as Richard Baxter, Francis Hutcheson, and Anthony Ashley Cooper, the Third Earl of Shaftesbury. On the other hand, Mitchell may not even have heard of some of those theologians, as the Dartmouth curriculum and the literature available on campus provided no specific introduction to their works. None of those writers is mentioned in his student essays, nor did he include references to other philosophers and theologians, even those whose works he surely had read, such as Calvin, Edwards, and Paley. His awareness of the thoughts and works of theologians of earlier centuries, and of the controversies among pre-Reformation and early Protestant theologians, may have been quite limited at that point, more so, probably, than he realized. Staughton, who promoted the Calvinist Baptist theology and who would not likely have considered it necessary or appropriate to give equal attention and status to other schools of theological thought, had introduced Mitchell to Christian theology.

The faculty at Dartmouth, although generally Congregationalist rather than Baptist, likewise identified themselves as Calvinists. They would have promoted the philosophy and theology that they espoused. Earlier theology to which Calvin had taken exception, or later theology that expressly diverged from that of Calvin, might seldom have been presented except perhaps as discredited ideas or even heresies, to which little attention need be given by the undergraduates. Consequently, the opinions that Mitchell expressed in his student essays probably did not depart significantly from what he had heard from Staughton and in his Dartmouth classes and encountered in assigned readings. Perhaps because of the relative uniformity of the theology to which he had thus far been exposed, from his freshman year onward he wrote on such subjects with remarkable confidence and, seemingly, even with a sense of authority.

Dartmouth Social Societies

Alpheus Crosby, of the Dartmouth class of 1827, reminiscing in 1869, observed that there had been at Dartmouth "much less of 'barrack life' than was usual for a college" in the 1820s. He attributed this in part to the college's provision of so few residential rooms; most of the students in the 1820s had been dispersed in boardinghouses around Hanover. Another factor was the average age of Dartmouth's students in Mitchell's years, which had been greater than that of students in most other colleges and universities. Because few of the students came from well-to-do families, they were generally frugal. "Great plainness in dress and furniture, and great freedom from all forms of expensive amusement and dissipation," prevailed, according to Crosby; "there was a strong public sentiment among the students in favor of good order, studiousness, virtue, and piety."[52]

No matter how strict and earnest the spiritual and religious tone of college life, Richardson observed, an outlet for "masculine companionship" was afforded through literary societies, "whose members vied to pledge, not brawn, but brains."[53] From the 1780s until the advent of Greek-letter fraternities in the 1850s, social life centered on the Society of Social Friends, of which Mitchell was a member, and the United Fraternity (the "Socials" and the "Fraters"). By the time of Mitchell's enrollment, the Dartmouth administration had become concerned that the escalating rivalry between the two societies had given rise to undesirable conduct detrimental to the college. Accordingly, every student, upon matriculation, was arbitrarily assigned to one or the other society, with the predictable consequence that their significance in the social life of the college waned.

Rather than owning "houses," these two societies, and all other student societies, shared the use of an assigned room in a college building. Dues were minimal, if any, but through donations (the members "taxed themselves to the utmost of their means")[54] and user fees, the societies assembled library collections that were, for a time, superior to the notoriously meager library of the college. By the 1820s the libraries of the two main societies included about three thousand volumes, giving students access to ideas of notable theologians of their own time and earlier. The societies offered a forum for "literary composition, oratory and debate" by individual members.[55] One of Mitchell's presentations to the Social Friends was on "The Age of Pericles"—for him, an unusual departure from subjects related to Christianity. He commented in the introductory paragraph that "Little can be written (by a freshman) within the limits of an essay." His next essay to the Social Friends was a "Memoir of Buchanan," concerning a Church of England missionary and educator in India. (Staughton had been especially interested in Baptist missions in India and had written a book on the subject.)

At least five other student societies existed at Dartmouth during Mitchell's student days, as well as several debating groups within the respective classes.[56] Programs of the Theological Society featured the presentation of "exercises" on theological topics and, beginning in 1824, discussions of such topics at the meetings.[57] For a time it had a library of its own. Whether Mitchell participated in this society is not known, although his interests suggest the likelihood. Mitchell did join the Society of Inquiry Respecting Missions, which had been organized in 1821 by students who felt "the importance of a more extensive knowledge of mission to enable [them] to ascertain [their] duty and prepare [themselves] to promote the Redeemer's kingdom."[58] Admission required the unanimous approval of the existing membership. Members presented exercises and dissertations generally related to the state and progress of Christianity in foreign lands. It, too, had a library. The society's minutes show that on November 4, 1825, Mitchell presented a dissertation on "Obstacles to the progress of Christianity in the Turkish Dominions," an essay preserved in the McCord Museum. On August 7, 1826, following a dissertation by fellow student Sherman Hall entitled "A comparative view of the old Spanish and the present system of government as they may affect the progress of the Christian religion in Spanish America," Mitchell was appointed to a committee to "confer on this subject." He also led the closing prayer at that meeting.

The Society of Inquiry was not free from dissension. In October 1826 it voted to dissolve and to donate any property it might have accumulated to the Theological Society. Shortly thereafter, some of its former members, along with other students, formed a new society with the same name, but with a new constitution and with its interests perhaps more strictly focused on bringing the gospel to the "Heathen." Mitchell may not have participated in this new society; he was not among the signatories to the constitution. Following the record of the dissolution of the old society in 1826, no minutes appear in the minute books until those for August 1831, by which time there was yet another constitution, suggesting that the society between 1826 and 1831 had been small and relatively inactive. Mitchell was probably not a member of the Handel Society, Dartmouth's and Hanover's "town-and-gown choral society" (with a tenuous historical connection to the present-day society bearing that name). Despite the stimulus to interest in sacred music provided by the Second Great Awakening, membership in the Handel Society was low during Mitchell's years at Dartmouth, never exceeding twenty-two during the 1820s.[59]

Mitchell was not a member of the New Hampshire Alpha Chapter of Phi Beta Kappa, which had not yet assumed its present role of honoring academic achievement. Before a national reorganization in 1845, it was, according to a history prepared by one of the chapters, "a society of kindred spirits, similar in its basis of membership to [a] present-day [social] fraternity, and in the character of its meetings to a debating or literary society." At Dartmouth, it was the first fraternity that was a chapter of an organization represented at other schools and was considered "exclusive" or "aristocratic," with dues of four dollars, presumably yearly. After 1819, according to John King Lord's history of Dartmouth, interest in this society declined, although recurrent attempts to perpetuate its presence at Dartmouth continued until other national fraternities displaced its social role.[60]

Tuition, Room, and Board

Mitchell, along with five other students, roomed at Mrs. Brown's during his first year as a Dartmouth student, in 1824. The Browns had moved in 1819 into the residence, a prominent colonial structure lying across from the Hanover Green and abutting a lane that led to the college cemetery. The house suited the needs of Mrs. Brown, her son, her daughter, and six Dartmouth student boarders. The following year, Mitchell moved to the home of Mrs. Brown's niece, Sarah Gilman, who had herself left the Browns' house in 1823 upon her marriage to William Chamberlain Jr., a professor of Latin and Greek.[61] Mitchell stayed in this house for three years, from 1825 to 1828. This continuity in his accommodations with the Browns and Chamberlains appears to have been amicable among all concerned.

William Chamberlain Jr. had graduated from Dartmouth in 1818 and joined the faculty in 1820. He was five years younger than Mitchell and the youngest member of the Dartmouth faculty. He had moved into a large house on College Street, which gave space for a growing family and student boarders.[62] Most Dartmouth faculty supplemented their "meager salaries" (seven hundred dollars annually) with rental income.[63] Chamberlain's wife, Sarah Little Gilman, was probably influential in the decision that brought Mitchell to her household, since the years she had lived with her aunt, Mrs. Francis Brown, overlapped Mitchell's time in the Browns' household. Mitchell was the Chamberlains' only boarder in the first year, and afterward two other students joined him.[64]

Chamberlain, the Greek and Latin studies faculty instructor for Dartmouth, may have taken a special interest in Mitchell's scholarly progress. For Mitchell, their association had a lasting influence. His exposure to the language and literature of the classical scholars deepened his lifelong scholarly study of biblical sources and references. At the time of his death, an obituary eulogized Mitchell's religious and scholarly devotion, noting that "in the very last years of his life you would find him reading the Bible in the original languages."[65] Chamberlain may have welcomed the opportunity to host a student of African descent. He held strong antislavery views, aligning his support with those who favored gradual over immediate abolition. The same year Mitchell joined his household, in 1825, Chamberlain rose to the podium of a Fourth of July celebration in Hanover to call slavery "contraband by the law of Nature . . . and forbidden by the whole tenor and spirit of the religion revealed in the Gospel," and to declare, "There is no property to a private man in the life and natural faculties of another." Shortly after Mitchell left Dartmouth, Chamberlain's rising stature on the Dartmouth faculty abruptly ended. He contracted tuberculous pneumonia and died in 1830, a severe loss to his students and the college community.[66]

Neither college publications nor newspapers of the time nor Mitchell's extant writings provide further information on his days on the Dartmouth campus, in or outside of his classes. The college, because of its small size at the time, neither needed nor produced many official publications, and no newspapers reported everyday events of Hanover and Dartmouth during Mitchell's years. The official catalogs of the era are preserved, but we find no other locally published items that might have offered glimpses of Mitchell and his classmates. (Several short-lived "student" and "village" periodicals, weekly and monthly, were successively published at Dartmouth or in Hanover at intervals of varying duration during the late eighteenth and early nineteenth centuries, but none were published during Mitchell's years as a student.)[67] Fortunately, the class of 1827 would later publish a commemorative memorial to their years at the college, which includes a passage describing Mitchell's trials at the time of his admission along with numerous vignettes that add insight to the character of the Dartmouth experience as lived by Mitchell in the mid-1820s.

Financially, the four years between Mitchell's arrival in Hanover and his enrollment at Dartmouth and his subsequent four years as a student were times of struggle and sacrifice. Whether or not he remained in Mrs. Brown's employ after arriving in Hanover is uncertain, but whatever his employment, it evidently provided at least for room and board. During his four years at Dartmouth, the tuition, which included a library fee, was $28 per year, and total expenses—including tuition, room and board, firewood, and the "usual incidentals"—were estimated by the college trustees at $101.87 per year.[68]

(The purchase of books, it would seem, was not among the major expenses generally faced by Dartmouth students at that time.) A five-dollar graduation fee, which went to the president of the college, was imposed at the completion of studies, and one dollar was charged for the diploma.

Mitchell would need outside help in meeting his college expenses, a predicament he shared with many of his classmates, who were typically sons of small New England farmers. Mitchell's Baptist brethren of Etna attested to the worthiness of his aspirations and the certainty of his financial need, writing on September 21, 1823, in a letter addressed "to any charitable or religious education society," that "it will aid the cause of Christ by granting him assistance . . . as he wishes to acquire an education the better to qualify him for the work of the ministry, for which work the church has given him licence, and knowing his entire inability to obtain it at his own expence."[69]

In response to this and possibly other entreaties, he received financial assistance from the Massachusetts Baptist Education Society, in May 1824, August 1825, May and December 1825, and August 1828—each time in the amount of thirty or thirty-four dollars.[70] The 1828 contribution was attributed to action on Mitchell's behalf by the president of the society, the Reverend Dr. Thomas Baldwin of Boston. The Baptists' ecclesiastical leadership had for more than a decade actively recruited "pious young men" for the ministry and funded their educational expenses through regional philanthropic societies, knowing how far their ordained pastors lagged in the attainment of formal training relative to other major denominations.[71] The Dartmouth treasurer's records note cash payments, mostly between six and seven dollars, received from Mitchell for college fees twice per academic year.[72] The addition of interest charges during Mitchell's last two years implies that meeting those expenses had been difficult. Also recorded are periodic receipts of fifteen or twenty dollars, designated "allowance from charity fund," a ten-thousand-dollar scholarship resource secured through the fundraising efforts of President Tyler to ensure that worthy indigent students could access a liberal classical education without straining the limited college treasury. This fund was long known as the Charity Fund, but later called the Ministry Scholarships.[73]

Even with basic tuition and fees supported from philanthropic or personal resources, most students required work to pay for other living expenses, and the college's schedule made appropriate allowances. The Dartmouth calendar comprised three terms per academic year, with a seven-week break in January and February and shorter breaks in August/September and May/June. Most students were permitted to extend their winter break to three months or sometimes more to earn more money where employment was available. Teaching in the public schools was a common practice among Dartmouth students. The students generally taught during the winter break, when the need for their pupils' labor on family farms was least pressing. Despite the low pay, such employment was "eagerly sought and competition was great."[74] Mitchell taught school at New London, New Hampshire, twenty-eight miles southeast of Hanover. In Crosby's opinion, by teaching in local schools, Dartmouth students acquired "new dignity of character, a new view of the relations of pupils and teachers, and a new sense of the objects of study."[75] A history of New London recalls the "predominance of the Baptist belief" in earlier times, and the town archives note that Dartmouth students had been employed as teachers during the early years of the town's school system (although not specifically mentioning Mitchell, but later confirmed by Baptist).[76] Baptists there may have communicated with their college-town coreligionists in seeking a teacher for the town's schools, or Baptists in Etna may have communicated with those in New London on Mitchell's behalf.

A Distinguished Class of Ministers and Antislavery Advocates

Nearly all of the students at Dartmouth in the 1820s were from the northeastern States—most from New Hampshire and Vermont, with a good representation from Massachusetts. Although antislavery sentiments were emerging in New England, the students more likely would have heard or read disparaging generalizations and "scientific" racial theories that ranked African races as inferior to Caucasians in the "Chain of Being."[77] The majority of Mitchell's classmates would enter postgraduate fields as clergymen, educators, and missionaries. Many appear to have shared a common bond to the moral, ethical, and religious calling to serve for the improvement of the human condition. The religious climate (discussed below) would inspire the initiated and convert some minds and souls still open to influence. While the liberality and isolation of Hanover and Dartmouth may have sheltered faculty and students from societal prejudices, most students were from rural environments and would have had very few real examples of slavery and bondage to inflame or confuse whatever intellectual or emotional attachments they held. Above all, few would have encountered African Americans in non-servile positions before coming to Dartmouth, and none could have known of or met any college-graduated black students, as one of the first would live among them in their college years.

Mitchell's example as a person of color would not have turned any against the race, and may have developed or reinforced positive attitudes among some. To his classmates, Mitchell embodied a new representation of persons of color, derived not from the relationship of master and slave or employer and servant, but from a fellow student granted claim to an equal educational status. Whatever their previous views and experiences, Dartmouth students were united in rallying to Mitchell's defense when he was denied admission. Over the next four years, they would recognize Mitchell's seriousness of purpose, academic success, and religious faith, which for some would strengthen any abolitionist persuasions and moderate attitudes on racial issues.

Some of Mitchell's classmates became prominent in government, in academia, and among the clergy. The best known, and the most notable in the context of abolitionist history, was Salmon P. Chase (1808–73). Chase became a leading opponent of slavery in the US Senate and later, as secretary of the Treasury, was the most passionately abolitionist member of President Lincoln's cabinet. He was sixteen years old when he came to Dartmouth, entering the college at the same time as Mitchell. Admitted with advanced standing, Chase graduated in 1826. He had spent his early years in Cornish and Keene, New Hampshire, northern inland towns where he would have seen few if any African Americans (although some African American families lived near Cornish, in Croydon and Newport) and possibly harbored the negative racial sentiments and attitudes common to small New Hampshire and Vermont towns.[78] Before coming to Dartmouth he had worked and studied with his uncle, Episcopal bishop Philander Chase, in Worthington and Cincinnati, Ohio, on the Ohio River, a forward battleground in the pro- and antislavery conflict.

Ten personal letters written by Chase during his student days at Dartmouth, including originals and published versions, survive: three to his cousin Joseph A. Denison Jr. in Royalton, Vermont, and seven to fellow student Thomas Sparhawk. Later letters to Sparhawk have also been seen.[79] Mitchell is not mentioned in these letters, but on one occasion Chase did refer to people of color. While Sparhawk was teaching school in Concord,

New Hampshire, Chase wrote, "I hope you will meet with no difficulty in the management of the *blacks* which are entrusted to you to shape out after a workmanlike manner" [emphasis Chase's]. According to Frederick J. Blue, one of Chase's biographers, "While at Dartmouth, [Chase] had indicated no awareness of the one black student among the undergraduates."[80] Chase had entered Dartmouth as a junior and probably had limited contact with Mitchell since there was no significant curricular overlap across the classes. They both belonged to the Social Friends literary society, and Chase was its president for one year. Chase did not aspire to ordination to the Christian ministry and probably had not participated in theological discussions to the extent that Mitchell and many other students did. His views on American slavery were not fully formed (or at least not yet declared). In the early 1830s, according to Blue, Chase "remained a colonizationist and showed little sympathy for the abolitionist position. . . . He did not believe that the two races could live together 'except under the constraint of force, such as that of slavery.'"[81]

Chase "expressed no special interest or sympathy for anti-slavery concerns until the summer of 1836," when, on July 31, he became acutely aware of the harassment of James G. Birney, the white abolitionist editor of the *Philanthropist,* by anti-abolitionist mobs in Cincinnati, where Chase was practicing law. Chase's sister, Abigail Chase Colby, alarmed by a rampaging mob looking for Birney, had taken refuge in Chase's home. The next day Chase rescued Birney from a mob that, with at least the passive acquiescence of civil authorities, was out to tar and feather him. Even then it was the cause of freedom of the press rather than the abolition of slavery that moved Chase to activism.[82] Although, in Blue's view, Chase's "early associations indicated none of the intensity with which he was about to join the anti-slavery crusade," an almost Pauline conversion ensued. It was "at that time," according to Chase himself, that he "became a dedicated opponent of slavery and the Slave Power."[83]

Among Mitchell's other fellow students, Alpheus Crosby, who later wrote so favorably of Mitchell in his memoir of student life in the 1820s, became a professor of Greek at Dartmouth. He was known as a "radical anti-slavery man."[84] Henry Shedd, who had represented the class of 1826 in signing the petition to the trustees on Mitchell's behalf, steadfastly supported abolition as a frontier minister in Ohio, denying communion to slaveholders and on at least one occasion "not hesitating . . . to brave the rotten eggs of a howling mob."[85] Charles Dexter Cleveland, who had signed the petition on behalf of the class of 1827, became a professor of classical languages. He was an active abolitionist who served as president of the Anti-Slavery Society of Philadelphia and was a lifelong friend and confidant of Chase. Benjamin Labaree became a minister and Middlebury College's longest-serving president. In the 1840s, the college became embroiled in a public controversy over the rejection of a black student from Philadelphia, which Labaree justified with the statement that "Middlebury is not inclined particularly to encourage negroes from all parts of the country to resort here for education. . . . Colored young men in Vt. and States adjacent, who would naturally fall to us, we will cheerfully receive."[86] In 1849, Middlebury did admit its first self-identified black student.[87] Asa Dodge Smith, a future president of Dartmouth, was in the class of 1830 and also became known as an abolitionist. In contrast, Ebenezer Allen (class of 1826) moved to Texas and became a "radical secessionist." Charles Backus Dana (class of 1828) became the rector of an Episcopal church in Alexandria, Virginia, in 1834, where he was Robert E. Lee's pastor and became a close friend of Lee and members of his family; in 1861, he moved to Mississippi. Moses Norris Jr., from Mitchell's own class, became a US senator from New Hampshire. He supported slavery and once dragged a Baptist minister from his pulpit when that minister spoke in favor of abolition, but he was also noted for his hospitality to Frederick Douglass when the latter visited Pittsfield, New Hampshire. William Thurston Boutwell, Mitchell's classmate and fellow boarder at Professor Chamberlain's, became a Presbyterian missionary to people of the First Nations in Michigan and Minnesota.

Graduation and Reverberations

Mitchell graduated from Dartmouth College with thirty-nine classmates on August 20, 1828. A lengthy news item prepared by the college and copied to national presses detailed the events and rosters for the two-day exercises: guest speakers, student orations, faculty names, graduating class lists, and the ascendancy of Rev. Nathan Lord to the presidency, succeeding Bennet Tyler. The news from Hanover carried an upbeat tone reflecting renewed confidence in the college's mission a decade following the favorable outcome of the Dartmouth College case argued before the US Supreme Court in 1819. Now it was claimed that "the advantages afforded by this ancient Institution for the prosecution of a thorough course of classical and liberal education are . . . not inferior to those held out by any other in our country."[88] The news reports listed all graduates of the class of 1828 without reference to race, hometown, or birth origin. Nor was attention invited to the unique circumstances of Mitchell's contested admission. For the times, this would have been the norm. The society had not yet swollen with passion over the fate of Africa's children enslaved on American soil. The voices of antislavery and abolitionism had not fully awakened. Few would have noticed or cared about the improbable event of a black man graduating from college in a small New England village. At that time, Dartmouth had no interest in drawing attention to this particular milestone.

Only after he had left the United States on his missionary call to Canada did public notice appear recognizing the trailblazing steps taken by Mitchell and, before him, the two self-identified black college graduates of 1826, John Brown Russwurm of Bowdoin College and Edward Jones of Amherst College.[89] The year was 1834 when Rev. Calvin Stowe mentioned the three college graduates in a speech before a gathering of the Cincinnati Colonization Society in Ohio. Reverend Stowe is better remembered as the husband of Harriet Beecher Stowe, his second wife, but he had been closely affiliated with Dartmouth when he met and married his first wife, Eliza Tyler, the daughter of Dartmouth president Rev. Bennett Tyler, who led the college throughout Mitchell's four years and presided at the graduation. Stowe was an 1824 graduate of Bowdoin and a professor of Greek at Dartmouth from 1830 to 1832.

In June 1834, Stowe came to the podium a day after a lengthy address by Rev. Lyman Beecher, his future father-in-law. Both spoke in opposition to the radical abolitionists' call for immediate emancipation and defended the aims of the African Colonization Society, which in Stowe's view offered "immediate relief" from the prejudicial degradation of blacks, which, "unjust and wicked as it is, will not be subdued at once; nor will the negro find *immediate emancipation* from the oppression of public sentiment." He recognized that the pace of change might be slow but cited positive signs that racial "prejudice is not universal and unbroken": "I have known three black men, Russwurm, of Bowdoin College, Mitchell of Dartmouth, and Jones of Amherst, to study without insult, and graduate with honor. . . . I once myself introduced a black man (a Mr. Butler, of Canada) to the students of Dartmouth college, whom he wished to address; and they listened to him with the utmost decorum and attention and sympathy."[90]

As Stowe spoke, over two million American blacks, almost 90 percent of the black population, were in bondage. And the three college-educated blacks he named had already left the country—Russwurm to Liberia, Jones to the British Colony of Sierra Leone, and Mitchell to Lower Canada. The story of three black college graduates was barely noticed. Mitchell had moved on, away from the pressing concerns of a nation increasingly at odds with its Constitution's humanitarian ideals. Stowe's wife, Eliza, died a few months later. Years later, his second wife, Harriet Beecher Stowe, would lend her pen to a novel, *Uncle Tom's Cabin* (1852), that would awaken Americans to the brutality and suffering of American slavery.

Emancipator Article of 1837 and Responses

In 1837, nearly a decade after Mitchell's graduation, only two more black men had graduated from American colleges, and none from schools in New England. Various factions of antislavery protest and activism had gained momentum. The wealthy abolitionist Arthur Tappen perhaps thought it useful to remind the public that educational attainments were indeed still possible for the oppressed blacks. As editor of the antislavery newspaper *The Emancipator*, he published a short article under the title "An Interesting Fact" that was reprinted in numerous local and national newspapers:

> Edward Mitchell, a colored man, was brought from the South by President Brown of Dartmouth College. He soon indicated a desire for mental cultivation, on being brought within its influence at college. He was prepared for entering the Freshman Class, was received as a regular student, and went through all the classes to a full and honorable graduation. He was uniformly treated with respect by his fellow students throughout the course. He was graduated in 1828, and is now a settled pastor of a Baptist church in Vermont. It is refreshing to meet such a fact: it should be mentioned in honor of Dartmouth. –Ib.[91]

No one seemed to notice the several inaccuracies (for example, Mitchell had left Vermont four years earlier), but radical abolitionists objected to its congratulatory portrayal of New England liberal largesse. The first volley came from the editor and publisher of the *Vermont Telegraph*, Orson S. Murray, a controversial antislavery activist. In republishing Tappen's article, he appended a sharply worded protest accusing the *Emancipator*'s editor of giving undeserved praise to New England and its private colleges for purporting to advance the cause of education among free blacks. In fact, Murray argued, it was a demonstrably flagrant misrepresentation "to make it believed that colleges in general, in New-England, open their doors to students without regard to color." He rebuked the Dartmouth trustees for their initial denial of Mitchell's admission, labeling them "slaves to prejudice," and commended the students, who had, in his view, "to the honor of human nature be it said—resolved at once that Mitchell should be returned and replaced among them, or they would withdraw from college."[92] Murray was attacking conservative antislavery advocates for overstating claims of progress based on such rare and isolated events as Mitchell's graduation. His criticism had a good factual basis. In the decade after Russwurm, Jones, and Mitchell had graduated from Bowdoin, Amherst, and Dartmouth, only two self-identified black men were confirmed to have graduated from a US college: John Sykes Fayette, from Western Reserve College (today, Case Western Reserve University) in 1836, and William G. Allen, from Oneida Institute in 1844. In the ten years since Mitchell's graduation in 1828, there had not been one self-identified black graduate from a New England college.[93]

The controversy continued across four successive weeks in the *Vermont Telegraph*'s columns, from July 12 to August 2, 1837, drawing statements from antislavery organizations and free blacks who described an intractable landscape of opposition to educational access. Reverend Joseph Tracy, also a newspaper editor, concurred with Murray but from an entirely different perspective. An 1814 Dartmouth graduate, Tracy worried that public "agitation on the subject" might discourage New England colleges from considering blacks for admission. His brothers, Ira Tracy and Ebenezer C. Tracy, were also Dartmouth graduates—Ebenezer in 1819 and Ira in 1829, one year after Mitchell. Tracy claimed that only one New England college was known to have rejected a black man because of color[94] and further public "excitement" might encourage other schools to "close their doors against them." Exaggeration of progress would only inflame public opinion, he added;

> We know Mr. Mitchell. . . .Very early in his ministerial life we invited him to our pulpit at our table. He preached for some weeks to the Baptist church where we then resided [Windsor ca. 1831]. The country had not then been thrown into a ferment about the complexion of its inhabitants, and, in the interior of New England at least, a sensible, modest man, like Mr. Mitchell, might pass for what he was worth.[95]

Another respondent reminded readers of how much the country already had been "thrown into a ferment." Rev. Theodore S. Wright, a respected African American seminary graduate of Princeton Theological Seminary (not affiliated with Princeton University), recalled incidents of white community outrage and opposition: "Look at New-Haven, at Canterbury, Conn., at Canaan, N. H., and you will see how they treat the attempts to give the colored any thing like a fair chance . . . They keep us down, drive us out of their schools, mob and break up our own schools, and then point at us in scorn as an inferior race of men."[96]

In 1831, citizens of New Haven, Connecticut, had voted 700 to 4 and blocked the construction of a "Negro College" for industrial training. Three years later, Prudence Crandall of Canterbury, Connecticut, attempted to open her small private day school to young black women but ultimately fled to Kansas to escape the militant backlash. In 1835, the townsfolk of Canaan, New Hampshire, ended the brief operation of an integrated private school established by white abolitionists. The men of the town hitched a team of ninety-five oxen to the wood-frame school building and dragged it a hundred yards from its foundations, forcing the students to flee.[97] Among the retreating black students escaping the ire of the Canaan mob was Thomas Paul Jr., son of Rev. Thomas Paul, pastor of the First African Baptist Church in Boston. Paul Jr. would return to New Hampshire in 1837 as a freshman at Dartmouth College and graduate four years later as Dartmouth's second black graduate of the college (Samuel McGill, an African American of Baltimore and Liberia, graduated from Dartmouth's medical school in 1839). In 1841, the year of his graduation, the young Paul spoke before an assembly of Boston's abolitionist community. His friend and early mentor William Lloyd Garrison published Paul's remarks in the *Liberator*. Whatever benefits he may have enjoyed from his Dartmouth education, Paul was unmoved by any sense of progress in America's regard of free men of color:

> The great characteristic of American slavery, and that which distinguishes it from all other species of oppression, is that hatred of the free colored man which makes his condition little superior to that of servitude itself. . . . Though his flesh is not bared to receive the lash, and his limbs are unfettered, yet he feels his immortal mind dragged to the dust by a weight far more galling than chains, and more torturing than fetters.[98]

In contrast to Mitchell, Thomas Paul Jr. had a community of African American support in his hometown of Boston, where he returned after graduation. Even there he would encounter divisive currents of racial discord among blacks and between blacks and whites. Ultimately, he left his position as headmaster of the Abiel Smith School for black children.[99]

President Lord and Nineteenth-Century Dartmouth Record on Blacks

In this welter of inertia among colleges and universities, increasing societal animus toward blacks, and opposing ideals espoused by abolitionists, Dartmouth seemed to find a way. In the decades before the Civil War, Dartmouth would admit twenty black men to pursue baccalaureate and medical degrees—eight to the college and twelve to the medical school. Nineteen entered during the administration of President Nathan Lord. Under his thirty-five-year leadership, the college expanded its faculty ranks, substantially enriched the endowment, and increased the physical dimensions of the campus to a size that would be recognizable today. He also took the unusual step of reversing his once liberal position in the slavery debate and issued a divinely inspired counterpoint to arguments of Garrison abolitionists.

But first, President Lord was known as a moderate antislavery advocate, a position consonant with the progressive climate of the Dartmouth campus. Alpheus Crosby pointed out that Lord

> was actually a "firm" Calvinist, and had been significantly involved with various abolitionist groups, opposing even the plan of colonization. He was even elected to the position of Vice President of the American Anti-slavery Society in 1833 (Kirsh). He felt strongly for

> the enslaved and oppressed, and his thinking lied with Rogers, Pillsbury, and Garrison—the "most intense radicals in the anti-slavery movement."[100]

In 1841, Lord was quoted in Charles Stuart's antislavery publication: "This Institution has no [dis]respect of nation or colour. . . . In 1828, a coloured gentleman, named Edward Mitchell, graduated at this college."[101] Lord's statement came the same year of Thomas Paul Jr.'s Dartmouth graduation.

Later in the 1840s, Lord became troubled by statements from radical abolitionists who questioned the infallibility of the Bible. Garrison wrote that to say "the Bible is divinely inspired" and stated that "to say that everything contained within the Bible is to be believed . . . [is] absurd and pernicious."[102] Appalled by such heretical statements and the strident tone of abolitionist rhetoric, Lord retreated from public view and turned to the Bible in search of God's word on the subject. He emerged from a period of reflection with changed views and on a mission to proselytize his newly enlightened opinions. Lord reversed his previous stance—that slavery was wrong because it was contrary to moral behavior and contrary to God's "Law to Love"—and sanctioned the publication of his freshly authored proslavery tracts, which were happily circulated by Southern slavery proponents. Crosby, first a student and then a colleague of the president, concluded that Lord was "honestly convinced that slavery is not, of itself, a moral evil, or, by necessity, politically injurious, but is essentially an ordinance of the God of Nature and Revelation for the ends of his general government."[103]

Lord's divinely inspired personal views, now broadcast to a national audience, could not be ignored by the Dartmouth community. Far out of step with students, faculty, and trustees, and under pressure from his Presbyterian colleagues, he resigned the college presidency in 1863. Despite his outright proselytizing that "Divine Providence" blessed America in its embrace of slavery, Lord's tenure as president is noteworthy for the nineteen black men who absorbed the classical literature taught in Dartmouth's classrooms and learned anatomy, physiology, and clinical care at its medical school. By way of explanation without apology or censure, Crosby noted, "Although he believed that a curse rested upon the negro race, he was yet ever ready to lift it, as far as human power could accomplish that end. He was anxious for their elevation and Christian education. Christian culture, and not mere political emancipation, he was sure, offered the race the best opportunity for improvement."[104]

Lord died in 1870, two years before Edward Mitchell. Lord, of course, knew all the black men who came to Dartmouth in the antebellum years, including Mitchell, and established close personal ties to several. During his tenure, of the twenty men of African ancestry who were admitted to Dartmouth, sixteen graduated, and the four nongraduates each pursued careers as educators during Reconstruction in the South and Midwest. Among these men were abolitionists, physicians, educators, Reconstruction-era politicians, a lawyer, and a daguerreotypist.

Selected Sketches of Antebellum Dartmouth College Black Students

Samuel Ford McGill (class of 1839), a Liberian colonist originally from Baltimore, secured funding to study medicine in Baltimore. Medical students there successfully opposed his admission, which prompted hasty arrangements by the Maryland Colonization Society to send McGill north, first to Vermont and then to a warmer reception in Hanover. In 1839 he graduated from Dartmouth Medical School, the first African American to receive a medical degree in the United States. He returned to Africa as Liberia's first black physician. Later in his career, he served for five years as acting governor of the Maryland colony in Liberia.[105]

Edward Draper (1855) received a bachelor's degree from Dartmouth in 1855. He studied law in Baltimore before sailing to Liberia with great expectations to become the colony's first college-educated lawyer. Unfortunately, he died young. His wife, Charlotte Gilburg Draper, published a volume extolling the virtues of African colonization.[106]

Augustus Washington (1846) during his Dartmouth years mastered the daguerreotype photographic technique. He too emigrated to Liberia. Many of his photos—a remarkable portrait series of black men and women in the early days of the Liberian republic—are preserved in the National Portrait Gallery in Washington. In 1846, before going to Liberia, he also captured the first known photo of John Brown, the rage-filled abolitionist who led the raid on federal troops at Harper's Ferry.[107]

There were abolitionists. In 1835, *Thomas Paul Jr. (1841)* of Boston, the son of a pioneering Baptist cleric, joined white and black classmates at Noyes Academy in Canaan, New Hampshire, thirty miles north of Hanover (briefly referenced above). Established by abolitionists, the academy attracted twenty black students, including future black leaders Henry Highland Garnet and Alexander Crummell. After its abrupt closure, Paul returned to New Hampshire for studies at Dartmouth. Following graduation in 1841, he was named headmaster at the Abiel Smith School for black children in Boston, another ambitious effort that was continually threatened by civic controversy. Perhaps reflecting on these events and, more generally, the plight of free persons of color, Paul wrote in the fiery prose of an abolitionist, published in the *Liberator* and excerpted above.[108]

In 1848, another abolitionist, *Jonathan Clarkson Gibbs (1852)*, came to Dartmouth from Philadelphia, perhaps cursing the several other colleges that had rejected him. Upon his graduation, he delivered a class commencement address, as only the second African American to achieve this honor (Russwurm was the first). A white Dartmouth alumnus in attendance wrote that although he believed in the inferiority of the black race, he had to admit there were possible exceptions, Gibbs being one. About Gibb's speech he wrote, "Such was the deserved applause bestowed by the audience for the excellence of his performance that I was tempted to envy his position. He left the rostrum with loud and continued demonstrations of high approbation."[109] Gibbs went on to study at Princeton Seminary and in 1855 was called to the pulpit of the Liberty Street Presbyterian Church in Troy, New York, a northern hub of abolitionist activity. Strangely, he invited President Lord to deliver the sermon at his installation ceremony. Lord consented and came to Troy. Perhaps it was Gibbs's design to liberate Lord from his embrace of slavery. If so, he failed, but many future successes awaited the energetic Gibbs. In the early Reconstruction years, he rushed to the South with missionary zeal. In Florida, he was elected to the state's 1868 constitutional convention and afterward named secretary of state, signing its new constitution. While serving as Florida's superintendent of education, he died unexpectedly at age fifty-two, with questions and suspicions surrounding his premature death. Gibbs was remembered as "the best informed colored man of the state who stood in front of the ranks of his race anywhere. Negroes have lost one of their noblest representatives, our State one of its most valued citizens, and our public school system one of its most intelligent advocates and its best friend."[110]

All of the black medical students graduated and went on to practice medicine, seven in Liberia and five in the United States, including *William Baldwin Ellis (1858)*, one of thirteen black men who served as assistant surgeons in the Civil War. *Louis Charles Roudanez (1857)*, of Haitian and Louisiana Creole heritage, practiced in New Orleans, where he published the first black daily newspaper in the United States and became an outspoken advocate of civil and political equality for men and women of color.[111] *Isaac Humphrey Snowden (1851)* and *Daniel Laing Jr. (1854)* had started medical studies at Harvard Medical School in 1850 before being ejected because of student opposition. Their very public rebuttal was chronicled closely in the Boston newspapers and protested strongly by Boston abolitionists, with whom the two men were aligned. With little fanfare or notice, they quietly resumed studies at Dartmouth Medical School before sailing for Liberia under the sponsorship of the Colonization Society in Boston. They both pursued careers as medical practitioners.[112] These two cases and the known antislavery temperament of the Dartmouth campus suggest collaborations between Boston colonizationists and Dartmouth faculty and officers, but we know of no research or literature on this possibility.

Six of the Dartmouth men went to the South after the Civil War, holding positions of importance during the Reconstruction period, working exclusively in postwar black schools and affiliating closely with black churches. *John Randall Blackburn (1863)* became a professor of Wilberforce University, a black university established before the Civil War, and later a trustee of Ohio University. Three of the MD graduates came to Dartmouth as men of color and left to pursue careers in predominantly white or mixed neighborhoods without public notice of their race. The interesting case of *James Parker Barnett (1854)* illustrates the trials of black men pursuing medical degrees. He completed college at New York University and two years of medical studies at the College of Physicians and Surgeons of New York (now Columbia University's medical school) before being ejected because of his African ancestry. He contested the dismissal, refusing to acknowledge his African heritage and arguing his claims based on the "Rights of Man." The matter carried to the New York State Supreme Court, which ruled that the state had no right to interfere with the operations of a legal, private entity, the Columbia Corporation. Barnett was dismissed but gained admission to Dartmouth Medical School and completed his studies. He joined the practice of Dr. James

McCune Smith in New York; Smith had been the first black American to receive an MD degree, in 1836, albeit not in the United States but in Glasgow, Scotland. Together, Barnett and Smith worked in both private practice and New York public medical institutions. Barnett was also a master-level ranked chess player.[113]

Like Mitchell, the majority of the black men at Dartmouth in the antebellum years did not seek or could not find employment in the United States. Thirteen of the twenty left the country soon after their time at Dartmouth—twelve to the Republic of Liberia, and Mitchell to Canada. For black men with talent and education, few opportunities existed in the United States. Most blacks were enslaved, living out the final chapters of legally sanctioned American slavery. After the Civil War, almost all black Dartmouth alumni remained in the United States. Despite persistent racial barriers in a uniformly segregated society, they successfully pursued careers on American soil. By the mid-twentieth century, 133 African American men had attended Dartmouth, comprising the second-largest number of blacks to enroll in a New England college, after Harvard.

Part II

A SERVANT OF GOD

FIVE

Indefatigable Exertions

I made an appointment for preaching. I have felt since, that this is all that I wish to live for. The assistance that I have often found, I trust from God, together with my early impressions and his providential direction have induced me to believe that it was his will that [I] should preach the gospel of his Son.
—*Edward Mitchell, "Outlines," 1829*

Mitchell had come to Hanover in 1820 fully awakened to the call of the ministry and had been introduced to the Hanover-area Baptists as one possessing the rhetorical skill of a "smart preacher." Soon, as he later wrote, "the brethren began to invite and urge me to a more public exercise of my gift."[1] In the Baptist tradition, which sanctioned preaching by members who possessed motivational gifts, the church leaders on January 20, 1822, prepared a letter stating that Mitchell had "for more than one year improv'd with us upon the tallant which God heath given him by way of prayer, exhortation & doctrine," and that they considered it their duty "to approbate him with his religious gift to any people where God in his providence may call him."[2] This endorsement carried Mitchell to other pulpits in the Hanover area, including the Baptist Church of New London. Five years later, while a student at Dartmouth, he received the anticipated call from the Etna congregation. On April 29, 1827, the congregation voted "to call [him] to ordination as an evangelist." Now designated a "licentiate," or one who was licensed to preach, he could now anticipate formal ordination.[3] Then as now, ordination generally ensued after one had first been settled as the pastor of a congregation.

Most Dartmouth graduates entering the ministry (one-half of Mitchell's graduating class) progressed smoothly from the academy to a settled pastorate. It must have given Mitchell some pause to contemplate in what direction to turn. Most free African Americans in the northern United States lived in black communities in the larger cities where churchgoers could and did attend black churches. Nearly all of the African American clergymen in the North at that time served such congregations. Against the grain of prevailing expectations, Mitchell would seek and find a different course. Perhaps he knew of the example of Rev. Lemuel Haynes (1753–1833), a Congregational minister of African ancestry who preached to and led white congregations in Vermont and New York despite occasional resistance and controversy.[4] Mitchell also may have known of Rev. Alexander L. Twilight (1795–1857), a Middlebury College graduate in 1826 and Vermont Congregational minister with undisclosed remote African ancestry that was not discovered until the twentieth century.[5] But Mitchell could not pass for a Caucasian. As a youth in Martinique and while in Philadelphia for a decade before coming to Hanover, Mitchell had lived as a man of color among blacks. Once relocated to the near-monoethnic world of New Hampshire and Vermont, he had communed daily among whites for some eight years and found in his religious and educational labors acceptance and occasional strong support. Could he count on a similar reception as the settled pastor of a New England white congregation?

The membership of the Congregational and Episcopal churches in the larger New England towns and cities, and to some extent that of the Methodist churches, drew from the middle and upper socioeconomic classes and were served by ordained seminary-trained ministers with college degrees. Baptist churches, in contrast, typically recruited their membership among the rural poor. Their congregations were smaller, and fewer of their ministers were college graduates. A Baptist minister's pastoral charge often included two or more churches. Many Baptist congregations were served by unpaid lay preachers, and those ministers who were ordained were often expected to have supplementary means of supporting themselves—as were many men in diverse occupations and professions at that time—usually through farming. Sometimes a minister's remuneration included the use of farmland in partial substitution for a cash salary. Conversely, the expectation that ministers would have other support made it feasible for many small congregations to call ministers.[6] As we shall see, Mitchell in no way resisted this course, his pious and missionary spirit conditioned by experience and faith to sacrifice and service.

In the ministerial profession he now entered, the demand for educated Baptist ministers was strong—as was the religious fervor of the era, where many souls were "destitute of religion" and at risk for eternal condemnation. Such times aroused the missionary spirit of many religiously trained men, and Mitchell had been called to service where it was desperately needed. Half of his graduating classmates also entered the clerical ranks. Although, like others of the class, he was now formally clothed in the academic cloak of a prestigious colonial college, he must have been hyperaware of the negative reception he might receive in predominantly white congregations. In Sutton, New Hampshire, where his formal religious exertions as a settled pastor would begin, he stepped away from the cloistered life of Dartmouth to test the moral conscience of America.

Sutton, New Hampshire, and Ordination

Following his Dartmouth graduation in 1828, Mitchell became the minister of the Calvinist Baptist congregation at Sutton, the next town south of New London, the scene of his college summer employment when he must have made a very favorable impression. By twenty-first-century standards, Sutton might seem to be a rural byway chosen by Mitchell because the isolation would protect against racial animus. Even if true (and it was not), the call to pulpit in Sutton was not unlike that of other Dartmouth graduates who entered the ministry in the early to mid-nineteenth century, whether of Baptist, Congregationalist, or other denominations. If not immediately embarking upon further study at a theological seminary, they likewise began their ministry with small-town congregations or in sparsely populated frontier regions. Francis Brown, after graduation from Dartmouth, had become a minister in the small Maine town of North Yarmouth, and it was from North Yarmouth that he was called to the presidency of Dartmouth. Bennet Tyler, likewise, had been called to the presidency of Dartmouth from a small town, South Britain, Connecticut. The smaller towns were more self-sufficient than today, differing less from the larger towns and cities in having readily available amenities, diverse businesses, and the presence of such professionals as physicians and lawyers.

The population of Sutton in 1830 was 1,424, while that of Portsmouth, New Hampshire's largest city at the time, was 8,032 and that of Manchester, now the state's largest city, was 837. Sutton was considered a promising town, strategically situated on roads to Manchester, Boston, and Portsmouth, and favored with an abundance of fertile farmland, mineral resources, and potential waterpower. The Sutton Baptist congregation traced its founding to 1803 and had nearly a hundred members, although it had been without a minister for the two years prior to Mitchell's arrival. As in many small New England towns, African Americans had established a small presence in Sutton dating back to the 1780s. Several black families lived there and in adjacent Warner while Mitchell was serving the Sutton Baptist congregation.[7] The published history of Sutton gives no indication that they were involved in his call to the pastorate or active in his congregation.

Already a licentiate, Mitchell was ordained an evangelist on August 18, 1829. (The word "evangelist" was commonly used at that time when clergymen were ordained, not only by the Baptist Church but also by the Congregational and Presbyterian churches and other denominations.) Although Mitchell was already a minister at Sutton, the ceremony was held at the church in Etna (thirty-five miles on the northwesterly road toward Hanover), the congregation that had sponsored his candidacy. The ceremony included a sermon by Rev. Ira Person, the Baptist minister at Newport, with several other clergy and notables present.[8] Three days before his ordination, Mitchell wrote the "Outlines of [his] religious experience," probably as a requirement and a statement of his personal creed. At Sutton, Mitchell "preached . . . to good acceptance" for about two years. Despite the brevity of this pastorate, he made a lasting impression. Decades later it was said that "in addition to his natural gifts, he was a thoroughly educated man" and "a fine speaker, by good judges said to be the best ever" to have served Sutton as a minister.[9]

According to a history of Sutton, Mitchell left that town for a "better position in Vermont."[10] Brief pastorates were not unusual at that time, and nothing suggests that either race or theology was relevant to his departure. A history of nearby New London published in 1899 deplored the allegedly "hasty, inconsiderate, hap-hazard way," prevalent among Baptist churches in the nineteenth century, of "not settling, but [merely] employing" a minister, often for a specific, relatively short term. In the 1820s and 1830s many towns in northern New England were in the early stages of their development, and spurts of optimism may have led to expectations for their churches that could not be sustained. Indeed, many small-town congregations could not support a minister year after year—if they paid him at all—especially among the Baptists.

From Sutton, Mitchell crossed the Connecticut River in 1830 to join the Baptist Church of Grafton, Vermont, about sixty miles southwest. Grafton was typical of the Connecticut River Valley villages that Mitchell would serve in the next few years. Favorably situated at the junction of two major stagecoach routes amidst fertile farmlands, water power, and soapstone quarries, Grafton was a flourishing small town by the standards of the time and more populous than today. Although served by Baptist ministers for several decades with little interruption, in 1830 the congregation was without a settled minister. The Vermont State Baptist Convention recruited Mitchell and his immediate successor, Rev. S. A. Estee, to serve as supply ministers.[11] (It was and is a common practice for a church without a minister to arrange with a higher court of the denomination for a supply minister to be appointed until a minister to be settled becomes available.)

A Call to Missionary Work

As Mitchell labored in southern Vermont, the Baptist Convention of the State of Vermont became concerned that the Danville Baptist Association of northeastern Vermont was "nearly destitute of ministerial labours," with only four ordained Baptist ministers to serve eighteen churches. All of the towns and churches were small and the people less prosperous than those in towns to the south and west. In such sparsely settled regions, providing pastoral services was a challenge for all denominations. Provision for the Baptist ministerial needs of the Danville Association would require the services of "missionaries" supported in part by the state convention.

Mitchell's attraction to missionary work had a strong foundation. His principal mentor, Rev. William Staughton of Philadelphia, had long been involved with the missions of the Baptist Church in England and America. In Philadelphia, Mitchell had joined with black coreligionists in forming the African Bible Society in a manner of missionary outreach for the "distribution of sacred scriptures" to black individuals and churches. In that time of spiritual conversion, Mitchell had "felt a peculiar pleasure in reading and researching the scriptures" and "a calmness in believing in Jesus Christ, and a delight in him to which I had before been a stranger."[12] Later, in Hanover,

Mitchell wrote approvingly in two essays about the Christian work of two eighteenth-century British missionaries to India, Rev. Claudius Buchanan and Rev. Henry Martyn. In his junior year at college he had reviewed the missionary work of the Baptist Home Missionary Society in evangelizing "native Indians" of the American West and reported on the church's progress, noting the "very considerable good which has been done by the labours of missionaries."[13]

Thus prepared in mind and spirit, in 1830 Mitchell turned to the north in response to the missionary call of the Danville Baptists. By that time, he probably had no motivation or desire to seek pastorates in America's black communities. Any psychological or emotional ties to America's blacks developed while living in Philadelphia had inevitably eroded with the loss of his family and the subsequent abrupt transition from a diverse urban life into the rural byways of northern New England. As he progressed further northward, he was unlikely to hear or learn of the emerging self-conscious identity among black Americans as expressed in broadsides, public celebrations, and organized meetings and protests. As Elizabeth Rauh Bethel points out in *The Roots of African-American Identity*, the antebellum period provided opportunities for both whites and blacks "to publicly proclaim a collective identity . . . and to strengthen and solidify the boundaries of class and ethnicity that buttressed and circumscribed American politics of self-interest."[14] But such developments were occurring far south of Mitchell's field of labor and were not immediately relevant to his daily personal or pastoral concerns.

Absent direct testimony from Mitchell, we cannot know if he would have been moved by evidence of an emerging activist spirit among American blacks. In Boston, a free man of color, David Walker, published in 1829 a four-part pamphlet, "Walker's Appeal," that called for uplifted consciousness and radical resistance in order to secure the freedoms earned after years of "blood and tears." In Philadelphia, African American leaders, who included Mitchell's former colleagues, rallied to the call of the 1831 First Annual Convention of the People of Color. The assembled attendants manifested an aroused and assertive posture of vigilance and activism among African Americans in demands for equality. The convention denounced the American Colonization Society's African resettlement projects but did endorse black emigration to

Upper Canada, where fugitive slaves and free blacks had established small communities in Toronto and neighboring communities. Mitchell, on the other hand, was headed toward the Eastern Townships of Lower Canada (later Canada East and Quebec) that bordered northern Vermont. This Canadian region would never become a final destination for slave fugitives or free black settlements.

Completely isolated in his northern Vermont–bound world, Mitchell was physically and possibly emotionally unable to respond to the rising concerns in black communities of America. Recognizing nothing but conflict in American racial discourse, Mitchell was moving toward a different vision of future rewards, and he was not alone. In 1831, as he headed toward the Canadian border, the two other college-educated black men, John B. Russwurm of Bowdoin and Edward Jones of Amherst, emigrated from the United States to join blacks at foreign destinations on Africa's shores: Liberia and Sierra Leone, respectively.

BURKE, VERMONT

In 1831, a year after his ministry in Grafton, Mitchell accepted the missionary call to the northern Vermont village of Burke, about forty miles from the Canadian border. His field of labor would encompass several other towns within a radius of about ten miles. In this new role he quickly showed the zeal and dedication that would be recognized as "indefatigable exertions." At the Seventh Annual Meeting of the Baptist Convention of the State of Vermont, in October 1832, it was reported that

> The Rev. E. Mitchell has labored for twelve weeks in the towns of Burke, Newark, Sutton [Vermont], Lyndon, Wheelock and Kirby. He reports that he was cordially received by the people, and that in consequence of his appointment they enjoyed the preached word more extensively than would otherwise have been practical. He has had three Bible classes under his care; one in Burke, one in Newark and one in Sutton. He has not been able to effect much in Sabbath school instruction only in connexion with Christians of other denominations. Since his report last year, some addition [in membership] has been made to the church at Burke, and, he hopes, that the seed sown

> will in due season bring forth fruit. He has received from the before mentioned churches and from individuals about forty dollars, in part pay for his services.[15]

The State Baptist Convention added sixty dollars to his income that year.[16] Although Mitchell's attempts to provide Sabbath school instruction in other denominations achieved little success, it was characteristic of his seemingly boundless energy to go beyond his primary objective of ministering to the widely scattered Baptists in his charge, demanding as that was. Mitchell represented the Danville Association of northern Vermont at several annual meetings of the Vermont State Baptist Convention, served as a trustee of the state convention in 1833, and led one of the prayers at its annual meeting that year. The "untiring" Edward Mitchell was one of the two original members of the state convention's committee on tracts when it was formed in 1833. He preached the opening sermon at the Danville Baptist Association's annual meeting in Coventry, Vermont, that same year, basing his sermon on Hebrews 3:1: "Wherefore, holy brethren, partakers of the heavenly calling, consider the Apostle and High Priest of our profession, Christ Jesus."

MARRIAGE TO RUTH CHENEY

On March 4, 1832, while based at Burke, Mitchell married Ruth Cheney, a daughter of Elder Moses Cheney (not to be confused with the abolitionist from Peterborough, New Hampshire, of the same name and family origin) and Abigail Leavitt Cheney. Moses Cheney was the Baptist minister at Derby, near the Canadian border, about twenty-eight miles north of Burke. The marriage evidently had Ruth's family's blessing, as her father performed the ceremony. The marriage was not recorded by the Derby town clerk, but a public marriage notice was published in the *Northern Osiris* newspaper of Derby on March 15, 1832.[17] State laws prohibiting interracial marriage (so-called anti-miscegenation laws) were common in the United States at that time, but neither Vermont nor New Hampshire had ever enacted them. Local customs in Vermont seemed to be permissive to black-white marriages, which over time, because of the scarcity of people of color in the state, led to a progressive "whitening" of some mixed-race progeny.[18]

Ruth Cheney, born September 10, 1803, in Sanbornton, New Hampshire, was twenty-eight years old at the time of her marriage to Mitchell. She and her twin sister, Naomi, were the second and third of the nine children (not including one that was stillborn or died soon after birth) born to Moses and Abigail Cheney after the deaths of their first two in early childhood. On her mother's side, Ruth was a fourth cousin of the "evangelical abolitionist" Joshua Leavitt. Mitchell's father-in-law was a self-taught minister who had grown up in Sanbornton, New Hampshire. He was regarded as "one of nature's preachers, magnetic and irresistible," and an effective evangelist and revivalist.[19] Moses Cheney had originally been associated with the Free Will Baptists, having worked with the founder of the "northern line" of that denomination, Rev. Benjamin Randall, in New Durham, New Hampshire. After twelve years, following "a most singular vision," he had transferred his affiliation to the Calvinist Baptists. After briefly serving churches in Sanbornton, Meredith, Gilmanton, and Brentwood, New Hampshire, he had come to Derby in 1823 to serve as the first minister of the Baptist Church following its reactivation. While minister at Derby he continued to travel around Vermont, New Hampshire, and Massachusetts as a visiting preacher and revival leader.

Cheney remained the Baptist minister at Derby until about 1838 (beyond Mitchell's departure). His decision to resign at that time was due in part to increasing dissatisfaction with theological trends in the Baptist Church and consequently deteriorating relations with the denominational organization in Vermont. Also, his son Nathan, with whom he had operated a farm in Derby, had left for the superior farmland and more benign climate of Illinois in 1835. When Moses Cheney "sold out at Derby" he renounced formal denominational affiliation. He served as supply minister of the Baptist Church in North Sanbornton for about a year, around 1840, after which he retired from the pastoral ministry and, in 1843, moved to Sheffield, Vermont, where one of his sons resided.[20] Others of Moses and Abigail Cheney's children settled in northeastern Vermont and northeastern New York as adults. It is unlikely that Moses Cheney significantly influenced Mitchell's theology, or vice versa, but it does appear that the families remained close.[21]

According to Moses Cheney's son Simeon Pease Cheney, all of the children of Moses and Abigail Cheney "could sing before they could remember."[22] From 1845 through 1847, five of Ruth's siblings, although not Ruth herself, performed as "The Cheney Family Singers," led by Ruth's brother Moses Ela Cheney. The four male members of that group also became teachers of singing or singing-masters in churches, and some became composers or otherwise contributed to Vermont's musical heritage. Moses Ela Cheney is credited with organizing the first musical convention in the United States. A comprehensive account of the musical activities of the family, however, does not mention Ruth.[23] After Ruth's death, obituaries tell of her strong support of Mitchell's pastoral duties, and his papers contain musical scores and song lyrics, transcribed and preserved, perhaps with her influence.

Resident Minister in Lower Canada

Although he was already charged with the pastoral care of the Baptists in six Vermont towns while based at Burke, Mitchell responded positively to the Baptists' concerns for the spiritual well-being of the increasing population of immigrants in the Eastern Townships of Lower Canada (now Quebec), directly across the border from Vermont.[24] At that time, the Danville Association included not only the Baptist churches of the Caledonia and Orleans counties of northern Vermont, but also some in northern New Hampshire and in several Eastern Townships of Lower Canada.[25] Mitchell occasionally preached to Baptists in townships lacking a resident minister, especially to those in Stanstead and Hatley, where he would later settle. The Baptist congregation in those townships had been organized in 1799 but remained small and with only occasional ministerial guidance.[26]

New England immigrants had come to the Eastern Townships between 1790 and 1830, first as Loyalists to the British Crown and later attracted by the desire to establish farms on affordable, unsettled land. Immigrants from New England far outnumbered those from Britain by 1830. Baptists, who were relatively numerous among the immigrants, sought their own ministers for their newly founded congregations. For a time most of the Baptist ministers in the Eastern Townships and elsewhere in Lower Canada came from New England, although some (not including Mitchell) may have been deterred from coming during the years of the Canadian Rebellions of 1837 and 1838 provoked by various factions contesting British Crown authority over local rule. International events elsewhere strained US–British North American relations during the 1830s but did not affect Canadian residents of the Eastern Townships and Americans of northern Vermont who accorded little significance to the international border between them, often treating commercial transactions as a free-trade zone.

In 1832, the first year of Mitchell's new missionary pastorate based in Burke, the Danville Association held one of its quarterly meetings in the Eastern Township village of Georgeville. Mitchell wrote of three days of "prayer, exhortation, and preaching," in which he had a leading role. "The season was owned of the Holy Spirit," he reported; "Souls were hopefully converted, and twelve persons were baptized on a profession of faith, and added to the church."[27] In the following year, Mitchell returned to Lower Canada with an appointment to serve in Eaton Township and vicinity. He quite likely welcomed, and may have sought, his new position. A history of the Baptist congregation at Burke notes that Mitchell was one of a succession of ministers who had been "employed to preach" but had not been "settled as pastor . . . for the want of a permanent place of worship, and the lack of means to sustain a settled minister among them, they did not prosper as they otherwise might."[28] Prospects were likely brighter in Eaton, and Mitchell's concerns now included the support of his wife as well as the family they anticipated.

The years 1832 and 1833 had been fateful for Mitchell—marriage and now the move to Lower Canada as a settled pastor. Left far behind were any memories of the hectic port cities of Saint-Pierre, Portland, and Philadelphia. Ahead of him lay a largely unexplored landscape of picturesque lakes, virgin forests, and tiny hamlets now filling up with hearty New England families forging self-sufficient communities, far distant from modern conveniences and conventions. To this world that moved slowly and patiently Mitchell brought the passion of the itinerant preacher now harnessed to an expectant pastoral flock. Although he probably needed no additional inducements, in 1833 the British Parliament did vote to abolish slavery at home and in most of its colonies, including Canada. Mitchell may have felt that whatever injuries he had endured from prior racist insults could now begin to heal. Perhaps we can understand that in marching north to a new drumbeat, he never would or could look back.

Edward and Ruth Mitchell moved from Vermont to Lower Canada in the autumn of 1833. Racial factors may have been a factor in their relocation. Notwithstanding perceptions of Vermont as an Underground Railroad gateway to Canada, rural Vermont was far from abolitionist in its sentiments, nor free from hostility toward African Americans. The radical white abolitionist Rev. Samuel J. May, a Unitarian minister who made a lecture tour of the larger towns of Vermont in October 1835, reported that "everywhere [he] was met with contumely and insult"; he was mobbed five times, and his meetings were "dispersed with violence" in Rutland and Montpelier.[29] In rural northeastern Vermont, there were scant numbers of African American residents (although one family from Sutton, New Hampshire, had settled in Derby). But in contrast to these reports of hostility toward abolitionists, neither the reports of the Vermont State Baptist Convention and the Danville Baptist Association nor histories of the antislavery movement in Vermont note any objections to Mitchell's ministry. Nor is it likely that Mitchell's new mission to Lower Canada reflected any change in pastoral relations or a significant break with the Baptists of Vermont. Although he took up residence in Canada, his status remained that of a Vermont missionary bringing pastoral services to Baptists in the Eastern Townships.

Mitchell would never return to America. The other American missionaries sent out by the Danville Association in the mid- and late 1830s all resumed their American lives as settled pastors and raised families. Only Mitchell remained in Canada. Realistically he could not have returned to the United States, where the racial fault line had widened and within his lifetime would fill with the blood and tears of anguished Americans irreconcilably divided on the slavery issue. Mitchell had no personal connections to family, close friends, or communities in the States, and before him lay the opportunity to grow a new family in a community of believers and friends—a place he would call home.

EATON TOWNSHIP

Moving from Burke, Vermont, to Lower Canada, Ruth and Edward Mitchell established their first home in Canada in the village of Sawyerville, Eaton Township, where they remained from October 1833 to November 1837. The church at Sawyerville was one of the oldest Baptist churches in Lower Canada, founded in 1796 by its earliest settlers.[30] It was flourishing in the 1830s, as reflected in the number of baptisms entered into the church minutes. The records of this church state that "On October 1, 1833, Edward and Ruth Mitchell were received into membership by letter, the same day we chose brother Mitchell to be our Pastor." (The authors of the respective reports put different emphases on who decided what. Then as now, it would seem, congregations referred to "having called" or "chosen" an individual to be their minister even when the choice was actually that of a higher court of the church.) Mitchell had had a previous association with the church, having served as the moderator of the ecclesiastical council convened to examine the qualifications of Amos Dodge, a member of the congregation, and recommended him for ordination in 1832.[31]

While attached to Sawyerville, Mitchell was one of four ministers who took turns preaching to a Baptist congregation at Barnston, just over twenty miles southwest of Sawyerville and across Lake Memphremagog from Georgeville. He was also one of two pastors who served the Baptist congregation in the western part of Stanstead and Hatley townships. The other was Rev. Jonathan Baldwin, a missionary from Coventry, Vermont, who became a member of the Hatley congregation in January 1834 and was called to ordination forthwith. Mitchell served on the ministerial council convened to examine Baldwin and approve his ordination. Like Mitchell, Baldwin shared pastoral responsibilities for several small congregations before returning to Vermont after 1840.

HIS MANY LABORS

Although settled in Eaton as pastor, Mitchell's missionary labors had multiplied. In 1834 he traveled "many hundred miles and preached a number of hundred sermons," baptized thirty persons upon confession of faith, and "promoted Sabbath school instruction." After his first year, the Vermont State Baptist Convention reported that "a goodly revival [was] enjoyed in Eaton" and that "in relation to this missionary and the field of his labours, we have reason to praise God, and continue our exertions." That year, in addition to his continued support from the convention, Mitchell received $236.50 contributed by his parishioners.[32] In 1835, under Mitchell's leadership, the Eaton church held a "protracted meeting," or revival, from September 21 through October 5. The church records say that "the session was precious, we have had the presence of the Lord and the out pouring of the Holy Spirit and many souls were hopefully converted unto the Lord, for which we feel truly thankful." The blessings of this "special awakening" continued into 1836, and eleven new members were added by baptism.[33]

In October 1835, in response to a request from a visiting Baptist from La Prairie, Lower Canada, Mitchell traveled to that town, ten miles above Montreal, where he "spent two Lord's Days." He reported that there were many Protestants in that area and a need for evangelical instruction in both English and French. His ability to speak both languages may have been a consideration in this invitation. He found, however, that there were four Protestant denominations near La Prairie, and the "ground [was] not so clear for Baptists as [he] had hoped." In the same communication to the Vermont State Baptist Convention, he called attention to the need for a resident Baptist minister in the west part of Hatley Township.

Although occupied with his pastoral duties in 1836, Mitchell did pause to send forty-three dollars to the Northern Baptist Education Society (successor of the Massachusetts body) in partial repayment of his Dartmouth scholarship. Under the headline "Bread upon the Waters" in the *Christian Watchman*, the society's financial secretary reported, "The moneys acknowledged from him are the more valuable from the fact, that his income is but limited; and . . . that at the time Mr. M[itchell] was a beneficiary, the Society took no obligations of their beneficiaries to refund at any time the amount received."[34] Perhaps Mitchell's pastoral flock in Sawyerville had been especially supportive that year because he and Ruth had welcomed their first child, Edward Staughton.

In 1837, to better support Mitchell and the five other Vermont Baptist ministers in Lower Canada,[35] the Vermont State Baptist Convention arranged with the American Baptist Home Mission Society for funds raised in Vermont for home missions to be directed first to the support of Vermont's own missionaries in Lower Canada, with the national society to receive any funds not thus required (not that there ever were any). Oversight of the missionaries in Lower Canada initially remained with the Vermont State Convention, but chronic financial difficulties, exacerbated by the financial panic of 1837, rendered this arrangement too much for the Vermont Convention to sustain. Oversight of the missionaries was "practically transferred" to the national Home Mission Society based in New York City.[36]

Early Years with the Stanstead-Hatley Calvinist Baptist Society

Of all parts of the Eastern Townships, the west part of Hatley Township—the vicinity of Georgeville and Magog along Lake Memphremagog ("beautiful waters")—seems always to have been closest to Mitchell's heart. This region was the first he had visited while based in Burke, and since the area Baptists were included in the Danville Association, he had had further opportunities to meet congregants. The area was close to the home of Ruth Mitchell's parents in Derby, Vermont, and to the homes of her siblings living in northeastern New York. The early American settlers of the Georgeville area, in the late 1790s, came from New England to take advantage of the relatively cheap, uninhabited land. The Baptists were the first to establish a congregation, some coming from the oldest towns of Massachusetts and Connecticut where settlement and expansion had exhausted the immediate supply of affordable farmland. Those who came to the Georgeville area clustered along Lake Memphremagog, a thirty-three-mile elongated lake basin draining north to the Magog River and nestled amidst first-growth forests, rolling hills to the east, and mountain peaks to the west. The southern third of the lake overlapped northern Vermont in the vicinity of Derby. Midway along its eastern shore was the small village of Georgeville.

In all directions from the village, medium-sized farms interrupted a densely forested landscape, giving the area an unmistakable picturesque character. A road linked Georgeville to the lake's northern terminus at Magog Outlet, a route well known to Mitchell's ministerial labors. It was the same road traveled by the artist William Henry Bartlett in the 1830s and 1840s to record "drawings of the Lake Memphrémagog region [that today] remain some of the most familiar historical images of this area."[37] Served only by mail routes, few concerns of the world interrupted daily life in the community. The first railroads arrived after 1860 to link Georgeville and other Eastern Townships to Montreal and the US Eastern Seaboard.[38] Georgeville's quaint charm and peaceful serenity attracted vacationing Canadians and Americans seeking cool, leisurely summer retreats. One was the nineteenth-century journalist Samuel June Barrows, who wrote, "Georgeville is one of the most stable villages in Canada." Nothing disturbed "the perfect tranquility and peace prevailing there. . . . The purposely constant deliberations of the inhabitants sometimes exasperate the nervous American, but this is exactly the calming he requires!"[39]

Mitchell was another appreciative visitor lulled by Georgeville's isolation and rugged self-sufficiency that awaited religious guidance. He suggested to the Vermont State Convention after his trip to La Prairie that Georgeville and the surrounding West Hatley area should have a resident Baptist minister, expressing tacitly a hope that he would be able to relocate there. Such a hope would not have been unrealistic. The increasing numbers of

Baptists in the Eastern Townships would require more Baptist clergy. At that time, a small, scattered congregation visited by Mitchell, Baldwin, and occasionally other clergymen constituted the Baptist Church of Stanstead and Hatley townships that enclosed Georgeville. The local brethren met in "Conferences," as they were called in the church minutes—meetings for the combined purposes of worship and church business, convening more or less weekly, usually on Fridays or Saturdays in Georgeville. Occasionally members gathered at residences in the Ives neighborhood north of Georgeville, in Magog Outlet, or in homes elsewhere in the area. Entries in the church minutes were very brief, generally noting only when and where a "conference" had met, except for the occasions when Mitchell ("from the Eaton church"), Baldwin, or another clergyman had been present to preach and serve communion. A few entries also record baptisms by Mitchell.[40]

Mitchell's hope, if such it was, of primarily serving the Stanstead and Hatley church was realized in 1837. From the American Baptist Home Mission Society, he received a letter of appointment:

> Dec. 20, 1837
> To the Rev. Edward Mitchell,
>
> [We] appoint you to publish the Gospel in the Province of Lower Canada for the term of twelve months from the time of your late appointment by the Ver Bap. Convention in Oct last to receive from this Committee through the Treasurer of the said Convention three hundred dollars including such sums as you may receive from the people to whom you shall minister.
> By Order of the Committee,
>
> S[pencer] H[oughton] Cone, Chairman
> Luther Crawford, Corresponding Secretary[41]

After four years at Sawyerville, and coinciding with the new arrangements with the American Home Mission Society, Mitchell, although still a missionary from Vermont, became minister to the Calvinist Baptist Society in the townships of Stanstead and Hatley, which included the village of Georgeville. The oldest organized church of the region, dating to 1799, its congregation had experienced the usual trials of small rural congregations, some known to

Mitchell from his prior service as a visiting preacher.[42] In November 1837, he, Ruth, and their newborn, Edward Staughton, moved to a small house and farm along the "Lake Shore" of Lake Memphremagog, three miles north of Georgeville on the road to Magog Outlet.[43]

Baptist services in the Stanstead and Hatley pastoral charge became increasingly concentrated in Georgeville. In later listings of Baptist clergy in Canada, Mitchell was listed as the minister in "Georgeville" or "Magog" rather than in "Stanstead and Hatley," all locations referencing the same congregation. But despite its growth during Mitchell's ministry, the Baptist congregation in Georgeville never had a church building of its own. It met initially in the brick "academy" building in Georgeville. After that building burned in 1848, the congregation met in the "red schoolhouse" that replaced it and still stands today. The school was situated between the larger buildings of the Church of England in Canada and the Wesleyan Methodist Church.[44] The academy building and schoolhouse it replaced were village landmarks that frequently signaled the end of a completed journey.

> Eighteen miles passed on, three of which were on the Lake Memphrémagog (one of the finest lakes of its size, and encompassed by the noblest scenery I have seen in Canada) the sweet little village of Georgeville lying on the shore of this lake, was reached there I spent the night. A very neat school house, which, because of its tower and other appurtenances, might be mistaken for a Church, graces this village. Divine service is occasionally held therein.[45]

Supplementing meetings in the schoolhouse, the Baptists convened in the smaller Ives schoolhouse north of Georgeville and quite close to Mitchell's home.[46]

Although settled with the Stanstead-Hatley congregants, Mitchell continued to serve a wider locus of missionary outreach. This was familiar terrain for him, having served earlier as a "messenger" from the Stanstead and Hatley congregation to the meetings of the Danville Association.[47] Though in Georgeville, Mitchell remained vital and active with Vermont-based Baptists. In 1839 he preached the opening sermon at the Danville Baptist Association's annual meeting in Barnet. When the Danville Association established the Derby Literary and Theological Institute in 1840, Mitchell was named a trustee. The academy envisioned an international role, with its site selected in part because of its proximity to the mission fields in Lower Canada. Several Canadian students were in its early classes.[48] In 1838 the Sixth Report of the American Baptist Home Mission Society recorded that "Brother Mitchell has laboured [in the Eastern Townships] since 1832. At that time there were but two Baptist Churches, and less than sixty members between Durham [a township just west of Richmond] on the west and the great wilderness on the east. Within the same limits, there are now seven churches, and three hundred and sixty communicants."

These fruits of ministerial labors came with sacrifices. In 1841, while traveling, A. H. House, a lay leader in the Barnston congregation, expressed regret that the work of the Baptist ministers in the Eastern Townships was hampered by their need for secular employment to adequately support themselves and their families. He referred to Mitchell as "being in more comfortable circumstances [than a minister previously mentioned], and being blessed with a liberal education, [who] has it in his power to do much good. . . . I doubt not he aims to glorify the great head of the Church, by making the best use of the advantages with which he is favored."[49] But, for Mitchell, there remained significant challenges.

Students from the Baptist Theological Institute in Montreal who toured the Eastern Townships in 1840 reported, "The state of things in the Georgeville church is encouraging, but the field traversed over is too large to be filled up by the indefatigable exertions of brother Mitchell."[50] Although factually true, the students may have underestimated Mitchell's capacity for missionary labors. Mitchell preached to the six other congregations of the Baptist Home Mission Society, most of which he had organized.[51] As was reported at the 1842 meeting of the Vermont State Convention, "It is now nine years since brother Mitchell commenced his labors in Canada under the patronage of the Convention. Through his instrumentality a portion of the desert has been made to bud and blossom as the rose." In those nine years he had traveled by foot, horse, and sleigh 16,646 miles (more than two-thirds the earth's circumference), preached 2,207 times, and baptized 103 persons.

DANVILLE ASSOCIATION WITHDRAWAL

At the 1842 Danville Association meeting it was also reported that Mitchell, "[our] highly esteemed missionary proposes, while he continues in the vicinity where he has so long been, to derive his whole support in [the] future from the people where he may labor," thus relieving his Vermont sponsors from the "burden" they had borne so long. Not surprisingly, the Vermont Convention—already in decline and financially embarrassed—acceded to this proposal, and after 1842 Mitchell received no further financial support from the Vermont State Baptist Convention or the American Baptist Home Mission Society. By this time the numbers of Baptists in Upper and Lower Canada had increased to the extent that the work of several small missionary societies was consolidated in the formation of the Canada Baptist Union in 1844 (which survived only to 1850). Thereafter, the churches in Canada East were no longer included among those in the Danville Association. When the Canadian churches withdrew, the Danville Association resolved

> that we cherish with pleasure the memory of the past years in which we have been associated, the precious seasons of our gatherings, the spirit of Christian love and sympathy, never bounded by any political lines, nor marred by the thought that we were the citizens of different governments . . . we pledge to them a continuance of our love, and pray that God may make them fruitful to every good work.[52]

The weaning of Canadian Baptist churches from their American sources of financial support, although projected as a sign of progress among the Canadian churches—growth in membership and resources to the extent that they could be self-supporting—was in fact necessary given the financially stressed circumstances among northern Vermont churches. After 1842, Mitchell was no longer listed among the ministers in the Danville Association. His affiliation thenceforth was with the Baptist Convention of Canada East, and his pastoral charge became part of the Ottawa Association. He was a Canadian minister, no longer a Vermonter working in Canada.

American Slavery Issues in Lower Canada

In 1841, Mitchell did participate in the committee work of a Vermont Baptist group convened to consider antislavery issues in the nation and before the church. It was during this time that abolitionism in the United States among the white population became active and openly confrontational. Eloquent black abolitionists came to prominence. But Mitchell had left the States in 1833. Racial issues seldom came to the fore in the Eastern Townships of Lower

Canada/Canada East during his years. In the townships of his ministerial work, there were no more than a few blacks.[53] Black Americans and Caribbeans who did come to Canada settled in other Canadian provinces. Before the American Civil War, the first black settlement in British North America was concentrated in the Maritime provinces of Nova Scotia and New Brunswick, where black Loyalists of the American colonies, both free and escaping slavery, had come by sea following the American War of Independence. From approximately 1835 to 1860, Upper Canada/Canada West became a haven for thousands of fugitives of Southern slavery. The small colonies established by free American blacks in Canada, like the ill-fated Wilberforce Colony of London, Canada, also were settled in Upper Canada. The momentum of black flight to Upper Canada increased after the passage of the Fugitive Slave Act in 1850 and the Dred Scott Supreme Court decision in 1857.

In contrast to Upper Canada and the Maritime provinces, the townships of Lower Canada attracted very few American and Caribbean blacks in Mitchell's field of work.[54] The few census-enumerated blacks of Lower Canada were likely descendants of black families that had accompanied some early European settlers and white Loyalists from the United States who brought slaves into the Canada during the late eighteenth century. Some slaves were sold across the border into Canada when slavery was outlawed in Vermont in 1777. Any of their still-enslaved descendants acquired freedom in the stepwise abolition of slavery in British North America that became complete in 1834. Some fugitives from the southern United States did travel to Canada via New Hampshire and Vermont, but most of them, if they entered Lower Canada/Canada East, did so in the vicinity of Philipsburg or Hemmingford, well to the west of Georgeville. On the whole, Lower Canada/Canada East, outside of Montreal, was far less significant than Canada West as a destination. Moreover, Baptists and their churches did not take a notably active role in secular issues in Canada before the 1860s. Studies of Canadian communities of the mid-1880s found that the Baptist followers living in "isolated areas of settlement" exhibited a "tendency to avoid concerns for worldly affairs" and showed little interest in political affairs.[55]

When the Civil War broke out in the United States in 1861, Mitchell was sixty-nine years old and had lived in Canada for nearly thirty years. Most of the Canadian and British North American involvement in that conflict, by sympathizers on both sides and by Confederate agents, was in Canada West and in Montreal and Halifax. Some participants in the Confederate raid on St. Albans, Vermont, fled to Frelighsburg, Canada East, but even that was about thirty miles west of Mitchell's farm in Georgeville. Following that raid, armed men representing the Union cause went to Newport, Vermont, at the south end of Lake Memphremagog, but encountered no Confederate activity.

In the Eastern Townships, where cultural and economic ties with the New England states persisted through the war years, sentiment favored the Union, and some men from the Townships enlisted in the Union army. Mitchell could hardly have been neutral in his reaction to the war, but there is no indication that he or members of his congregation took any active role.[56] Of some interest is the fact the editor of the *Stanstead Journal*—the favored local news source for the Georgeville area, first published on November 6, 1845—editorialized frequently in support of the Union, contrasting its cause to the "villainy" of the rebelling Confederacy. This was editor and owner LeRoy Robinson, who authored Mitchell's sympathetic final obituary and published occasional news items about Mitchell and his congregation. The *Stanstead Journal* never once noted Mitchell's African ancestry. The only census that captured nonwhite racial status in the Georgeville area was the 1861 Canadian Census, in which the census enumerator did not check the column "colored person, mulatto or native" for Mitchell or any family member. Indeed, no blacks were counted in 1861 in the entire Stanstead county of 12,258 souls.[57] One historian of black Baptists wrote that Mitchell "spent the rest of his life preaching to blacks in Eaton and Magog Canada" and erred by failing to distinguish what parts of Canada received the incoming streams of black immigration.[58] With perhaps one recent exception when attention was directed to an eighteenth- and nineteenth-century small slave community and burial ground in St. Armand,[59] researchers of the history of black Canadians have directed their attention to population centers settled by blacks in other Canadian provinces and territories.

Ordination and a Settled Pastorate

Mitchell's new status had civil as well as ecclesiastical significance. As a resident Canadian minister and no longer the itinerant missionary from Vermont, he needed a specific pastoral charge. Arrangements were made and explained in a letter dated December 11, 1843, from Avery Ives, clerk of the Calvinist

Baptist Society of Stanstead and Hatley, conveying an invitation from the church brethren to become their pastor. Mitchell had already served the church in a part-time capacity as a missionary and had been living in the area since 1837. On December 27, 1843, he was ordained a Calvinist Baptist minister and installed by an assembly of four Baptist colleagues in nearby towns, Rev. Archibald Gillies of Eaton, Rev. Israel Ide of Barford, Rev. Francis N. Jersey of Stanstead, and Rev. James Green of Barnston. Now that Mitchell had been formally endorsed by a religious council, legal formalities followed, in January 1844. The ministers who had been present at his ordination testified. Two of his parishioners, Samuel Brooks and Benjamin Hart Ives (of Georgeville), having satisfied the legal authorities that they were well-established residents of the United Province of Canada and had sufficient material assets to support the obligation they would undertake, swore to be "sureties for Edward Mitchell of the Township of Hatley, in the said district [St. Francis], minister or pastor of the Calvinist Baptist Society of the Townships of Stanstead and Hatley . . . for the due execution of the duties as minister or pastor as aforesaid, in conformity to the provincial statute." Mitchell himself, in Sherbrooke, swore before the Hon. John Fletcher, one of the judges of the Court of King's Bench for the District of St. Francis, that "as minister or pastor he would be faithful and bear true allegiance to Her Majesty Queen Victoria."[60]

One of the responsibilities that came with Mitchell's new legal status was recording the births, marriages, and interments of his parishioners and any others requiring the legal authority of a clergyman. He performed baptisms, but not in the context of his civic obligation. By the time Mitchell received his legal status as a Canadian minister in 1844, the restrictions previously enforced by Catholic authorities regarding which ministers could perform legally recognized marriages in Canada East had been removed. The Canadian Baptist Archives contain two bound volumes comprising twenty-eight annual journals in which Mitchell had entered these acts, dating from January 1844 to February 1872, each of the many entries signed "Edward Mitchell, Baptist Minister."[61] Among his first actions was to "present and register," on December 17, 1844, the births of his own children—Edward Staughton, Naomi Clark, and Nathan Cheney, who were at that time eight, five, and three years old.[62] That year, he officiated at nine marriages, thirteen baptisms (and registered the births), and three funerals. Over the next twenty-eight years of his ministry, he presided over 154 similar ceremonies. The many marriages registered in his record books reveal that he, like many members of the clergy, officiated at the weddings and funerals of non-Baptists in addition to those in his own congregation.

HOME AND FARM IN GEORGEVILLE

With his new status as a resident Canadian minister, and with a growing family, it became appropriate for Mitchell to expand his farmland along Georgeville's lakeshore. In January 1845—then aged fifty-four, with children nine, six, and four years old—he bought a farm of 175 acres from Russell Rexford Jr., one of his parishioners, who was moving to Minnesota. This land, for which Mitchell paid eleven pounds and five shillings, may have been part of or adjacent to his first residence on the Lake Shore.[63] The property is bounded by prominent families of the area—the Ives, Rexfords, and Merrimans.[64] Mitchell's pastoral responsibilities were becoming concentrated in Georgeville. As Baptist ministers in Canada East became more numerous, this trend would continue, requiring less of his time traveling and thus making the operation of a farm more feasible. The Mitchell farm on the Georgeville–Magog road would be the family's residence for the rest of Mitchell's life.[65] His home and farm, although closer to the village of Georgeville than to present-day downtown Magog, was in the southern part of Magog Township, and his parishioners were "scattered over a territory twelve miles in length." The names Georgeville, Magog, and West Hatley have been used more or less interchangeably in denoting Mitchell's parish and residence, as the place-names Eaton Township and Sawyerville, a village within Eaton, had likewise been used in that context earlier.

Years later, when eligible for Canadian Crown land grants, Mitchell purchased 100 acres in 1857 (£78 15s.) and his son, Nathan, added 50 acres in 1867 ($125), both subdivisions of Range 16, Lot 1 in Magog Township.[66] Aided by his two sons, daughter, and wife, Mitchell was able to place about one-third of his property under cultivation. By 1871, the year before his death, the family reported owning 280 acres, comprising several barns, livestock, fields of wheat, barley, and oats, peas and corn, potatoes, and turnips, along with honey and maple sugar that surely sweetened moments in the fading days of his life.[67]

PASTORAL LABORS

Periodically, Mitchell posted notices in the *Stanstead Journal*, for example, on January 25, 1866, "Marriage licenses can be obtained from Rev. E. Mitchell, Magog, C.E." Clergymen of that time routinely posted such advertisements and undoubtedly welcomed the fees and honoraria. One minister advertised that those who purchased a license from him would receive a "desirable present." Mitchell's record book contains no information on the religious heritage or the occupations of the people he married and other records are too few to disclose any patterns, but at least one of his later weddings suffices to engender speculation. The bride was from a Church of England family prominent in Magog's business and social circles, and the groom was a Roman Catholic laborer.[68] Perhaps latter-day Romeos and Juliets sought and found a compassionate reception from this Baptist minister whose own marriage had been "mixed."

Minute books and other records of Baptist congregations in the nineteenth century indicate that "Blessed are the peacemakers" applied directly to the role of a minister, as church members, in accord with Matthew 18:15–17, brought their disputes to the church, or as members of the congregation became aware of discord among their fellow members. Mitchell was thus called upon as a mediator. An item in the fonds at the McCord Museum, especially intriguing to Georgeville historians, concerns Mitchell's arbitration of a feud between two prominent members of his congregation. Written by Mitchell, but in words for the two parishioners to acknowledge as their own, the item states that after a conversation with Mitchell they agreed that their "difficulties [had] arisen from misunderstanding each other" and that they would "mutually agree to forgive and forget all past differences" and pray that the Lord would forgive them both.

In the same years, his parishioners regularly supported his physical comforts. Like other clergymen, Mitchell expressed thanks for such beneficence by publishing "A Card" of appreciation, in the *Stanstead Journal*. One year, he thanked his parishioners for providing him with a "Buffalo Coat," a suit of clothes, grain, and "what Solomon said 'answereth all things'"—money.[69] These and other bounties over time allowed the Mitchell family to maintain the comforts of their home dwelling and farm.

In contrast to the high regard for Mitchell consistently expressed by parishioners and fellow members of the Baptist clergy, a less favorable and biased assessment of his ministry was made in 1846 by George Jehoshaphat Mountain, Church of England Lord Bishop of Montreal. Mountain's apparent bias reflects a shared low opinion of the Baptists and Methodists then prevalent among the Anglican clergy in Canada. They perceived the Baptists' and Methodists' "plain style, egalitarian brotherhood, evangelical worship, and itinerant preaching," in the assessment of historian Alan Taylor, to be a "threat [to] moral and social order" and suspected the ministers and adherents of those denominations of harboring republican sentiments.[70] Mountain's attitude toward these churches was no doubt also influenced by protests by non-Anglican adherents against the status of the Church of England in his native England, and by their opposition to an established state church in Canada. He also seems to have held a dim view of persons of African descent. Following a tour of the newly designated Diocese of Quebec in 1846, he reported that at the "incipient village" at the outlet of Lake Memphremagog,[71] there was "a small place of worship, with a steeple, which might be taken for the church of the village, but it is assigned over to no religious body whatever, and is at present served only by a coloured man, a Baptist by profession, who comes from a distance to preach in it once in four weeks, exciting, from all that I could learn, very little interest, in any shape, upon the subject of religion. The building is much out of repair."[72] In the bishop's opinion, "If the Christian government of Britain had done its duty before God for its transatlantic subjects," such conditions would not have prevailed.[73] No such remarks appear in any of the Baptist publications of the time.

TEMPERANCE AND BIBLE SOCIETY WORK

While convening with his local Baptist congregants in homes and at the Georgeville brick schoolhouse regularly each week, Mitchell also engaged in broader outreach to his community for social gatherings, typically Yuletide celebrations, and, in a more serious vein, to promote spiritual and moral well-being. During a period of temperance revivals in the 1840s, Mitchell led regular meetings of the Georgeville area temperance group. At a January 1842 meeting, he hosted a visit by R. D. Wadsworth, the secretary of the Montreal Temperance Society, during his 280-mile tour of Eastern Township villages. Wadsworth braced the cold and a major snowstorm, as he reported in the *Canada Temperance Advocate* of that year: "Georgeville—In the evening had a good attendance at the school-house Elder Mitchell presided. A very respectable society here, to which 20 members were added on this occasion."[74] Mitchell's temperance work likely was short-lived since, as noted by J. I. Little, temperance activism waned after the "grounding" of Montreal Temperance Society agents and the withdrawal of the American Home Missionary Society from the Lower Canada scene in 1843.[75] Even so, the tenor of Mitchell's evangelism for temperance reform is evident in a sermon that he left among his surviving papers. Mitchell characterized the defeat of the "criminal services of Prince alcohol" as no less a Christian and patriotic duty than the call to arms against "an invading foreign army." His convictions carried into his home. His son, Edward Staughton, who died at a young age, was remembered as having "abstained from all stimulating drinks and from the use of tobacco, and on all occasions defended the temperance cause."[76]

Mitchell's work with affiliates of the American Bible Society, first begun with African American clergymen in Philadelphia, continued in Georgeville. The Georgeville Bible Society comprised Mitchell, other local clergy, and village merchants, who presumably served a philanthropic role. Meeting from 1850 until at least 1870, the society listed Mitchell as president or secretary in reports to the British and Foreign Bible Society.[77]

MILLERISM COMES TO LOWER CANADA

An important, albeit brief, chapter in Mitchell's Georgeville years developed when a preacher from New York brought his apocalyptic message to the Eastern Townships. In June and July 1835, when Mitchell was still based in Sawyerville, the millenarian evangelist William Miller (1782–1849) made his first tour of northern Vermont and the Eastern Townships of Lower Canada, preaching at towns that included Derby and Georgeville. Miller was from Low Hampton, New York, across the Poultney River from Fair Haven, Vermont (i.e., not part of "The Hamptons"), but his sister, Anna Miller Atwood, and her family lived at Magog Outlet (and, to Miller's dismay, her husband was a Universalist). These affiliations explain Miller's particular interest in Canada's Eastern Townships. His preaching emphasized the Second Coming of Christ, which, from his interpretation of the books of Daniel, John, and Revelation—especially his calculations based on Daniel 8:13–14—he expected to occur between March 1843 and April 1844 (later extended to October 1844). This would, in his prophecy, immediately be followed by "the destruction of the kingdoms of this earth and all the wicked, to allow the establishment of God's kingdom." In the few years remaining before the Second Coming, Miller preached, humankind should prepare through repentance, commitment to Christ, and the rejection of such heresies (in his assessment) as Universalism.[78]

In the "early phase" of Miller's evangelism, from 1835 to 1840, he preached in response to invitations from existing churches, mostly Baptist and Methodist. Mitchell was much impressed by Miller during this period. In 1836 he traveled to Lansingburgh, New York (now part of Troy), to attend a series of lectures by Miller. This trip was about 270 miles each way, a major undertaking before railroads reached his area. Following these lectures, Mitchell was one of twenty-one clergymen who endorsed Miller's preaching and signed an oddly litotic statement: "Having heard the above mentioned lectures, I see no way to avoid the conclusion the coming of Christ will be as early as 1843."[79]

Miller revisited the Magog area in 1838 and preached twelve sermons. He was again in the area in 1840, after Mitchell's appointment to the Baptist ministry in Georgeville. Beginning on June 20 of that year, Miller lectured at Magog Outlet and nearby. From June 28 through July 5, he presented a series of fifteen lectures to large crowds that gathered around the Georgeville schoolhouse in which Mitchell's congregation met.[80] Miller considered Georgeville a place where "much good work would be done." Mitchell welcomed Miller's visit, calling this "a time of refreshing to us," when "The Holy Spirit, we trust, was present in his enlightening and renovating grace." Further, he wrote in a passage that indicates his own theological emphasis as well as Miller's, "Many souls felt anxious to be prepared for death, judgment, and eternity; and quite a number have manifested hopes of pardoning mercy." Thirty new members joined Mitchell's congregation following Miller's lectures, bringing the total membership as of October 1840 to 104. The Free Will Baptist Church in Stanstead added about 200.[81] In his report quoted above, Mitchell noted that Miller's "favourite theme was the second coming of Christ," but he said nothing further with regard to Miller's parousial and millenarian predictions. According to Daniel Walker Howe, "Many evangelical clergy"— whether or not they were convinced as to those predictions—"gladly accorded Miller's views a hearing because he shook people up and interested them in religion."[82] With the initial impact of the Lansingburgh lectures having subsided, Mitchell probably valued Miller's visit primarily for its evangelical and revival potential rather than for its millenarian predictions.

Miller preached at Georgeville during the "early phase" of his evangelism. After 1840, when his health declined and Joshua Vaughan Himes assumed a majority role in the movement, Miller's evangelism became less restricted regionally, more aggressive, more specific in its predictions, and consequently more controversial. In contrast to the earlier salutary effects on membership in existing churches, this later phase of Miller's evangelism, according to the Adventist historian Denis Fortin, "created such an excitement in the Eastern Townships that many Methodist and Baptist members left their respective churches to join this new movement," and "as a result these churches were shaken to their very foundations."[83] The new churches founded by some of Miller's followers included precursors of the Advent Christian and Seventh-Day Adventist churches.

Although Mitchell wrote favorably in 1841 of Miller's early preaching in Georgeville in the *Canada Baptist Magazine and Missionary Register*, on the whole, the Baptist clergy soon became disillusioned with Miller. He is not mentioned in any of the reports of the Vermont State Baptist Convention or in the minutes of the Danville Baptist Association, with which the churches in the Eastern Townships were still affiliated in 1838. Nevertheless, many people in the Eastern Townships remained convinced. In April 1843, on the date of Miller's most specific prediction thus far for the Second Coming, according to an account published eighty-nine years later, "a large number of persons, in white robes, assembled on Morrill Hill, Stanstead, in momentary expectancy."[84] (How many of those who assembled, if any, had then or formerly been members of Mitchell's congregation is not indicated in that account.)

For some of those who had heard Miller's prophecies, 1844 probably brought a sense of reprieve and relief, but for Miller himself and his most thoroughly convinced and devoted followers, that year brought the "Great Disappointment." Most returned to their former denominations, others remained with the Adventist churches they had founded, and some became skeptical about Christianity in general. For Mitchell, life seems to have continued with no such trauma. His association with Miller does not appear to have been of major significance when Mitchell's life and career are considered in their entirety. He seems not to have been closely involved, if at all, with the "second phase" of Miller's evangelism. In Sylvester Bliss's *Memoirs of William Miller*, neither Mitchell nor Georgeville are mentioned in connection with Miller's activities after 1840, despite Miller's earlier enthusiasm for that area.[85] Nor does Fortin's study of Miller and Millerism in the Eastern Townships mention Mitchell or Georgeville in connection with events after that date. The Mitchell family fonds at the McCord Museum contain nothing in which Miller is mentioned. It is unlikely that Mitchell's confidence in Miller's millenarian predictions was long sustained. He adhered steadfastly to his Baptist affiliation and continued without interruption as minister to his Baptist congregation at Georgeville. All three of the Mitchell children were conceived between 1835, when Mitchell first heard Miller preach, and 1843, the year in which Miller had predicted that the Second Coming would occur.

FINAL YEARS

Until his death in 1872, Mitchell continued as spiritual leader of the Calvinist Baptist community, whose membership declined as Georgeville and other Eastern Township villages transitioned from the original Anglophone settlements dominated by New England immigrants to the Francophone communities of today. He lived to see the Georgeville area become a retreat for visiting and vacationing New England families. Edwin Cassander Manning, a Kansas newspaperman and politician, was a boy of eleven in 1849 when he spent a year in the Georgeville area with his relatives and attended Baptist church services. Reminiscing as an adult, Manning recalled that "the preacher in English broadcloth was a marvelous person" whose children tested him closely in grammar school exercises.[86] Such were the sentiments accorded to Mitchell and his family by colleagues, parishioners, and friends. Rev. Edward Mitchell died on March 21, 1872, in his eighty-first year. A nineteenth-century Baptist historian judged him to be "the most profound theologian ever to have resided in this region."[87]

SIX

A Profound Theologian

The Second Great Awakening at Dartmouth

When Mitchell arrived in the United States in 1810, the Second Great Awakening was in its ascendancy; when he was ordained to the ministry in 1829, it was at its zenith. This, as characterized by historian James M. McPherson, was "a wave of Protestant revivals [that] swept the country during the first third of the nineteenth century."[1] Payson and Staughton were leading figures in this movement. Popular interest in and enthusiasm for religion soared. Churches became more active in revivals and in reaching out to rural and newly settled areas that had been unchurched. So great was the impact of the Second Great Awakening, in its diverse aspects, that any biographical study of a Protestant Christian minister or theologian in North America during this period should consider the phenomena that characterized this epoch, how that individual was affected, and where he or she stood with regard to the diversity in theology that came so much to the fore. This is especially significant in Mitchell's case, because he was recognized and respected as a theologian by his contemporaries in the Baptist clergy, and because in the present day the implications of his designation as a Calvinist Baptist minister might be misunderstood.

Religious revivals occurred at most of the colleges and universities in the United States during the Second Great Awakening, including Dartmouth, as noted in chapter 2. With the Dartmouth College trustees having envisioned an increasingly evangelical role for the college, and with its president, Bennet Tyler, being another prominent figure in this movement, the Second Great Awakening had a significant impact at Dartmouth.

Mitchell studied for and entered the ministry in a time of great optimism among the clergy, but in the academic sphere it was also a time of turmoil. Not only was the Second Great Awakening a time of renewed popular interest in religion, but, as noted by Daniel Walker Howe, it was also a time when "learned theological discussion flourished" among intellectuals, who "were philosophically sophisticated and determined to apply reason to religion."[2] Although theological differences were by no means new to North American Protestant Christianity, inevitably, with this increase in "learned theological discussion," more and more individuals became embroiled in controversies.

Mitchell, before he came to Hanover, would already have been aware that more than one denomination existed within Protestant Christianity and that views on infant baptism were a major difference between the Baptists and most of the other denominations. Otherwise, he had probably heard little about theological differences. In view of Mitchell's newness to the study of Christian doctrine during his years in Philadelphia, it is unlikely that his early mentor, William Staughton, confident in his own Calvinist Baptist theology, would have said much to him about theological controversies. At Dartmouth, as Mitchell became aware of greater diversity in Christian theology than he could have imagined when he first considered becoming a minister, he might at first have been startled. Undoubtedly the theological activity and debate during the Second Great Awakening would have greatly interested him, challenged him, at times distressed him, and required some difficult decisions. But these developments, and his increasing awareness of them, did not divert him from his pursuit of becoming a Baptist minister.

Some prominent theologians of the time were faculty members at universities and seminaries and became known for their scholarly works. Others among the clergy disdained academia and contended that an aptitude for preaching was a divine gift that no amount of schooling could bestow. Some of the best-known American theologians and ministers of the nineteenth century, including Staughton, sensed no incompatibility between academic theology and preaching, or competition for their energies, but established reputations both as erudite theologians and as charismatic preachers. Among the Baptists, Staughton had been a leader in asserting the value of scholarship in combination with piety for the clergy.[3] Mitchell's decision to study at Dartmouth, despite the challenges that doing so would present, indicates that he accepted Staughton's views in this respect.

Calvinism: Old and New School

The influence of rationalistic academic theologians brought new attention to Calvin and led to the reexamination of his theology. Some Christian denominations traced their religious heritage from or through Calvin, but his works had received relatively little attention during the previous century. Although in the public mind "Calvinism" is sometimes equated almost coextensively with the doctrine of the predestined salvation (sometimes in combination with emphasis on a work ethic), this, according to the historian of religion James R. Payton Jr., is a distortion or a least a misplacement of emphasis. Calvin accepted the doctrine of predestination as a legacy from his precursors of the previous two centuries, but, according to Payton, he was not "fixated on predestination," nor was it central to his theology.[4] Nevertheless, the doctrines of determinism and predestined salvation figured prominently in perceptions of Calvinist theology during this period. Adhering to Calvinism, or more specifically to those doctrines, became a struggle—or more of a struggle than ever—for some of the clergy. Those North American theologians and clergymen who continued to identify themselves as Calvinists, whether Baptist, Congregationalist, or of other denominations, became divided into Old School and New School Calvinists. Those of the New School saw and respected Calvin not as a doctrinaire but as a "champion of piety," as Payton characterizes him, piety in this context being defined as an intimate relationship with God that shapes all life. It is in this context, rather than in that of the present-day misplaced emphasis noted by Payton, that Mitchell's identification as a Calvinist Baptist minister should be viewed.

For those of the New School, their concept of Calvinism was sufficiently broad that they could continue to identify themselves as Calvinists even though they rejected the theology of predestined salvation. In New School theology, as exemplified by Nathaniel William Taylor of Yale University, one of its most influential advocates, the reinterpretation of the doctrine of original sin, as expressed by Howe, was that "Although all human beings sinned, they possessed 'power to the contrary,' that is, the moral power to refrain from sinning if they chose."[5] Taylor, as interpreted by W. A. Hoffecker, believed that "God promotes moral action by a system of means and ends in which man can respond to ethical appeals for repentance."[6] In some cases, however, those of the New School were disowned as Calvinists by those of the Old

School. Some Old School Calvinists considered the revival emphasis of the Second Great Awakening to be hostile to their theology. Those of the New School, in contrast, being freed from the doctrine of predestined salvation, perceived very good reasons for revivals and evangelism. Taylor encouraged revivalist preachers to, in Howe's words, "emphasize the importance of making a conscious choice for Christ."[7]

Bennet Tyler, who had been president of Dartmouth during Mitchell's student years, became so concerned about the growing influence of the New School that, after resigning from the presidency of the college in 1828 and then serving five years as pastor of Payson's former church in Portland, he became one of the organizers of a conservative Calvinistic faction within the Congregational church. This faction, called the East Windsor [Connecticut] Pastoral Union, and its affiliated seminary were formed explicitly in opposition to the allegedly Arminian (or, in some disparaging characterizations, Semipelagian) theology of Taylor and the New School Calvinists.[8] But although Tyler professed to adhere to Old School Calvinism, he is noted for having led a revival at Dartmouth while Mitchell was a student. His beliefs even then may have been closer to Arminian, or to those of the New School, than he recognized. Later, a division would arise within the East Windsor Pastoral Union, with Tyler contending that "Man has understanding and natural strength to do all that God requires of him," whereas another of the founders, Joseph Harvey, countered that God does "require of impenitent men what they have no power to perform."[9]

Some aspects of the theological divergence that proliferated during the Second Great Awakening were correlated with geography. In the northern United States, according to McPherson, the evangelical enthusiasm of this era "generated a host of moral and cultural reforms."[10] Lyman Beecher, a renowned revivalist preacher of the time, proclaimed that "the great aim of the Christian Church in its relation to the present life is not only to renew the individual man, but also to reform human society."[11] Reformers in the North, according to McPherson, generally "repudiated Calvinist predestination, preached the availability of redemption to anyone who truly sought it, urged converts to abjure sin, and worked for the elimination of sins from society."[12] Slavery was regarded as "the most heinous social sin." Other churches and individuals, predominantly but not exclusively in the Southern states, regarded societal reforms as "distractions and corruptions of the pure gospel message."[13] As summed up by the historian of American religion Sydney E. Ahlstrom, the societal reforms of the Second Great Awakening were to them "only side effects of efforts that were ineffable and beyond mundane measuring . . . to bring word of amazing grace to wretched souls."[14]

Theological diversity became especially marked among the Baptists. Some, forming such sects as the Primitive and Two-Seed-in-the-Spirit Baptists, remained so strongly predestinarian in their theology that they opposed Sunday schools, seminaries, tracts, and missions as unbiblical and useless, because in their belief, salvation had been determined prior to birth. Other sects, notably the Missionary Baptists, arose in explicit opposition to that theology. Although to some extent the divergence in theology among Baptists extended into Canada, the proliferation of sects was largely limited to the United States, where the issue of slavery superimposed a further schismatic influence upon that of theology. In Canada, both Regular and Free Will Baptist churches were present, but the much smaller numbers of Baptists precluded further divisions.

Denominational historians have noted that whereas strictly Calvinistic theology had prevailed among the earlier Baptists in North America, a theology closer to that of the Free Will Baptists gradually came to predominate, except in the most conservative (predominantly Southern) sects.[15] It was the Baptists and the Methodists who were most zealous in holding revivals in areas where churchgoing had fallen off and in establishing new churches in rural and frontier areas. In the mid-nineteenth century the designation "Calvinist Baptist" was replaced by "Regular Baptist," although the latter name continued to imply a theology more conservative than that of the Free Will Baptists. Mitchell, in the later years of his ministry at Georgeville, was designated a "Regular Baptist" minister.[16]

Mitchell, Staughton, and New School Evangelism

Mitchell's religious mentor, Rev. William Staughton, although he regarded himself as a Calvinist, had rejected predestinarianism. An ardent evangelist, he founded the Baptist Board of Foreign and Domestic Missions. Nor did Mitchell, although he may have struggled with the issue of predestination in the early years of his ministry, ever fully accept that doctrine. In his personal creed written in 1829 he expressed a belief "that there are those given to Christ before the foundation of the world, who are known to us by their repentance, belief of the truth, and obedience of the Gospel." But while this wording, based on Romans 8:29–30, might appear predestinarian, it is similar to that of Arminius on "conditional election"—that "God's choice of certain individuals unto salvation before the foundation of the world was based upon His foreseeing that they would respond to His call."[17] In Arminian belief, all can and do sin, and salvation requires willful repentance and willful acceptance of God's grace, whereas Calvinism, in its strictest form (or Old School interpretation), considers sin to be theoretical, because of the inability to choose to sin. Although Mitchell would not have identified his own beliefs as Arminian, his use of the term "repentance" in the context noted above represents at least a compromise with Arminian theology. The "Outlines," written at the same time as the creed, indicate that he believed a spiritual metamorphosis had occurred in his own life, and that he, like many of his contemporaries who identified themselves as Calvinists, was convinced that his and others' ministries could make a difference for those they reached. With his theology being centered on Christ's sacrifice as the basis of salvation, and with his preaching being focused on individual morality, a personal relationship with God through prayer, and salvation through faith in and commitment to Christ—in Beecher's terms, on the renewal of the individual rather than the reform of society—his ministry contrasted, to various degrees, with the greater emphasis on social issues among some other clergy and their churches in his time.

As his ministry continued, Mitchell became unequivocally identifiable with New School theology. His enthusiasm for the revival movement and his New School belief that evangelism could be effective, leading to salvation through decisions for Christ, are illustrated in a manuscript paper he wrote in 1840.[18] Referring to Baptist missionaries who had visited the West Hatley area some twenty years before his arrival, he wrote, "In a reformation that followed their preaching, many of this early band of settlers experienced the pardon of sin through the blood of Christ, [and] souls were converted." Beginning in essays he had written as a student, such as those on knowing oneself and on the perceived benefits of the Reformation, and recurrently in his later notes and manuscripts, Mitchell emphasized that humans have an innate moral sense and a mind capable of rational thought and learning. This mental capacity, he contended, carried with it the obligation to use it in study and prayer, which should lead one to a conscious decision to become a Christian. One's mind, with that innate moral sense, should then be used in a search for guidance from the Bible in Christian living. This emphasis on the moral sense and the obligation to use one's mind is fully developed in Mitchell's later writings.[19] This emphasis on humans' moral sense is clearly in harmony with that of the New School, and specifically with that of Taylor, as paraphrased by Hoffecker, that "God promotes moral action."

Mitchell's Scholarship

Mitchell's passion for Christian theology and philosophy remained with him throughout his life. The fonds at the McCord Museum contain many notes, essays, and other items written by Mitchell throughout much of his ministry. It was his practice, in his studies of the Bible and in developing his thoughts on theological subjects, to put his thoughts into writing. Among the contents of the fonds is a notebook containing a large number of citations of biblical verses from both Testaments, with brief notes as to their implications for salvation and the Christian life.

According to the *Baptist Encyclopaedia*, quoted below, Mitchell became regarded as a "profound theologian" by his contemporaries in Canada. This was especially remarkable considering the absence of universities and libraries—and Mitchell had an enviable library—in the Magog area in his time. This reputation appears to have been established orally and through personal communications, rather than through published works. The resources in both the Canadian and US Baptist archives are extensively indexed for references to individuals as their names appear in church publications, and at neither institution is there a record of any publications by Mitchell other than his report on the rise and progress of the church in Stanstead and Hatley townships.

Three manuscripts by Mitchell in the fonds at the McCord Museum are theological treatises: one on God's grace and salvation; one on pedobaptism (denounced as being "from Popery," as Baptists often characterized the practice at the time), with comments on its history and the biblical case against it; and one on the Christian life, with discussions of many passages from the New Testament. What use Mitchell may have made of these treatises is not stated, but they may have been presented at regional Baptist meetings. At least one such indication appears in the Baptist publication *Montreal Register*, in which it was recorded that at the quarterly meeting of the Baptist churches of the Eastern Townships in Eaton Township, September 1846, Mitchell was one of the "brethren" who delivered a "discourse."[20] (The subject was not reported.) Another item in the fonds is a message—perhaps a copy of a letter written to a congregation he could visit only infrequently—resembling a sermon but with the opening line "You look for our annual epistle." Its topic is the importance of family worship and the inculcation of Christian principles in one's children, a recurrent theme among Mitchell's notes.

CONCLUSION

Final Days and Next Generations

Mitchell continued his ministry to the Baptist congregation in Georgeville and vicinity until his death, March 21, 1872, after a short illness at the age of eighty in his home on the Georgeville–Magog road. Interment was in the Ives Cemetery, near his home of thirty-five years. On the gravestone erected by his parishioners is carved the first verse of the hymn "The Christian Soldier" by James Montgomery: "Servant of God, well done/Rest from thy loved employ/The battle fought, the victory won/Enter thy Master's joy." This is followed by Hebrews 4:9: "There remaineth therefore a rest for the people of God."[1]

In an obituary in the Newport (Vermont) *Express and Standard*, attributed to "L." (probably LeRoy Holmes Robinson [1821–1901], for many years editor and publisher of the *Stanstead Journal*), it was said that "a man of steadfast integrity; a preacher of marked ability; a scholar that retained his love of learning—the very last years of his life you would find him reading the Bible in the original languages; a true friend; a kind and affectionate husband and father has been called from the scenes of earth. He has fought the good fight and has gone to receive his crown."[2] The last sentence was based on II Timothy 4:7–8, a passage that Mitchell himself had used as his text at funeral services. A similar, slightly shorter obituary, also by "L.," was published in the *Stanstead Journal.*

Mitchell had been the minister of the Baptist congregation in Georgeville for nearly thirty-five years. He appears to have been content in that pastorate and to have considered his ministry there a success, as indicated in his article on the "rise and progress" of the church in his area. He did not aspire to a more prestigious pastorate in the Baptist Church in Canada. After his death, the Eastern Canada Baptist Convention, upon motion by the Rev.

J. W. Truesdell, resolved "that this Convention with devout thankfulness as well as deep sorrow, record the recent departure of our highly esteemed and worthy Brother, Rev. Edward Mitchell, of Magog—thankfulness for his long service—sorrow for our present loss." The editor of the minutes, Rev. Duncan McFarland, added that "Brother Mitchell was, by general consent, one of the most able and faithful of our country pastors. He labored in the Eastern Townships for 44 years, both as missionary and pastor. We feel the loss which the churches have sustained, and sincerely sympathize with the afflicted family in their sorrow."[3] A tribute quoted in the *Baptist Encyclopaedia* stated that Mitchell "was regarded as the most profound theologian ever settled in the section in which he passed so many years of his useful life."[4] It was obviously the pastoral and evangelical ministry to which Mitchell's life was primarily dedicated.

Mitchell Family and Descendants

After the death of Mitchell, his wife, Ruth, remained in Magog Township until 1882, when she was seventy-nine years old. Then the farm was sold[5] and Ruth and Naomi moved to Laconia, New Hampshire, near Ruth's birthplace, where by that time Nathan, the third of Edward and Ruth Mitchell's children, was living, as were other members of the Cheney and Leavitt families. Ruth died November 12, 1889, in Laconia. A long obituary published in the *Stanstead Journal* and excerpted here offers testimony to her Christian devotion:

> LACONIA, N.H., NOV. 12, 1889, MRS. RUTH C. MITCHELL
>
> . . . In 1837 [the Mitchells] removed to the Ives neighborhood in Magog, P. Q. As this tiny home grew to a farm, it became necessary to combine in one, the pastor's and the farmer's wife. . . . [F]amily cares were never so great as to prevent her rendering her husband the invaluable assistance in the discharge of his pastoral duties. . . . With a cheerful, hopeful disposition she was a welcome visitor to the bedside of the sick and the unfortunate. . . . Honest and openhearted, she made no enemies and won friends wherever she made acquaintances. . . . Throughout the vicissitudes of her long life her Christian character was ever marked by a simple, unanswering faith in God.[6]

Edward and Ruth Mitchell had three children.[7] The oldest, Edward Staughton Mitchell, was born July 14, 1836, in Eaton Township, Lower Canada, and died unmarried December 1, 1878, of consumption, in Pilot Grove Township, Illinois, while visiting his mother's brother Nathaniel before continuing a planned trip to California. He had left Georgeville and farming to pursue other ambitions. His talents were very apparent to others. As mentioned earlier, Edwin C. Manning, who had as a boy spent a year with relatives in the Georgeville area, recalled that his "chum" Edward S. Mitchell had been the champion speller at the Ives School that year and his closest rival. From Edward Staughton's obituary we learn of the high esteem he had earned in Georgeville and the many fine attributes he gained as the child of Rev. Mitchell.

> Though his father was a minister and a graduate of Dartmouth, the opportunities of the deceased for public instruction were limited to the common school. Yet, through his love of reading, his extraordinary memory, his access to his father's library, (an excellent one) he made acquirements not second in importance to those of professional men generally. He discovered a genius for drawing, but brought up a farmer, he only developed his tastes in agricultural pursuits, intermingled with various mechanical work for which he had great tact. His intellect was exceedingly clear and talents remarkably balanced. He was social and genial to an uncommon degree; chaste and inoffensive in demeanor, and in his sense of appreciation, exquisite. His honor and integrity were without blemish. He ever abstained from all stimulating drinks and from the use of tobacco, and on all occasions defended the temperance cause. He was well informed upon all questions of the day and an able debater.[8]

Naomi Clark Mitchell was born November 11, 1839, in Magog Township. She became an elementary school teacher of the township. (Her teaching certificate, now at the McCord Museum, attests to her moral character but does not mention academic qualifications.) Several essays by her on topics of morality are in the Mitchell family fonds at the McCord Museum. After the death of her father, Naomi and her mother remained in Magog Township until 1882, when the farm was sold and Ruth and Naomi moved to Laconia, New Hampshire. Naomi maintained close ties with her friends in the Georgeville-Magog area, returning to visit nearly every summer. She died unmarried June 1, 1902, in Lowell, Massachusetts, where she had been staying with her nephew Edward (see below) and his family during her final illness. Her brief obituary emphasizes her continuing relationship to the Georgeville community: "Miss Naomi Mitchell died at Lowell Mass., June first. She was the only daughter of the late Rev. Edward Mitchell, a Baptist minister, for many years a resident of the Ives neighborhood in the township of Magog. She will be brought and buried by the side of her parents in the Ives burial ground on Wednesday. Miss Mitchell had visited her friends in this vicinity nearly every summer."[9]

Nathan Cheney Mitchell, the third of Edward and Ruth Mitchell's children, was born August 26, 1841, in Magog Township. In 1866 he bought Crown land in Magog Township, expanding the Mitchell homestead and farm. In 1871 he married Ruth Hunkins Frye (née Leavitt), a widowed first cousin once removed, who had been born in Sanbornton, New Hampshire, April 27, 1839. There are discrepancies in dates given in obituaries and other records, but a census record stating that Nathan had immigrated to the United States in 1868, considered with the birth of their first child in Laconia in 1872 and their second and third children in Magog Township in 1874, suggests that he had established a residence in or near Laconia prior to the time of his marriage without immediately severing his connections with Magog Township. Records at the McCord Museum indicate that in 1874 he was back in Magog Township, operating the farm and serving as a road inspector for part of that township. By 1878 or 1879, following the death of his father, Nathan and Ruth established a home in Laconia, from which he traveled to work as a brick mason in diverse localities of New England. Successive Laconia city directories, which were first published in 1895, indicate that he worked in Lowell, Massachusetts, but he continued to be listed as a resident of Laconia and was said in obituaries in the *Laconia Democrat* and the *Laconia News and Critic* to have been "for many years a resident" of that city. Nathan died from complications of prostate surgery on June 10, 1909, at the New England Sanitarium, a long-term care facility in Stoneham, Massachusetts. News of his death was recorded back home in Quebec: "We learn of the death of an old landmark in the person of Mr. Nathan Cheney Mitchell, formerly a resident in the Ives neighborhood in old days."[10] His wife, Ruth, died May 13, 1919. Nathan and Ruth had three children, Edward, Mary Josephine, and Nathaniel Leavitt.[11]

Edward Mitchell, the first of Nathan and Ruth Leavitt Mitchell's three children and the only one who was survived by descendants, was born in Laconia May 4, 1872. In 1893 he married Flora McDonald Gold (March 5, 1873–April 20, 1937), a Laconia resident originally from Melbourne, Quebec (now part of Richmond). According to his marriage record, he was a "polisher" in Laconia; he likely worked with wood products, in view of his subsequent employment as a "rubber" by a manufacturer of pianos in Concord, New Hampshire, or perhaps with stone, as might be suspected from his father's association with the building trades. Edward and Flora later lived in Lowell, Massachusetts, Baltimore, and Takoma Park, DC. They had eight children, of whom seven survived beyond infancy, and as of this writing numerous descendants are living throughout much of the United States. In 1938, Edward married Anna Brubaker, a widow, in Camden, New Jersey. Edward died from complications of colon cancer on March 13, 1947, in Philadelphia.[12]

The second of Nathan and Ruth's children, Mary Josephine Mitchell, was born in Magog Township on January 29, 1874, and came to Laconia with her parents. As a young adult she was employed by a paper-box manufacturer. After her father died in 1909 she moved to Needham Heights, Massachusetts. She returned to Laconia in 1915 and, except for a brief residence in Boston around 1922, spent the rest of her life there, where she was employed by a manufacturer of industrial needles. She became interested in genealogy and traced her ancestry back to *Mayflower* passenger Richard Warren. The line of descent was either through her great-grandfather Rev. Moses Cheney or through her great-grandmother Abigail Leavitt Cheney, both of whom had Pilgrim ancestors. She also became a member of the Daughters of the American Revolution. Her great-great-grandfather Nathaniel Cheney, father of Rev. Moses Cheney, and another great-great-grandfather, Moses Leavitt, father of Abigail Leavitt Cheney, had been soldiers in the American War of Independence. Josephine Mitchell died unmarried in Laconia, September 4, 1965.[13]

The third of Nathan and Ruth's children, Nathaniel Leavitt Mitchell, was born in Magog Township on March 3, 1879. He spent his adult life in Laconia, where he became assistant postmaster. In 1913 he married Louise Hattie Edwards, who had been born in Indianapolis, September 3, 1878, but had grown up in Laconia. Nathaniel Mitchell died December 23, 1918, in the influenza epidemic that swept the world that year, and Louise Mitchell died in 1956, both in Laconia. They had no children.[14]

FAMILY RELIGIOUS AND SOCIAL AFFILIATIONS

In 1888, at the age of fourteen, Mitchell's granddaughter Mary Josephine Mitchell was baptized by the minister of the First Free Will Baptist Church in Laconia, and in 1909 the minister of that church officiated at her father Nathan's funeral. Assuming that Nathan and Ruth Leavitt Mitchell arrived in Laconia before the First [Regular] Baptist Church was established in 1888, the family may have attended the Free Will Baptist Church because it was the only Baptist church conveniently available and remained with that church after the First Baptist Church came into existence. The congregations merged in 1919. Josephine Mitchell remained a member of the merged congregation for the rest of her life and attended services regularly.

The contents of the fonds at the McCord Museum are evidently from the estate of Mitchell's granddaughter Josephine, as indicated by such items as a postcard sent to her by a friend in Needham Heights in 1925 after she had returned to Laconia. To her friends in Laconia and Needham Heights, Josephine Mitchell emphasized her descent from a passenger on the *Mayflower* and from patriots who had fought in the American War of Independence, but privately, at least, it would seem that she also took pride in her descent from Rev. Edward Mitchell. Josephine Mitchell moved to new quarters on at least nine occasions after her mother's death in 1919, twice moving from Laconia to the Greater Boston area and twice returning to Laconia. Such relocations are often occasions for "downsizing," when potential archival material is likely to be discarded, but she nevertheless preserved her grandfather's "Outlines," his student essays, his theological notes and discourses, and other papers. Then, 136 years after Edward Mitchell's ordination and 94 years after his death, or perhaps even later, his great-grandchildren presumably donated this material to the McCord Museum, or to McGill University, which administered the museum at the time.[15]

Naomi Mitchell, who had until then retained her membership in the Baptist Church of Magog, affiliated with the First Baptist Church when it was founded. She was said to have been a "prominent worker" in that church, of which the theological and liturgical heritage was similar to that of the churches of which her father had been minister. As a Baptist minister officiated at the funeral of Josephine's younger brother, Nathaniel, it seems likely that he, too, had remained with the Baptist faith throughout his life. The religion of her older brother, Edward, as an adult has not been determined. He and Flora McDonald Gold were married by the minister of the First Free Will Baptist Church in Laconia, but later records indicate that Flora and their children were, while in Takoma Park, Seventh-Day Adventists.[16]

As noted above, Naomi Mitchell's obituary in the *Laconia Democrat* mentioned her service to the First Baptist Church. In the same newspaper, Nathaniel L. Mitchell was said to have been one of Laconia's "best known and most popular young men," active in the Masonic Order, the Elks, and the Grange. The *Laconia Evening Citizen* reported that representatives of the Daughters of the American Revolution and the Laconia Senior Citizens' Club had attended Josephine Mitchell's funeral. None of those obituaries, nor those of Nathan C. Mitchell in the *Democrat* and the *News and Critic*, mentioned their Afro-Caribbean heritage. As Mitchell's children were only one-eighth of African descent, and his grandchildren half that, this component of their racial heritage was probably not known widely, if at all, among their friends and acquaintances in this city. Census reports and registers of deaths in Laconia list all members of the family as "white."

In many families, once one member has "gone to college," subsequent generations expect and are expected to do so, but this did not happen in the Mitchell family until later generations. By contemporary accounts, his children were bright and academically talented. But their household was one of Christian thrift and economy. Comfortable and self-supporting on their farm, there would have been little discretionary income or family resources to support the expense of higher education. But although Mitchell's children did not pursue college education or ordination to the Christian ministry, and his grandchildren were born too late to have known him, a family tradition seems to have persisted, impressing upon later generations that Mitchell had been a remarkable person in whom posterity would be interested.

EPILOGUE

Dartmouth's memorialization of Edward Mitchell began a quarter century after his graduation. The class of 1827—graduates one year ahead of Mitchell—printed a forty-page twenty-fifth reunion booklet highlighting achievements of class members and recalling youthful days on the Hanover campus. The editor, Dr. Jonathan Fox Worcester, wrote with obvious pride in retelling the Mitchell controversy and noting his class's united support in the student protest that "won one of the brightest honors for the College, its freedom from distinctions on account of color." Class members later voted to publish an updated second edition of the original 1853 booklet in time for Dartmouth's centennial celebrations, in 1869. By that time, twenty black men had attended Dartmouth College and the medical school—far more than at any another school of higher education. The American Civil War had decided the slavery question, and the US Congress was busy constructing constitutional amendments to guarantee freedoms and expand civil rights to all citizens. It was a timely moment for the college to acknowledge its stance against racial caste exclusion. Professor Samuel Gilman Brown, president of Hamilton College, delivered a keynote address celebrating Dartmouth's one hundred years of enviable institutional growth in size, prestige, and wealth. Brown had been the seven-year-old-son of President Francis Brown in 1820 when he first met Edward Mitchell in his father's household. Later, he was a precocious Dartmouth freshman during Mitchell's senior year. About Mitchell, he said,

> I believe that no student was ever excluded from the College on account of color. . . . In 1824, Edward Mitchell, a native of Martinique, W. I., a young man with some African blood and color . . . accompanied President Brown on his return from the South. . . . Many young men of African lineage have since entered the College, [and they have been] subjected to no special disabilities, nor has one, so far as can

now be recalled, been treated by his fellow students or by others, with disrespect on account of his race.[1]

When the Dartmouth Press printed Brown's speech in 1870, Mitchell was married with three children, living comfortably one hundred miles north of Hanover. He was not present to hear Professor Brown's testimonial. He died two years later.

In 1913, Frederick Chase and John King Lord, coauthors of the definitive Dartmouth College history, recalled Dr. Worcester's and Professor Brown's personal accounts and proclaimed that Mitchell's admission to Dartmouth established a precedent in 1824, which "from that time governed the College, which has shown an unfailing hospitality to the Negro, even when the doors of other institutions were closed against him. Many of that race have entered here, and many have graduated."[2] Later Dartmouth presidents reaffirmed the significance of Mitchell's admission in sustaining the college's open admission policy. President James Wright in 2006 said to an alumni gathering, "Our current commitment to diversity is . . . part of the legacy of Samson Occum, Edward Mitchell, E.E. Just and so many others. Dartmouth admitted its first African American student, Edward Mitchell in 1824, forty years before the next Ivy League school and over eighty years before the last did so."[3]

However profound Mitchell's legacy may have been, as late as the first decade of the twenty-first century Dartmouth had almost no record of Mitchell's life.

Remembered but Lost

Dartmouth has a deserved reputation for its tenacity in maintaining contact with alumni. But as late as 1868, when Mitchell's graduation class was organizing its fortieth reunion, the college had no recent contact address.[4] As Mitchell moved from one stage in his life to another—a youth in Martinique, a young man in Philadelphia, a student at Dartmouth, a minister in Vermont and then in Canada—he seemed to put each new stage of life behind him. In the longest and final stage, Mitchell settled in a small Canadian village with limited lifelines to the outside world. He had no reason to maintain ties with America and its volatile cauldron of conflicted, untempered passions. Slavery had been abolished the year he settled in Canada. Few men or women of African descent inhabited his field of ministry. As a community of the faithful embraced Mitchell and his family, Dartmouth lost its slender purchase on the life of its first black graduate. His resurrection has come in fits and starts.

The Mitchell family archive at Montreal's McCord Museum was unknown to researchers of Dartmouth history until the twenty-first century. As late as 2015, the Dartmouth archives had only a small file on Edward Mitchell—a thin folder whose size contradicted the importance given to his memory.[5] A few historians in the early twentieth century had recognized Mitchell as one of the first black American college graduates but referenced no new sources. During and after the civil rights era, as black students took seats at Dartmouth in increasing numbers, Mitchell was nearly forgotten. In 1983, Raymond Hall, a Dartmouth professor of sociology, reviewed the more than two-hundred-year history of blacks on the Hanover campus. In *A Reaffirmation of Mission: The Saga of the Black Experience at Dartmouth*, a rich story of struggle and triumph written in 1983, Hall recalled Mitchell's life and the legacy he spawned but added no new information, which at the time was thought to be nonexistent.[6]

Late in the twentieth century, Robert Bruce Slater, editor of the *Journal of Blacks in Higher Education*, published an article titled "The Blacks Who First Entered the World of White Higher Education," a more or less complete listing of black men and women who had crossed ivy-covered thresholds of the nation's predominantly white colleges and universities. Edward Mitchell was listed, with a note that there was "very little information" about his life.[7] In a reply to the article, Caldwell Titcomb, professor emeritus at Brandeis University, reported that "deep in the bowels of a Harvard Library" he had found additional biographical information on Mitchell. He submitted to the journal a short biographical sketch of Mitchell, a reworking of the entry in William Cathcart's 1881 *Baptist Encyclopedia*.[8] For a time, Titcomb's biosketch stood as Edward Mitchell's concluding epitaph.

Unacknowledged Racial Identity

American observers often labeled Edward Mitchell a Creole, a generic designation applied to mixed-race individuals of blended French, European, and African ancestry from the Caribbean islands or francophone migrants from Canada. He was neither white nor conventionally black. Vincent Byas of Howard University points out that when applied to people of color, "the 'Creole' has been variously defined in the United States so as to avoid connotations of Negroid ancestry."[9] Whether by this device or other means, we found consistent attempts to minimize Mitchell's African ancestry. As a Dartmouth student in the mid-1820s, Mitchell was espied by Sarah Parker Parrott, for whom the sight of a man of African descent walking casually with white college mates was an exceptional experience. She described Mitchell as "very highly respected" and "nearly *black*" (emphasis hers), that is, almost white but with discernible African heritage.[10] Similarly, others consistently distanced Mitchell from his African ancestry by describing him as "not extremely dark," as having "some African blood and color," or as being "somewhat tinged with African dye."[11] In America, Mitchell's African heritage and its complementary European component never went unnoticed and constantly exposed him to unacknowledged biases and false presumptions about black racial inferiority. From what we know, Mitchell bore up well under this constant scrutiny, recurrently making a good impression and gaining the confidence and respect of others at a time when people of color were consistently denigrated and ignored.

Mitchell's extant writings contain no mention of his racial identity or heritage, nor of that of anyone else. Yet, he had been raised on a Caribbean island where nothing more than race mattered. He only refers obliquely and without emphasis to his Caribbean origins—his mother, a "native of the Island," his father "French." No reports from the Vermont Baptists refer to Mitchell's racial or geographic origin. Mitchell did serve on an antislavery committee, but there is no evidence that he had a significant role in the committee's deliberations. Reports in news items from Canadian sources rarely mention his ethnicity. His maternal racial background is not disclosed in his obituaries or *Baptist Encyclopaedia* biographical entry.

Perhaps guided by ingrained habits developed early in life, in the community of *gens de couleur* in Martinique, Mitchell appears to have selectively negotiated opportunities for advancement by alliances with prominent and socially well-placed whites. From Prentiss in Portland to Staughton in Philadelphia, the Baptists of Vermont, and finally the original Baptist settlers of the Georgeville area in Canada, Mitchell mapped a route of progressive personal advancement and social assimilation. But he was not immune to American racial animus. Philadelphia Baptists refused to inter the body of his young child. Dartmouth trustees rejected his admission to the college, exposing the nearly universal practice among American colleges to deny blacks access to white classrooms. Mitchell did not mention either of these incidents in his "Outlines," nor, it would seem, to his friends and parishioners, fellow students, Baptist leaders in Vermont, college or church historians, or the press—who would have been especially likely to take note and report them.

After moving from Portland, Maine, Mitchell took steps to find his place among people of color in Philadelphia, where the energies of blacks had already begun progress's long journey. He encountered the most charismatic white Baptist clergyman of that time and received his mentorship. Even so, Mitchell's first marriage was to a woman of color and he settled his family among other black Caribbeans and Americans. While in Philadelphia he broke bread with the city's most prominent black religious and civic leaders. But after the deaths of his first wife and family, he was drawn to the allure of employment with the president of Dartmouth and, shortly afterward, the promising reward of a college education.

Mitchell gained a new footing at Dartmouth in the world of educated and informed men of progressive moral bent and humble means. But he was far from invisible in the whiteness of northern New England. From Dartmouth sources, we hear nothing but contexts, incidents, and identities connected to race, ethnicity, and birthplace. Even as Mitchell left the United States for Canada, American observers, news editors, memoirists, and historians continued to view and discuss him in a racial context. In every direction and at each turn, Mitchell witnessed the divided soul of America's racial birthright. Once on the path of religious salvation, and with encouragement to use his rhetorical and evangelical talent, he had no interest in reliving the taunts and insults of his days in Philadelphia. He left the City of Brotherly Love on a northbound journey and pursued a religious ministry in a social context that would comfort and protect his life.

We came to better understand Mitchell as a free man of color traversing the Atlantic World in different contexts of racial oppression and resistance. During his formative years in the French Antilles, he witnessed an incompletely contained cauldron of black protest and rebellion by free blacks and slaves. In the United States he would learn of short-lived slave rebellions on Southern plantations and the early signs of organized protest among free people of color.[12] Unable to breach walls of white resistance, American blacks were building self-governing religious, social, and educational organizations within increasingly segregated communities. Over time, such actions would lead to the expression of a distinct identity, self-consciousness, and culture among American and Caribbean peoples of African ancestry. But these developments gained momentum in the years after Mitchell had settled in Canada.

We conclude that in the productive years of his life, Mitchell assimilated into the nearly uniform Anglo-French-Caucasian world of the Eastern Townships of rural Quebec. He found acceptance in small villages first populated by Anglo-Americans and later by Irish, Scottish, and French-Canadian immigrants. Mitchell, like other settlers, was foremost an *immigrant,* with Baptist religious and family associations entirely familiar to his community. He presented to these communities an impressive personal and professional résumé—the endorsement of influential white men, education from an elite American colonial college, and a record of impressive missionary field work in northern New England and Canada. He had married Ruth Cheney, the daughter of a respected white Baptist clergyman. To that religious community, Mitchell represented an *exceptional* child of the African race. Race as we know and understand it today had ceased to matter for Edward Mitchell. The slavery that concerned Mitchell was slavery to sin, from which the white residents of Canada were fully in need of deliverance. As a Dartmouth student he had written, "The Christian orator would indeed inspire with the love of liberty; but it is the liberty of the sons of God! He would urge [listeners] to break off the shackles of slavery; but it is the slavery of sin!"[13] He could not have felt right about agitating for black rights among whites of Canada in a community with no immediate examples of black oppression or enslavement. While the white editor of the local newspaper could rail against the sins and crimes of Americans during the Civil War, neither he nor his subscribers had a stake in the fight, more concerned as they were in preserving their historical and ongoing exchanges with northern New Englanders, with whom they shared a porous international but locally inconsequential border.

As noted by literary historian John Ernest in reviewing narratives from the early nineteenth-century narratives highlighting educational advances by individual blacks in America, "Behind the list of firsts that so often represents African-American progress is a longer record of those who faced severe trials in their efforts in collective struggle and isolated achievements." Ernest found that nineteenth-century black writers could not assemble these examples into a coherent narrative because "there was no larger story of educational progress to tell, and the individual tales were themselves *complicated*."[14] Indeed, Mitchell's story is complicated and it is incomplete. No men of African descent in Mitchell's time followed his path. And no matter how earnestly we attempt to understand this Caribbean man of white and black ancestry, detached from his cultural roots and imperfectly planted on American and Canadian soil, our final understanding and conclusions are equally imperfect. In writing these chapters of the life of Rev. Edward Mitchell, we have renewed our appreciation of the complexity of the black experience here and everywhere.

Legacy

Before Edward Mitchell in 1828, only three other men of African descent had graduated from American colleges, all from New England schools: Alexander L. Twilight of Middlebury (1823), Edward Jones of Amherst (1826), and John B. Russwurm of Bowdoin (1826). Russwurm and Jones self-identified as black men. Twilight's ancestry was recognized through research conducted well after his death. As for the self-identified black men who attended college in the same years as Mitchell, few noticed these utterly improbable signs of black progress in small New England villages. Only at Dartmouth did one black man's achievement arouse supportive student protest that reversed an institution's course. A decade later, in a small village of northeastern Ohio, the trustees of Oberlin College endorsed an institutional commitment that opened educational opportunities for generations of black men and women.[15] But these isolated examples of progress had few contemporary counterparts. Other Ivy League schools did not follow for another four decades, and not until after the Civil War. The next self-identified black college graduate was Richard Theodore Greener of Harvard College, in 1870.[16] By that year, twenty-one men of African ancestry had visited Dartmouth on the Hanover Plain, all leaving to pursue successful careers as Liberian colonists, physicians, lawyers, abolitionists, teachers, and clergymen.

Whatever the motivations and circumstances that permitted or encouraged the entrance of black men to Dartmouth, the college's isolation shielded them and Dartmouth from public scrutiny. Moreover, as President Ernest M.

Hopkins pointed out in 1931, Dartmouth was the only Ivy League school to establish itself before "inviting the village in to grow up around it." Its sister colleges had developed in "centers of population."[17] In this insular climate, Dartmouth students could gaze critically at the outside world while enjoying the prerogatives of privacy, seclusion, and self-governance. Upon leaving their studies, Dartmouth students appreciatively returned to the college a strong measure of loyalty, harkening knowingly to Daniel Webster's words: "It is a small place . . . yet there are those who love it."

Mitchell undoubtedly possessed a measure of love for Dartmouth, even beyond that offered by the obvious compassionate soul that guided his life. His life's work reflects the training and opportunities gained from his time at the college. We further understand that whatever the rewards and disadvantages he inherited at birth as the mixed-race child of a Caribbean slave society, his birthright ultimately became the source of his energy and ambition. At Dartmouth he crossed a once impenetrable threshold to taste the fruits of a classical college education. Once graduated, he accumulated acceptance, respect, and affirmation at every turn to realize improbable dreams and goals. In one of the few published works written by Mitchell—commissioned by the American Baptist Home Mission Society to rejuvenate a struggling church in lower Quebec—he reflected on his ministry: "At present [in 1841], we number one hundred and four, scattered, however, over a territory twelve miles in length. Many of the first members of the church have lived to see their children and grand children embracing the Savior. . . . Thus did the Lord plant a vine in this wilderness, did prepare room before it, and we trust has caused it to take deep root."[18]

In a well-lived lifetime, Mitchell would see the reward of many planted roots with sturdy ascending vines in Quebec and at Dartmouth. He is the original source of Dartmouth's legacy in educating men and women of African ancestry. While avoiding confrontations with others on racial issues, he repeatedly confronted white society's prevalent views of what could be expected of persons of color. He earned a college degree at a time when doing so was a rare achievement for persons of any race.

Throughout his life he found great satisfaction in learning, especially from the study of the Bible and theology. He was ordained to the ministry. He was respected by the faculty and by his fellow students at Dartmouth, the members of his congregations, and the people of northern Vermont and the Eastern Townships of Quebec. Fellow members of the Baptist clergy considered him to be outstandingly effective as a missionary and evangelist. While he retained his respect for Calvin and remained grateful to Staughton, he thought independently about salvation and the Christian life and became regarded as a profound theologian by his contemporaries in the Canadian Baptist clergy. And always he offered a favorable representation of human potential unfettered by arbitrary shackles and impediments.

In accounting for Mitchell's success in reaching his goals, it is legitimate to acknowledge that he repeatedly benefited from extraordinarily good luck—a resourceful mother, Olive *dite* Cazabon; the white and colored Creoles of Martinique who gifted him the spirit of an adventurous sailor and the inquiring mind of a young scholar; Captain Prentiss of Portland, Maine; the Baptist divines Payson and Staughton; the Brown and Gilman-Chamberlain families of Hanover; Dartmouth faculty and students; members of the Baptist congregation in Etna, New Hampshire; colleagues in the Baptist ministry; and parishioners in New England and Canada. We would guess that the African American colleagues he met in Philadelphia—the city's most prominent black leaders—also had some important influence in his life, perhaps comforting some of his sorrows and, almost certainly, exemplifying what Christian energy and faith could bring to a community in need of religious guidance. But as the historians of Sutton, New Hampshire, emphasized, although he was assisted by others, both individuals and organizations, "he helped himself also."[19] Mitchell's learning to read at an early age, his quick acquisition of an excellent knowledge of English grammar and vocabulary, and his success as a student at Dartmouth cannot be dismissed as gifts from others. His achievements must be attributed to qualities that included intelligence, an aptitude for and a dedication to study and learning, initiative, courage, goodwill toward others—and to his perseverance in his "noble and independent course."

Our research on the life of Edward Mitchell has been consistently refracted through a racial lens, and we readily acknowledge being guilty of interpreting Mitchell as a man of color, even as he taught us that, in the end, he was a man of God who understood his own faults and imperfections without reference to his ethnicity. Having now reviewed his life's journey in some detail, we are convinced that although providential fate led him to test the soul of Dartmouth's moral ground, once having secured the high ground of educational attainment, he served the best instincts of his restless spirit, deeply religious faith, and strong moral bearing. In so doing, he served a larger cause. This seafaring immigrant from a French-Caribbean slave colony opened a door of opportunity through which many Dartmouth men and women of color have followed. A policy of no racial bar to Dartmouth admission endured. Between 1824 and 1950, before the era of civil rights, 131 men of African descent became alumni of Dartmouth, the second-largest number of blacks to enroll in a New England college. They came from foreign shores, rural byways, and crowded urban streets to inscribe their mark on the institution of the granite state of New Hampshire. Their dreams and aspirations were honored despite the racial biases and politics that even today continue to inflame passions. Dartmouth's history on the American race question is arguably unique, even distinguished among American colleges and universities.

ACKNOWLEDGMENTS

In the course of this research, we have greatly appreciated the cooperation and helpfulness of staff members at the McCord Museum of Canadian History, Montreal, Quebec, especially Nora Hague, for the opportunity to study the material in the Mitchell family fonds, and Céline Widman, who organized and digitized a large portion of its content. Jeffrey Horrell, dean of Dartmouth libraries, encouraged our efforts to bring this work to publication. Peter Carini, Sarah Hartwell, and Barbara Krieger, staff of the Rauner Special Collections Library of Dartmouth College, were consistently helpful in identifying and retrieving archival materials and encouraging our efforts. Thanks also to the Canadian Baptist Archives, McMaster Divinity College, Hamilton, Ontario, for access to historic church records, published and unpublished; the US Baptist Historical Society Archives, Mercer University, Atlanta, Georgia, for access to many additional historic published and unpublished church records—especially Betsy Dunbar, who not only provided access to resources but also did some searching on our behalf and called our attention to the entry in the Samson Street Church minutes on Mitchell's admission to membership in that church; the Eastern Townships Research Centre and the John Bassett Memorial Library, Bishop's University, Lennoxville, Quebec, for access to library resources; the Historical Society of Pennsylvania, Philadelphia, for access to books and microfilms; and the Laconia Public Library, Laconia, New Hampshire, for access to the resources in the New Hampshire history room and newspaper microfilms. Thanks to Kathy Curtis at the Stanstead Archives for recovering obscure newspaper articles. We are grateful to Anne-Marie Dionne of the South Baptist Church of Laconia for information on the Mitchell family from church records. John Scott, of Georgeville, Quebec, provided vital information from and copies of material in the archives of the Georgeville Historical Society and from his compilation of local sources important to Edward Mitchell's life in and around Georgeville. We thank the late Caldwell Titcomb for bringing our attention to the information on Mitchell in the *Baptist Encyclopaedia*. Others provided timely input when needed, including David LePitre of Stanstead, Quebec, who pointed our research to important documents. Ross Revelle and his family, descendants of Newton Brookhouse, helped sort through the acquisitions and sales of the properties purchased from the Mitchell family and provided some historical context for life on the Mitchell farm property.

Several academic historians helped guide our discoveries and interpretations of the parish records of Martinique and offered helpful leads to the works of French and Caribbean scholars. We especially thank Catherine Desbarats of McGill University, Rebecca Hartkopf Schloss at Texas A&M, Vincent Cousseau of the Université de Limoges, Pauline Remy of Hope College, and Reena Goldthree of Dartmouth College, who was an invaluable resource throughout. Geoffrey MacLean, who has thoroughly researched the Cazabon family of Trinidad, provided critical historical documents and constant feedback and comment as our research progressed. Elise Guyette and Susan Dunbar offered valuable comments and documentation on the lives of early African American individuals and families of Vermont and Lower Canada. Lucas Clawson, reference archivist at the Hagley Museum and Library in Wilmington, Delaware, kindly helped in finding and interpreting Mitchell's Philadelphia Savings Fund Society records.

The Black Alumni of Dartmouth Association (BADA) injected constant encouragement and energy into this project, especially presidents Ellis Rowe and Leah Bojnowski and members Dennis Young, Lesa Walden-Young, and Benjamin Moynihan, each of whom provided critical feedback. As Dartmouth students, Tai Antoine, Crishuana Y. Williams, and Derikka K. Mobley assisted by conducting original research and organizing discussions and presentations important to grounding our work in the history of African American experiences at Dartmouth College. Tailour V. Garbutt, another Dartmouth student, wrote an award-winning essay that fully captured the pain and the rewards of tackling research on Mitchell in the Dartmouth archives.

We are also grateful to the staff of the Baker-Berry Library, Dartmouth College, Hanover, New Hampshire; the Brown Library of the Maine Historical Society, Portland; the Mills Library of McMaster University, Hamilton, Ontario; the Ohio Historical Society, Columbus; and the public libraries of

Needham, Massachusetts, and Concord and Rochester, New Hampshire, for access to books, journals, and archival materials.

Our families were constant in their patience and forbearance, applauding our small discoveries and weathering all momentary disappointments. Thanks especially to Tanner and Melissa, who lived through every moment.

APPENDIX I

Selected Birth, Marriage, and Death Abstracts from Catholic Parish and Civil Registers of Martinique and Guadeloupe

Olive *dite* Cazabon (1761–1808), Mother of Edward Mitchel (born Édouard Michel)

YEAR	DATE/PLACE	EVENT	ÉTAT CIVIL TRANSCRIPTION AND TRANSLATION	SOURCE[a]
1761	12 Apr 1761 Fort Royal, Martinique	Baptism Olive *dite* Cazabon (1761–1808)	Baptized Olive, a three-week-old natural daughter of Marguerite, a *nègresse* who says she is free, living in this parish, after seeing the certificate of Le Procureur du Roy, dated the ninth of this month, the godfather Jean and the godmother Pauline. Signed Jean Ambroise, a Capuchin parish priest.	BNPM view 110 no 569
1790	6 May 1790 Fort Royal, Martinique	Baptism of son Jean Philippe Casabon (1790–1846)	Baptized Jean Philippe, born 24 Apr 1790, natural son of the *mulâtresse* Olive, free as she says by her act of enfranchisement registered 21 Sept 1789, godfather Isaac free *nègre*, godmother Elisabeth mulâtresse libre, Jean Isaac [Soubeiran], Father Jean Louis cap.	ANOM view 17

YEAR	DATE/PLACE	EVENT	ÉTAT CIVIL TRANSCRIPTION AND TRANSLATION	SOURCE[a]
1792	25 Feb 1792 Saint-Pierre, Martinique	Baptism of son Édouard Michel (1792–1872)	Baptized Édouard Michel, illegitimate *métis*, born the thirtieth of last month to Olive, a free *mulâtresse* woman as indicated by her duly certified act of emancipation of the 17th of July 1789. The godfather was Michel, free *métis*, the godmother Magdalaine, free *mulâtresse*, in attestation of which I signed with the godfather, the godmother being unable to sign. M[ichel]. Cazabon, Father Maunier.	ANOM view 18
1804	14 Nov 1802 Basse-Terre, Guadeloupe	Birth of son Joseph Honoré (1802–1817)	Born Joseph Honoré, a *mulâtre*, free by birth, born on the twenty-third brumaire of the year eleven [14 Nov 1802] of this city, natural and illegitimate son of Olive *dite* Cazabon, a free *mulâtresse* confirmed by a certificate of liberty, witnesses Madame Roux, wife of Mingot, Pierre . . . and Lazare Buissière, merchant. Signed Buissière, Roux Mingot	ANOM view 173
1808	7 Dec 1808 Basse-Terre, Guadeloupe	Death Olive Cazabon (1761–1808)	Came forward the named Joseph Billouin, a merchant, a *mulâtre* free and patented, who reported the death of the named Olive Cazabon, a *mulâtresse*, free and patented, the nineteenth pluviose in the year thirteen [8 Feb 1805], aged 50 years, native of Fort Royal, Martinique, on the declaration of the named Joseph Tourneaux and Antoine René, free *mulâtres*.	ANOM view 171 no 115

YEAR	DATE/PLACE	EVENT	ÉTAT CIVIL TRANSCRIPTION AND TRANSLATION	SOURCE[a]
1817	29 Apr 1817 Basse-Terre, Guadeloupe	Death of son Joseph Honoré (1802–1817)	Death of Joseph Honoré man of color, free by birth, native of this city, almost 15 years old, the natural son of the late Olive *dite* Cazabon, a woman of color, free by birth, and resident of Joseph Laboliere, a man of color, on the declaration of Joseph Laboliere and Victor Monrose.	ANOM view 21 no 7
1846	1846 Saint-Pierre, Martinique	Death of son Jean Philippe Casabon (1790–1846)	Died Sr. Jean Philippe Casabon, at a house located in this city, rue du Précipice, aged 56, a native of Fort Royal domiciled in Saint Pierre, son of unknown parents, witnesses Sir Louisy Modeste 31, merchant clerk, and Sir Charles Victor Jules Berion 21.	ANOM view 115 fol 363

[a] BNPM = La Banque numérique des patrimoines Martiniquais; ANOM = Archives Nationales d'Outre Mer.

Sources: Les registres d'individualités et les registres de population esclave de Martinique en ligne, La Banque numérique des patrimoines Martiniquais, www.patrimoines-martinique.org; Dépôt des papiers publics des colonies, Martinique and Guadeloupe, FR ANOM 1DPPC, Archives Nationales d'Outre Mer (ANOM), Aix-en-Provence, France, anom.archivesnationales.culture.gouv.fr/caomec2/.

Michel Cazabon (1778–ca. 1809), Godfather of Édouard Michel

YEAR	DATE/PLACE	EVENT	ÉTAT CIVIL TRANSCRIPTION AND TRANSLATION	SOURCE[a]
1778	16 Jun 1778 Sainte-Luce, Martinique	Baptism Michel Cazabon (b. 1778)	Baptized an infant born of the legitimate marriage of Dominique Cazabon, a resident of this parish, and Mme. Charlotte Elizabeth Fort Beauchaine, the godfather Michel Fort and godmother Dame Manet Bernard Brazdonna, signed D. Cazabon, Michel Fort.	ANOM view 5

YEAR	DATE/PLACE	EVENT	ÉTAT CIVIL TRANSCRIPTION AND TRANSLATION	SOURCE[a]
1792	10 Jan 1792 Saint-Pierre, Martinique	Witness at marriage Rose Jeanne Cazabon and Charles Louis Mourot	Married Charles Louis Mourot boulanger, native of [unreadable] in Lorraine, son of the late Sr. Jean Louis Mourot and Jeanne Catherine Robere, with Rose Jeanne Cazabon, native of St Esprit, minor daughter of Sr. Dominique Cazabon and the late Dame Charlotte Elisabeth Fort, signed by parents and others, including D. Cazabon, Rose Jean Cazabon, M[ichel] Cazabon.	ANOM view 15
1792	25 Feb 1792 Saint-Pierre, Martinique	Named godfather of Édouard Michel	Baptized Édouard Michel, illegitimate *métis*, born the thirtieth of last month to Olive, a free *mulâtresse* woman as indicated by her duly certified act of emancipation of the 17th of July 1789. The godfather was Michel, free *métis*, the godmother Magdalaine, free *mulâtresse*, in attestation of which I signed with the godfather, the godmother being unable to sign. M[ichel]. Cazabon, Father Maunier.	ANOM view 18
1793	15 Jun 1793 Saint Pierre, Martinique	Named representative for Godfather of Jean Baptiste Pointerai	Baptized Jean Baptiste born yesterday of the legitimate marriage of citizen Jean Baptiste Pointerai, native of Bordeaux, and citizen Anne Madeleine Robert, native of this parish, the godfather was citizen Jean Robert Pointerai, uncle of the baptized, represented by Michel Cazabon, and the godmother Catherine Robert, aunt of the baptized, signed Michel Cazabon, Maunier, priest.	ANOM view 16

YEAR	DATE/PLACE	EVENT	ÉTAT CIVIL TRANSCRIPTION AND TRANSLATION	SOURCE[a]
1795	23 Jan 1795 Saint-Pierre, Martinique	Named godfather of Rose	Baptized Rose, a *mulâtresse* born in the month of August of the previous year, natural daughter of Justine, a free *câpresse*, godfather Sir Michel Cazabon, and godmother Mlle. Marie Patrice. Signed M. Cazabon, Father Cairety.	ANOM view 15
1808	23 Apr 1808 Saint-Pierre, Martinique	Witness at death of Jean Dominique Cazabon	Died [Jean] Dominique Cazabon, native of Sainte-Luce, son of the late Dominique Cazabon and Mme. Rosette Fort Beauchêne, at the residence of his brother-in-law Mourot, residing at rue du Précipice, aged thirty-two years, on the declaration of Sir Michel Cazabon, baker in this town residing on rue du Précipice, aged twenty nine years, brother of the deceased, and Sir Augustine Rostenne, profession of mariner, residing on rue du Précipice, thirty-three years old, neighbor of the deceased. Signed M. Cazabon and A. Rostenne.	ANOM view 178
1808	20 Aug 1808 Saint-Pierre, Martinique	Witness at death of Rose Briançon	Died Rose aged 18 months, daughter of Sir François Briançon, master tailor residing rue du Précipice and Mme. Elizabeth Défis, on the declaration Sir Jose Joseph Benoit Bourguille and Michel Cazabon, baker, rue du Précipice, aged 29. Signed Bourguille, M. Cazabon.	ANOM view 209

[a] ANOM = Archives Nationales d'Outre Mer.

Source: Dépôt des papiers publics des colonies, Martinique and Guadeloupe, FR ANOM 1DPPC, Archives Nationales d'Outre Mer, Aix-en-Provence, France, anom.archivesnationales.culture.gouv.fr/caomec2/.

Dominique Cazabon (1737–1802)—Parents, Wife, and Children

YEAR	DATE/PLACE	EVENT	ÉTAT CIVIL TRANSCRIPTION AND TRANSLATION	SOURCE[a]
1765	12 May 1765 Le Vauclin, Martinique	Death of mother Jeanne Baudry (1710–65)	Died Jeanne Baudry, native of the city of Nantes, parish St. Nicolas, wife of François Cazabon.	ANOM view 8
1773	2 Nov 1773 Saint-Esprit, Martinique	Marriage Dominique Cazabon (1737–1802) and Elisabeth Charlotte Beauchaine Fort (1756–1781)	Marriage of Sir Cazabon, native of St. Pierre, resident in the parish of Vauclin, legitimate son of the late Sir François Cazabon and of Mme. Jeanne Baudry with Mlle. Charlotte Elisabeth Fort Beauchêne, native of the parish, baptized in Rivière Salée, minor age, legitimate daughter of the late Jean Baptiste Fort Beauchêne and of the late Mme. Rose Charlot Menet, signed Charlotte Fort Beauchêne, Noyer, Fort Villeronce, Ariant Fournier, Mme. Cazabon, Braseronce Fort Beauchêne, Father Paul, capuchin.	ANOM view 8
1774	6 Sep 1774 Saint-Esprit, Martinique	Death of son Unnamed Cazabon	Buried a child *ondoyé* of Sr. Casabon and Dame Beauchaine.	ANOM view 5
1775	17 Jul 1775 Saint-Esprit, Martinique	Baptism of son Jean Dominique Cazabon (1775–1808)	Baptism administered to a child *ondoyé* at home on account of infirmity by Goujon de Ruisseau, born on the 9th of this month of legitimate marriage of Dominique Cazabon and Dame Charlotte Elizabeth Fort Beauchaine, inhabitants of this parish, named Jean Dominique by Fortville Ronce, godfather Jean Charles Fort Beauchaine and godmother Mlle. Marianne Cazabon, uncle and aunt of the child, signed with Fortvile Ronce, Cazabon, Marianne Cazabon, Father Paul.	ANOM view 5

YEAR	DATE/PLACE	EVENT	ÉTAT CIVIL TRANSCRIPTION AND TRANSLATION	SOURCE[a]
1778	19 Jun 1778 Sainte-Luce, Martinique	Baptism of son Michel Cazabon (b. 1778)	Baptized an infant boy born of the legitimate marriage of Dominique Cazabon, a resident of this parish, and Charlotte Elizabeth Fort Beauchaine, named Michel by Michel Fort.	ANOM view 5
1780	Feb 1780 Le Vauclin, Martinique	Death of sister	Buried Marie-Anne Cazabon, died yesterday, aged 33.	ANOM view 2
1780	7 Jun 1780 Sainte-Luce, Martinique	Baptism of daughter Theresa Marie Cazabon (1780–1808)	Baptized a child born of the legitimate marriage of Dominique Cazabon and Charlotte Fort Beauchaine, named Thérèse Marie by Jean Baptiste Beauchaine and by Mme. Thérèse Cablian Ferre, godfathers and godmother, signed D. Cazabon, Beauchaine, [others], and the parish priest.	ANOM view 3
1781	Jan 1781 Sainte-Luce, Martinique	Death of wife Charlotte Elisabeth Fort Beauchaine	Buried Mme. Charlotte Elisabeth Fort Beauchaine aged 25 years, spouse of Dominique Cazabon, daughter of Jean Baptiste Fort Beauchaine and Rose Perrine Menet.	ANOM
1788	24 Jun 1788 Fort Royal, Martinique	Death of sister Luce Cazabon (1737–88)	Buried Mlle. Luce Cazabon, a native of the village of St. Pierre, died the previous day, aged 51.	ANOM view 24
1802	9 Jul 1802 Basse-Terre, Guadeloupe	Death Dominique Cazabon (1737–1802)	Died Citizen Dominique Cazabon, secretary at the military hospital of this city, native of St Pierre, aged sixty-four.	ANOM view 79 no 152

YEAR	DATE/PLACE	EVENT	ÉTAT CIVIL TRANSCRIPTION AND TRANSLATION	SOURCE[a]
1808	23 Apr 1808 Saint-Pierre, Martinique	Death of son [Jean] Dominique Cazabon (1776–1808)	Died Dominique Cazabon, native of Sainte-Luce, son of the late Dominique Cazabon and Rosette LeFort Beauchêne, at home of Sir Mourot, baker and brother-in-law, living on rue du Précipice, aged 32, not married, by the declaration of Sir Michel Cazabon baker of this city, living rue du Précipice, aged 29 years, brother of the deceased. Signed Michel Cazabon and Sir Augustine Rostenne, sailor by profession, living rue du Précipice, age 33, neighbor of the deceased.	ANOM view 178
1810	20 Sep 1810 Saint-Pierre, Martinique	Death of daughter Jeanne Rose Cazabon (1777–1810)	Died Mme. Jeanne Rose Cazabon, 33 years old, wife of Sir Louis Mourot, baker, by the declaration of Sir Géraud Chartrand, 42 years old, resident of Le Fort and Sir Jacques Dénis Villegente, 58 years old, resident. Maximin Cairety priest.	ANOM view 69

[a] ANOM = Archives Nationales d'Outre Mer.

Source: Dépôt des papiers publics des colonies, Martinique and Guadeloupe, FR ANOM 1DPPC, Archives Nationales d'Outre Mer, Aix-en-Provence, France, anom.archivesnationales.culture.gouv.fr/caomec2/.

APPENDIX 2

Edward Mitchell and Neighbors in Philadelphia

GASKILL STREET BETWEEN SOUTH THIRD AND FOURTH STREETS, 1820

NAME[a]	OCCUPATION/ IDENTIFICATION	ADDRESS[b]	
		South side	*North side*
Denham, Susan[c,d]	Widow	40/42 Gaskill	
Skinner, John[d]	Sea captain		43 Gaskill
Dewar, Susannah[c,d] Dungan, David[d]	Teacher Tobacconist	44 Gaskill	
Cirrell, Henry[e]	Carpenter		45 Gaskill
McAllister, Charles[d]	Tailor	46 Gaskill	
Ford, Deborah[d]	Widow of Robert Ford		47 Gaskill
VanMetre, John[d]	Paperhanger	48 Gaskill	
Soup Society House[d]	Society for Supplying the Poor with Soup Gratis	49 Gaskill	
Rose, Ann[d] Barriere, Peter[c]	Widow Baker		51 Gaskill (313)
Brown, Elenor[c,d]	Widow, tailoress		53 Gaskill (315)
Mitchell, Legome[c] **Mitchell, Edward**[c] **Sourwalt, Serrah**[c] **Sourwalt, Anthony**[d] **Burgoyne, Stephen**[d]	Wife Porter Wife Mariner (also silversmith, sailmaker) Mariner		55 Gaskill (317)
M'Connell, Eleanor[c,d]	Teacher		57 Gaskill
Cheeks, William[e]	MD		61 Gaskill
Colonel, John[d] Davis, Elizabeth[d] Davis, Thomas[c] **Barthelemy, Wm**[c,d]	Jeweler Widow, carpetweaver [Husband or son] Waiter	62 Gaskill [Back]	

NAME[a]	OCCUPATION/ IDENTIFICATION	ADDRESS[b]	
		South side	*North side*
Hopkins, John[c]	Carpenter		63 Gaskill
Mitchell, Joseph B.[c,d]	Accountant, future bank president	64 Gaskill	
Coates, Samuel, Jr.[c,d]	Accountant		65 Gaskill
Vesey, Edward[d]	Sawyer &c.	66 Gaskill	
Huddy, Hunlock[d]	Inspector of customs		67 Gaskill
Cook, Elisha. W.[c,d]	Turner		69 Gaskill
Rice Sarah[d]	Widow		71 Gaskill
Young, James H.[c,d]	Engraver		73 Gaskill
M'Neilledge, Alexander[d]	Mate of vessel		75 Gaskill
Lyndall, Samuel[d]	Cabinetmaker	80 Gaskill	

[a] Name in bold indicates free person of color.

[b] Number in parentheses refers to modern numbering.

[c] Source: 1820 US Census.

[d] Source: 1820 Philadelphia city directory.

[e] Source: 1819 Philadelphia city directory.

APPENDIX 3

Captain William Prentiss's Caribbean Voyages, 1803–11

TRIP NO.	YEAR/ SHIP	ROUTE AND DATES[a]	LEAVE/ RETURN	SHIPPING NEWS OR PORT SHIPPING LIST EXTRACT	SOURCE[b]
1	1803 Schooner *Clarissa*	Portland–Guadeloupe Jan 1803	►	Feb. 8th, latitude 26, 49 long. 63, spoke sch'r Clarissa, Prentiss, from Wilmington, for Guadeloupe, out 16 days	*Telegraph and Daily Advertiser* (Baltimore), 1 Mar 1803
		Guadeloupe–Portland 30 Apr 1803	◄	Portland, April 30. Arrived Schr. Clarissa, Prentiss, 35 days from Guadaloupe	*Daily Advertiser* (New York), 9 May 1803
2	1804 Brig *Edward*	Portland–Guadeloupe–Martinique 28 Aug 1804–Nov 1804	►	Sailed Edward, Prentiss, Guadeloupe	*New York Price Current,* 1 Sep 1804
			◄	Arrived brig Edward, Prentiss, Marin, (Mart.), 25 days	*Commercial Advertiser,* 30 Nov 1804
3	1805 Brig *Edward*	Martinique–Portland 4 Jan 1805–22 Apr 1805	►	Cleared, Prentiss, Guadaloupe	*Eastern Argus,* 4 Jan 1805
			◄	Portland, April 22 from . . . Edward, Prentiss, Martinique	*New York Price Current,* 4 May 1805
4	1806 Brig *Triton*	Portland–Martinique Aug 1806	◄►	The case of the brig Triton was determined . . . condemnation on the grounds of its being a circuitous route	*Virginia Gazette,* 8 Oct 1806

TRIP NO.	YEAR/ SHIP	ROUTE AND DATES[a]	LEAVE/ RETURN	SHIPPING NEWS OR PORT SHIPPING LIST EXTRACT	SOURCE[b]
5	1807 Brig *Ocean*	Portland–Havana 11 Mar 1807	►	Cleared Ocean, Prentiss, Havanna [*sic*]	*Eastern Argus*, 12 Mar 1807
		Havana–Portland 18 May 1807	►	At Portland, May 18. Arrived . . . brig Ocean, Printess [*sic*], Havanna[*sic*], 17 days	*New York Aurora*, 26 May 1807
6	1809 Brig *Tropic*	Portland–Surinam 20 Apr 1809–31 May 1809	►	Portland April 20, Tropic Prentiss, [for] Spanish Maine	*Baltimore Price-Current*, 29 Apr 1809 NOSL for Surinam, 31 May 1809
		Surinam–Boston 20 Jul 1809–28 Aug 1809	◄	Now landing, Cargo of brig Tropic, 262 hhhds, 36 tierces, 3 bbls first quality Surinam Molasses	NOSL for Surinam, 20 July 1809 *Boston Commercial Gazette*, 4 Sep 1809
7	1809 Brig *Tropic*	Portland–Martinique 4 Nov 1809–17 Jan 1810	►	Master Prentiss, Tropic, 161 tons, crew 7, Portland. Cargo: 35 kegs butter; 70 empty hhds	*Baltimore Price-Current*, 4 Nov 1809 NOSL for Martinique, 17 Jan 1810
		Martinique–St. Bart's–Boston 17 Apr 1810–17 May 1810	◄	Master Wm Burns, Tropic, 161 tons, crew 9, Portland. Cargo: Molasses Rum 276 hhds 43 brls, 35 kegs butter	NOSL for Martinique, 17 Apr 1810 *Federal Republican*, 21 May 1810
		Boston–Portland 17 May 1810–18 May 1810	◄	Bartholomew, 32 . . . from St. Bartholomew for Castine [ME]	*Charleston Courier*, 1 Jun 1810
8	1810 Brig *George*	**Portland–Jamaica 27 Sep 1810–1 Nov 1810**	►	Am Brig George, Wm Prentiss, 224 tons, 8 crew, Owner Albert Newhall. Cargo: 20 bbls bread, 10,000 staves	*Federal Gazette* (Baltimore), 27 Sep 1810 NOSL for Jamaica, pt. 4, 1 Nov 1810
		Jamaica–Wilmington (NC) 20 Nov 1810–Dec 1810	◄	Am Brig George, Wm Prentiss, 224 tons, crew 7, Portland, Owner Albert Newhall. Cargo: ballast	*Federal Gazette* (Baltimore), 23 Nov 1810 NOSL for Jamaica, pt. 4, 20 Nov 1810

TRIP NO.	YEAR/ SHIP	ROUTE AND DATES[a]	LEAVE/ RETURN	SHIPPING NEWS OR PORT SHIPPING LIST EXTRACT	SOURCE[b]
9	1811 Brig *George*	Wilmington (NC)– Jamaica 15 Jan 1811– 28 Mar 1811	►	Jan 15–22, for . . . George, Prentiss, West Indies	*Baltimore Price-Current,* 2 Feb 1811
		Jamaica– Yucatan (Mexico) 28 Mar 1811– Apr 1811	►	Brig George, Wm Prentiss, 224 tons, crew 8, Portland, built Portland 1806, Owner Albert Newhall. Cargo: ballast	NOSL for Jamaica, pt. 4, 28 Mar 1811
		Campeachy (Mexico)– Portland May 1811– Jun 1811	◄	Arrived—The brig George, Prentiss, of Portland, 38 days from Campeachy, with logwood to John Ferrers	*New-York Gazette,* 18 Jun 1811
10	1811 Schooner *Joseph*	Portland–Aux Cayes (Haiti) 6 Aug 1811– Oct 1811	►	Left at Aux–Cayes, Oct 10, schr. Joseph, Prentiss, of Portland, to sail in 12 ds	*American and Commercial Daily Advertiser* (Baltimore), 18 Nov 1811
		Aux Cayes (Haiti)– Portland Oct 1811– 11 Dec 1811	◄	Ar. schr Joseph, capt Prentiss, 34 days from Aux Cays, with Molasses, Coffee, &c to Deering, Newall & Watson	*Portland Argus,* 19 Dec 1811

[a] Route in bold indicates that Edward Mitchell was on board.

[b] NOSL = Naval Office Shipping Lists.

Sources: Naval Office Shipping Lists, British Online Archives; newspaper extracts are from reports typically found in "Shipping News" sections, *America's Historical Newspapers*, NewsBank.

APPENDIX 4

Outline of the religious experience of Edward Mitchell written August 13, 1829

On August 13, 1829, a year after his graduation from Dartmouth College, Edward Mitchell made his confession of faith to a member council of the Baptist Church of Hanover, New Hampshire. He related his experiences of religious awakening and baptism as the foundation of his faith, professed his belief in Baptist Church doctrine, and wrote his account of church ordinances. On August 18, 1829, the congregation ordained Mitchell as an evangelist. The following is a transcription of Mitchell's confession as written by his hand in a small booklet of folded manuscript paper. The holograph is preserved in the Mitchell Family Fonds (P044) of the McCord Museum, Montreal, Canada.

About twenty years ago, I was residing in Portland in the state of Maine. Not far from the time that the late Dr. [Edward] Payson was settled there. His preaching was instrumental to the conviction and conversion of many persons in Portland about this time; among whom, was the gentleman's wife with whom I then resided. Her faithful and pious conversation with me was that which made any serious impression[s] on my mind that were lasting.

I then seemed to myself as one who had been in a deep sleep all my days; I began to feel that I was and had been a great sinner against God. A sence of my sins often caused me to weep and to attempt to pray, but still there was an unwillingness to give up all my sins, nor had I any reference to the Atonement of Christ when I prayed.

For a considerable time, perhaps for eight or nine months, I was in a kind of slavish fear; sometimes my conviction was considerable pungent, at other times I would be in stupidity and carelessness.

I went to sea, with an intention of following the sea-faring life; In the first voyage I nearly, or quite lost my religious impression. I went a second voyage. The most of that I spent in my wicked course and carelessness about my soul.

Nearly at the close of this voyage on my passage home, it pleased God once more to awaken me. A violent storm arose, I thought myself just going to eternity in an unprepared state. A sence of my ingratitude to God, of the great aggravation of my sin, and the great opportunities I had neglected, all seemed to be placed before me and to fill me with horror. I saw and was constrained to acknowledge that it would be perfect justice in God were I to be cast off forever. It pleased God to spare me, and in a few weeks after we arrive[d] in safety.

About this time I heard two sermons, one on the solemnity of death and judgement, and on the other, the great reparation, which will take place on the day of judgement; The first from Math v. 25 by Mr. [Nathan S. S.] Beman. then of the 3rd Congregational Church, Portland, second from Math 21:40 by the late Dr. [Edward] Payson, of the 2nd Church

These made very solemn impressions on my mind, and I felt the solemn importance of being prepared for those same events. At this time I was impressed with the necessity of giving up the seafaring life on account of its numerous temptations to vice; although my prospect for worldly gain in that was every day brightening.

I went from Portland to Philadelphia, where I remained from 1811 to 1820. For 2 or 3 months of my first residence in the place, I attended worship with an episcopalian society, and for a while rested in the system of do and live.

I calculated to say over some forms of prayer, amend somewhat external conduct, to attend church in hope that by that means I should find acceptance with God. But hearing that on a certain Sabbath evening, Dr. [William] Staughton, a Baptist minister, was going to preach a funeral sermon, I felt a desire to go, which I did. His text was Math 11:28. 'Come unto me', etc. The holy rest of heaven which he spoke of in the course of his address made me feel that something deeper than an autumn reformation was necessary.

Several sermons which I heard at this time was blessed in making me acquainted with the sinfulness of my heart; and I was lead to pray to God for mercy, and ask the forgiveness of my sin, but I had no view nor idea of the way of salvation by grace.

One evening in the Spring of 1811, the Dr. preached from the verses, 'For ye know the grace of our Lord Jesus Christ', etc. 2 Cor. 8:9. The condescension of Christ in coming to save sinners was set to my mind with such light, that I was enabled to renounce all my self-righteousness, and to look to Jesus alone for righteousness and strength.

I do not recollect any sudden transition from darkness and distress to light and comfort. But I felt a calmness in believing in Jesus Christ, and a delight in him to which I had before been a stranger.

At this time I felt a peculiar pleasure in reading and researching the scriptures. I felt a love to prayer and to saints, they appeared to me the excellents of the earth, and when I saw them together commemorating the dying love of the Savior, I often felt strong desire to be among them.

After visiting Dr. Staughton few times for private conversation on the state of my mind, I went before the Church October 14th 1811; and having received their fellowship, I was baptized on the 19th and received into the Church on the 20th of the same month.

Exercises in Regard to Preaching

Soon after I was enabled to hope in the Saviour, I felt a desire to consecrate all my time and talents to his service. I thought if I only had the grace and gifts requisite for such an undertaking, how gladly I would go forth and preach to my fellow men the rich grace of a Saviour.

Thoughts like these would be more deeply impressed on my mind at sometimes than at other times. But when I examined myself by meditation on the scriptures privately to ascertain whether I had any gifts with which I might venture forward, I would find such barrenness in my mind, and the scriptures would be so much shut up, that I would think my thoughts about preaching was only the workings of a proud heart.

A few times in some small circle I would try to exhort, but I found my gift so small here, that I again and again gave up the thoughts of preaching. These were some reasons for the space of five years, when I was quite low in mind, then I thought but little on the subject. At other seasons in the same space, when being refreshed, it would lay with weight on my mind.

A scene of affliction I was called to pass through in 1816 awakened my mind much to the subject of preaching. Though I could not satisfy myself respecting the pain, I concluded that I would search the scriptures more diligently, and attain in reading such help as might be useful, and leave the event with providence. I concluded if I had any talents to preach, God would show it to the Church, and they would call me to it. In that way I left the subject and there remained.

In the year 1820 Providence so ordered, I came to Hanover. In the fall of the same year I visited the brethren in the east part of the town; then a feeble body, scattered and few. Through that fall and the following winter and spring I had some opportunity to exercise my gift with them in prayer and exhortation.

About this time when I attempted in conference and prayer meeting to speak from some passage of scripture, I often found my mind enlarged and could speak with some degree of freedom. At length, in the Spring of 1821, the one and another of the brethren began to invite and urge me to a more public exercise of my gift. At first I hesitated, but I soon found that I was brought to that very place where I had left the subject of preaching; viz., that if God designed that I should preach he would show it to his children, and they would call me out.

Accordingly in May 1821, I made an appointment for preaching. I have felt since, that this is all that I wish to live for. The assistance that I have often found, I trust from God, together with my early impressions and his providential direction have induced me to believe that it was his will that [I] should preach the gospel of his Son.

NOTES

Introduction

1. The distinction of first Ivy League graduate of African ancestry has sometimes been accorded Theodore Sedgwick Wright, who graduated from Princeton Theological Seminary in 1828. The seminary and Princeton University (the latter called the College of New Jersey until 1896) were then and are now distinct institutions, so Wright should not be designated a graduate of Princeton University. It has also been said that Prince Saunders attended Dartmouth some twenty years earlier than Mitchell, but Saunders was in fact a student at Moor's Indian Charity School, which was distinct from Dartmouth College and which did not confer or offer courses toward baccalaureates. The other self-identified men of color to graduate from an American college before Edward Mitchell were Edward Jones (Amherst College, 1826) and John Brown Russwurm (Bowdoin College, 1826). Alexander Lucius Twilight, who graduated from Middlebury College in 1823, is now recognized as the first US college graduate of African ancestry, but he did not self-identify as a person of color in his time at Middlebury. His African ancestry was uncovered by modern research, which established his link to a family of color counted in the US 1800 Federal Census of Vermont.

2. Mitchell was the first ordained clergyman of African descent to serve a wholly or predominantly white pastoral charge in Canada. Samuel Dunbar (1762–1832), likewise of biracial ancestry, who had come to Barnston, Lower Canada, from Massachusetts in 1800, was licensed as a lay preacher by the Methodist Episcopal Conference during the latter years of his life. He served as a pastoral visitor, caring for the ill, and preached on various occasions, but he was not ordained or settled as the pastor of a congregation. See Hubbard and Lawrence (1874) and Suzanne Dunbar, "Descendants of Sampson Dunbar," accessed March 25, 2011, www.olypen.com/tinkers/SampsonDunbar4gendescendancy.pdf. In the United States, some African American ministers in the early nineteenth century had been licensed to preach by predominantly white denominations (notably including the Rev. Richard Allen, an African American leader in Philadelphia, in the early years of his ministry), but nearly all of them, if they became pastors of churches, served black congregations. Of the very few African American pastors of predom-

inantly white churches during that period, the best known was the Rev. Lemuel Haynes, of African and English ancestry, who was, as noted above, an ordained Congregational minister in Vermont and New York from 1783 to 1833. See Saillant (2003) and Fernald (2007), who discusses Haynes in the context of slavery in New Hampshire. That Mitchell was likewise an ordained clergyman who served white congregations in New Hampshire and Vermont during the latter part of that same period is less well known, although it was noted by Fisher (1935).

3. Antoine (2012).

4. Chapman (1867, 244). See also annotated copy at "Sketches of the Alumni of Dartmouth College," Rauner Special Collections Library, Dartmouth College, accessed 23 August 2011, www.dartmouth.edu/~library/rauner/chapman/.

5. Slater (1994, 52).

6. Personal papers and ephemera of the Edward Mitchell family were deposited at the McCord Museum of Canadian History at an uncertain date, but probably in the 1920s. The Mitchell family fonds (1822–97) include originals of Mitchell's college essays and discourses, hand-copied words of sermons, pastoral letters, summaries of his thoughts on religious themes, biblical reference notes, and original newspapers containing his obituaries. A few hymns are included, none written by Mitchell. John Leland's "Evening Hymn," with the opening line "The day is past and gone," is copied with words and two-part music. Other hymns, for which only the words and the melody were copied, include "Rest for the Weary," by William Hunter, which was an old favorite of the time, and a hymn known by its opening line "There is a school on earth begun," by E. B. Sherwood, similar in its theme of salvation and the afterlife. There is an anti-alcohol "church ballad," with words only, by George Easton, an agent of the Scottish Temperance League (Easton had lectured at Sherbrooke and Eaton Corner, in the Eastern Townships, in March 1869, and Mitchell was quite likely present and may have met him on one or more of those occasions), and a few unattributed secular verses.

7. In testimony given to church elders prior to his ordination in 1829, Mitchell offered a confession of faith and statement of his personal creed. He committed his testimony to writing with the heading "Outlines of the religious experience of Edward Mitchell Written August 15, 1829 at Sutton, New Hampshire." The twenty-page booklet, written in his hand on folded manuscript paper, is preserved in the Mitchell family fonds, P044/A,6.1, McCord Museum of Canadian History, Montreal, Quebec.

ONE Birth and Baptism

1. Mitchell's birthdate in American and Canadian sources is January 27, 1794. The Saint-Pierre, Martinique, Catholic parish baptismal record gives the date as January 30, 1792. The minor difference on the January calendar is understandable,

but the year discrepancy required further investigation. Strong collateral evidence established that we had Mitchell's Martinique baptismal record. The 1794 birth year appears in American and Canadian records after 1860. Based on the 1794 date, Mitchell would have been thirty, not thirty-two, upon entering Dartmouth in 1824. At some point, he or someone responsible for his employment or enrollment may have wanted him to appear two years younger. In this book, Mitchell's age will reference the birth date stated in his baptismal record: January 30, 1792.

2. Description of Martinique and Saint-Pierre taken from varied historic and contemporary sources: Daney (1846), Chauleau (1993), Giraud (1980), Louis (2011), McCloy (2015), Moreau de Jonnés (1822), Pinckard (1816), and Lambolez (1905).

3. From Voyages: The Trans-Atlantic Slave Trade Database, a comprehensive compilation of slave cargoes from Africa to the Atlantic World, we obtained data on numbers of captives embarked at Africa and disembarked at Martinique: from 1653 (date of first arrival) to 1791 (just prior to Mitchell's birth in 1792), 157,804 slaves embarked in 548 voyages, and 132,805 survived passage (14.5 percent death rate) (www.slavevoyages.org/voyages/lJk4T6NW); and for the total up to 1831 (when the legal slave trade ended in the French colonies), 204,623 slaves embarked in 704 voyages, and 174,599 survived passage (14.95 percent death rate) (www.slavevoyages.org/voyages/1fVoZjag).

4. Descriptions and historical information are based on nineteenth-century texts (Coke 1808–11; Pinckard 1816; Moreau de Jonnés 1822; Monnier 1828; Daney 1846) and a history of Catholic priests in Martinique (Rennard 1951).

5. Several French and British sources recount details of the 1794 Battle of Martinique. We relied on Howard (2015), whose comprehensive presentation locates the Martinique conquest in the context of the British campaign in the West Indies from 1793 to 1815. For an earlier British account, see Fortescue (1906).

6. Cormack (2011) gives a concise summary and analysis of different interpretations of the shifting alliances among Creole whites (planters and *petits blancs*), *gens de couleur*, and black slaves in Martinique during the French Republican period. See Schloss (2009) for an informative study of ethnic, sociocultural, and political dynamics in Martinique society from 1802 until the end of slavery in 1848.

7. Tomich's (1990) comprehensive study of Martinique sugarcane production provides good information on the African territorial origins of Martinique's imported slaves and the attitudes of planters towards the different African tribal groups. A more detailed portrait has been developed from modern ethnographic studies of African populations and the findings of the collaborative Voyages database, which is the source of slave disembarkation numbers.

8. Worthen (1890); Mitchell obituaries in *Express and Standard* (Newport, VT), April 2, 1872, 2, and *Stanstead Journal*, April 3, 1872, 2. Material in the *Stanstead*

Journal has been located not only through issues in the Mitchell family fonds at the McCord Museum of Canadian History, and searches of back numbers now online, but also from Wilson and Tilton (1993), who had access to issues additional to those online.

9. In the French West Indies, Martinique and Guadeloupe had racial classification systems for mixed-race offspring that differed from other French possessions while employing the same labels. In the simplest terms, for Martinique/Guadeloupe, the proportion of black ancestry for selected racial categories was as follows: *mulâtre*, one-half; *métis*, one-fourth; *carterone*, one-eighth; and *mamelouc*, one-sixteenth. In Saint-Domingue/Haiti, the meanings of *carterone* and *métis* were reversed. In the French Antilles, the phrase *gens de couleur* typically applied to any person of mixed African and white ancestry. In some contexts, *mulâtre*/mulatto and *gens de couleur* are used interchangeably. For background, see Giraud (1980).

10. The Mouillage parish (la Mouillage paroisse de Notre-Dame de Bon-Port), one of several Saint-Pierre parishes, is the port district of the city served by the l'église de Notre Dame du Bon Port. *Mouillage* means anchorage and usually references a shipping port.

11. Prosperity of the Catholic Dominican friars and their slave plantation in the Saint-Pierre parish is noted in Rennard (1951) and McCloy (2015).

12. The Superior Council performed administrative and judicial functions in French colonial societies. The council's *huissiers*, or bailiffs, were responsible for notifications and enforcements of its rulings. The bailiffs established a self-funded "communal purse" to defend against harmful claims and acts. For a complete transcript of the legal proceedings of Cazabon's personal dispute with Noyer, which contains details about Cazabon's personal and family life, see "Noyer, Guillaume, habitant de la Martinique" (1784/1785).

13. Pinckard (1816, 331–32), a British physician and writer, traveled the West Indies and published astute observations on the social organization of Martinique's slave society. Quotes from his writings were later published by English abolitionists.

14. Mention of Father Joseph-Jean Maunier (1751–1803) is made in several studies of Martinique, including Daney (1846, 107, 364); in Rennard's (1951) history of the work of Catholic Parish priests; and in communications to the *GHC Bulletin* (Bardin 1990, 1998) that describe Maunier's central role in the 1790 patriotic raising of the tricolor flag at Saint-Pierre. Biographical notes are found in Salvarelli (1897) and Catholic parish birth records of Saint-Maximin-la-Sainte-Baume (Var, France) for March 11, 1751.

15. "Dom Cazabon, passenger," No. 205/277 (1795), ADM 103/510 part 1, Register of POWs, Martinique, 1797–1801, The National Archives, Kew, UK (hereafter, TNA).

16. At various times, priests were given different instructions for documenting

freedom status. At the time of Mitchell's birth, the Act of 1789 required priests to demand proof from blacks and *gens de couleur* claiming freedom status. These attestations did not always hold up under close scrutiny. Olive gave "proof" of her free status to parish priests or civil authorities on at least three different occasions during her lifetime.

17. While the French were in power and perceived a constant British threat, slaves who served the French in the military for a specified time were freed. Slaves could be freed by their masters under French rule, but not during the period of British rule, from 1794 to 1802. The requirements and restrictions for granting and receiving freedom status varied over time.

18. Remy (2015, 7, 158) analyzes the intersection of race and culture in the "open space" of French colonial cities as it influenced social and sexual power dynamics between free women of color and Creole whites. She devotes a chapter to Saint-Pierre (pp. 111–82).

19. Dominique was the son of François Cazabon, possibly the original habitant of Martinique. François's origins are obscure, but he appears to have come to Martinique around 1820 and is described in an 1851 marriage ceremony (probably his second) to Marie Jeanne Simon as a "*natif du Robert, paroisse St. Rose*" in Martinique. François's first wife, the mother of Dominique Cazabon, was Jeanne Baudry, born 1712, in St. Nicolas parish, Nantes, France. See appendix 1 for extracts of Martinique parish registers for the Cazabon family.

20. The term *habitant* and its complement, *colon*, used in the context of the French West Indies, refer to French immigrants and their descendants who owned land in the colonies. A *colon* is usually the original French settler.

21. Cazabon's appointment as bailiff is recorded in minutes of the Conseil Supérieur 1779–85: "1783, sixth month, Presented the name Dominique Cazabon bailiff in the *sénéchaussée* of this city to be provided with a commission of bailiff in the court granted to him by the general and intendant of this island dated March 12 by them signed and countersigned by their secretaries, below which is the act of registration of that in the seneschals of that city on the seventeenth of the same year." Author's translation from French text, transcribed by Geoffrey MacLean.

22. Mackintosh (2013).

23. "Dom Cazabon, passenger," TNA.

24. David Quénéhervé reported that on September 12, 1794, in Landerneau (outside Brest, France), Dominique Cazabon signed with other "*déportés*" from Martinique as a witness for Rose Boromée, who claimed abandonment by her husband, Frédéric Alexis. See "Trouvailles de David Quénéhervé" (2012).

25. Williams's (2009, 176) entry for the ship *Heart of Oaks* includes a description of four vessels (including the *Tiber*, carrying Dominique Cazabon) commandeered by the French to transport passengers from France to the West Indies.

26. See appendix 1.

27. The transcript of court records and legal proceedings, "Noyer, Guillaume, habitant de la Martinique," reveals Cazabon's ownership of the slave woman Pétronille. The original civil case was initiated by Noyer who had purchased Pétronille and her five children from Dominique Cazabon in 1775. By creative and perhaps unscrupulous maneuvers, Cazabon regained possession of Pétronille and her children. Noyer died in 1785 and his wife, Catherine Gujon, pursued the case. Pétronille and her children eventually achieved freedom, and at least three of the five children survived into the nineteenth century, each carrying the Cazabon or Casabon name.

In the court record, Cazabon acknowledges the sale of Pétronille and her family to Noyer and gives the names and ages of the children: "Je reconnais avoir vendu et livré à M. Noyer ma négresse Pétronille avec ses enfants mulâtre nommée Sophie âgé de huit ans, Hélène âgé de six ans, François âgé de quatre ans et Modeste âgé de deux ans, et Charlotte âgé d'un mois, pour prix et tournois de quatre mils cinq cents que je payé en quittance et reconnais me réservant Sophie et Hélène dont j'ai couru les risques jusqu'à la livraison, au St. Esprit, ce 13 février 1775; signé Cazabon." (From "Noyer, Guillaume, habitant de la Martinique" [1784/1785].)

"François" is likely the François Cazabon who emigrated to Trinidad and died in 1855. His son was the painter Michel-Jean Cazabon. Martinique and Guadeloupe parish civil records give details on the deaths of Pétronille, Sophie, and Hélène:

Pétronille: Died January 20, 1814, Le Vauclin, Martinique. "Pétronille métive libre, fille naturelle de feue Segrimaux, habitante de bourg du Vauclin est décède âgé d'environ 74 ans, témoins Charles et Joseph, hommes de couleur libres" (ANOM view 3).

Sophie: Died January 6, 1841, Basse-Terre, Guadeloupe. "Sophie Casabon, fille de Pétronille, Mlle. Sophie Casabon, âgé de 63 ans, sans profession en cette ville, native du Vauclin, Martinique, fille naturelle de la feue Petronille, par Pierre Joseph 33, maitre cordonnier, et Joseph Cailles 22, marin" (ANOM view 94, no. 4).

Hélène: Died August 11, 1848, Le Vauclin, Martinique. "Mort de Hélène Casabon, âgée 84 ans en sa maison sise au bourg du Vauclin, témoins Adolph Bouffard 36 géreur d'habitation et Mathieu Charny 46 marchand" (ANOM view 28, no. 94).

28. François Cazabon is likely the mixed-race, Martinique-born father of Michel-Jean Cazabon, the Trinidadian painter. See MacLean (1986) for background on the Cazabon family in Trinidad.

29. Ibid.

30. For an account of Trinidad's settlement by mixed-race families of the French Antilles lured by inducements of Spain's Cédula de Población, including a

reference to François Cazabon's land grant, see Campbell (1980). The article also discusses the growth of the free-coloured population in Trinidad.

31. MacLean (1986), the author and art collector, writes an excellent biographical sketch of Michel-Jean Cazabon (1813–88) in a handsome volume portraying a broad sample of Cazabon's preserved nineteenth-century landscapes, portraits, and illustrations.

32. Like Olive, the children of Olive and Pétronille took Cazabon or Casabon as a surname or "*dit* name." Jean Philippe died as Jean Phillip Casabon in 1846 in a dwelling on rue du Précipice. Joseph Honoré died in 1817, age sixteen, in the city of his birth, Basse-Terre, Guadeloupe; had he grown to majority age, he no doubt would have adopted the Cazabon name of his mother. Hélène Casabon and Sophie Casabon both died unmarried at advanced ages. François is likely the François Cazabon who immigrated to Trinidad.

33. Residents of rue du Précipice were found in Saint-Pierre parish *actes d'état civil*, which in the years 1807 to 1809 often identified residential addresses and occupations of named individuals. The Villegente family history is briefly recounted in Froidefond de Boulazac (1891, 412–13).

34. Madame Roux-Mingot is mentioned among the midwives identified in *Familles de Basse-Terre au 19e siècle*, between 1804 and 1809. *Sage-femme*, a midwife, is one of the oldest professions held by women.

35. See Cousseau (2011/12) on naming customs, practices, and legal restrictions during Martinique's colonial era.

36. The Michel surname is occasionally found among white Creoles of Martinique of noble origins. See Germain (1994) and Bruneau-Latouche, Cordiez, and Cordiez (2002). "Reynal de Saint Michel" is a family whose origins trace to a privateer and French noble, Laurent de Reynal de Saint Michel (1676–1744), who came to Saint-Pierre about 1700. His French ancestors were nobles of Launac, Haute-Garonne, in southwestern France—"de Saint Michel" references a nearby castle. Laurent's descendant, Édouard de Reynal de Saint Michel, resident of Saint-Pierre, came to the United States in 1872 as a Georgetown University student (Georgetown University [1873, 22]), following a small tradition of wealthy families who sent sons to Georgetown, which was founded by Dominican Catholics.

37. Laws and practices pertaining to surnames in the French West Indies varied from place to place and from time to time. In some areas, slaves were forbidden to have surnames, or to have surnames differing from those of their masters, although many secretly took surnames of their own choosing. Free blacks generally adopted surnames by the age of majority, choosing a name that may have been the mother's, an altered version of a white father's, a self-selected "*dit* name," or an acquired nickname. For a period beginning in 1802, persons of color in Martinique were required to have surnames but were not permitted to adopt family names held by

white Creoles. Mitchell would have been obligated to declare a surname at the age of majority (twenty-one) (Cousseau 2009, 2011/12).

38. Germain (1994); Roget and Bruneau-Latouche (2000).

39. Michel's Cazabon's godfather, Michel Fort, is noted in Michel Cazabon's baptismal record. See appendix 1.

40. Cousseau (2009).

41. Jean Isaac was the godfather of Olive's first son, Jean Philippe, born in 1790. Jean Isaac's role in the 1793 protest by Saint-Pierre men of color in the name of the revolution was reported by the early French historian Sidney Daney de Marcillac (Daney 1846), recalled more recently by the Martinique scholar Léo Elizabeth (1993), and further detailed by Abel Louis (2011). Olive named her third son after Jean Isaac's brother, Joseph Honoré, also active in the resistance movement. Jean Isaac fled Martinique in the time of the British occupation. His wife reported in 1809 that he had escaped to Baltimore.

42. In commenting on Meunier's "fidelity" and "sacrifice," Louis (2011, 438) recalls that Meunier had "insisted on the bravery of the French regimented troops clustered in the two forts of the capital, [and] saved the battalion of Bellegarde, in the front line and the companies of Hunters of Pelage at the redoubt Bouillé."

43. Meunier emerged once again on the side of the French forces during the Napoleonic Wars, suffering capture and imprisonment, but returned to Saint-Pierre and established himself as a *propriétaire* before his death in 1831.

44. Minutes of the Sansom Street Church, Philadelphia, microfilm, in the library of the Historical Society of Pennsylvania and at the American Baptist Historical Society Archives, Mercer University, Atlanta, Georgia (hereafter, ABHS Archives). The handwriting in the church minutes for this period is not always unequivocally clear. (The surnames that we interpret as "Witham" and "Frazier" in a passage quoted in the next chapter appeared to be "William" and "Francis" to Betsy Dunbar of the American Baptist Historical Society Archives.)

45. In the three next-earliest references that we have seen—the Baptist church minutes for April and May 1816, a list of subscribers to a new edition of *The History of Baptism* (R. Robinson 1817), and the Philadelphia directors of 1816 and 1817—and other public documents the spelling is "Mitchell." In 1818, Mitchell signed his name on a Philadelphia Savings bank transaction as "Edward Mitchell" with a distinctive cursive form that remained consistent in the many signature examples found in manuscripts and his official journals of Canadian civil acts in his later life.

46. The history of slavery and rebellion in the French Antilles has focused on Saint-Domingue, but several important works have uncovered significant uprisings among slaves and *gens de couleur* during the period of the French Revolution and Napoleonic Wars, the period of Edward Mitchell's residency. All were put

down relatively quickly. For good accounts of the uprisings of 1790, 1793, and 1800, see Elisabeth (1989), Geggus (1996), Moitt (2001), and Tomich (1990).

47. The population counts for Saint Pierre in 1807 are taken from Trani (2015), who references the "Map and Census of Martinique in 1808," fonds 3293, National Archives of Overseas.

48. Cormack (2011).

49. Guadeloupe held a distinct place in the history of French privateering during the French Revolution. Knight and Liss (1991) argue that the "1,800" enemy ships captured or destroyed during the first years of the French Revolution reflected the harnessing of Guadeloupe merchantmen's long experience and skill in coastal cabotage and contraband trade.

50. The legality of the *Eagle*'s capture was argued for many decades and not settled until after 1900, a not uncommon complication of prize captures that engaged some of the best legal talent of the age. A full account of the procedural twists and turns of the *Eagle* case is given in records of the United States Congress (1907).

51. Capture of *La Démocrate* corsair reported in compiled reports of Southey (1827, 168).

52. "Michel Cazabon, seaman," No. 1589 (1799), and "Paul Canaud, Captain," No. 1521 (1799), ADM 103/19, Barbados, French prisoners of war, 1793–1802, TNA.

53. Louis Mourot, a master baker, was briefly caught in the crossfire of ongoing disputes between Martinique's captain-general Villaret de Joyeuse and the French colonial prefect, Pierre-Clément Laussat, over an issue of bread supplies to Saint-Pierre troops. Laussat characterized the baker Mourot as *l'entrepreneur*. Mourot, the husband of Jeanne Rose Cazabon, survived the years of warfare and died in 1822. For an account by Laussat (who spelled Mourot as "Mouret"), see Laussat (1831); for a more general account of the tensions between Martinique's captain-general and prefect, see Johnson (2006).

54. Robert Surcouf (1773–1827), a French privateer and slaver, quoted in Norman (1887, 392).

55. For background and analysis of French naval strategy during the Napoleonic War, see Peifer (2013) and Sechrest (2003).

56. Lamothe was captain of the schooner *La Dione* in a cabotage voyage in 1803 to Spanish Caribbean islands: "État nominatif des bâtiments auxquels il a été accordé des actes de francisation et des congés de navigation entre le 1er vendémiaire (23 septembre) et le 30 brumaire 30 brumaire (21 novembre 1802)," No. 43, 8 Brumaire 1802, "La Gtte [*goélette*, schooner] La Dione, 50 tonnage, Denys Villegente propriétaire, Cabotage Trinité Espagnole." In 1810, Lamothe was named in St. Pierre parish civil records as a baker, affiliated with Louis Mourot (Michel Cazabon's brother-in-law): "Death of Jeanne Rose Cazabon," view 69, ANOM, 20 Sept 1810 Saint-Pierre Mouillage, Dépôt des papiers publics des colonies, Martinique

and Guadeloupe, FR ANOM 1DPPC, Archives Nationales d'Outre-Mer, Aix-en-Provence, France (hereafter, ANOM).

57. The naval scenes of battle in that period are recounted by de Poyen-Bellisle (1896). A retrospective account of the Guadeloupean corsairs is rendered in *Revue de Paris: Journal Critique, Politique et Littéraire* (1843, 182–85).

58. "Edward, boy," No. 4373, "François Marrisseaux, Captain," No. 4300, and "Auguste Rostenne, second Captain," No. 4301 (all 1807), ADM 103/3, Antigua and Barbados, French prisoners of war, 1803–1808, TNA. After his release to Martinique, Rostenne was a neighbor of the Cazabons on rue du Précipice. On *La Démocrate* and other French ships, men of color were commonly recorded by a single name, as was "Edward" whom we identify as the young Édouard Michel. He was fifteen years old, a common age for the rank of "boy" (typically fourteen to sixteen). Many of the men aboard the *Démocrate* clearly were recruited from Martinique, and no other Édouards of an appropriate age with connections to the Cazabons were recruited as a "boy" on this voyage.

59. For Captain Ballard's report of *L'Hortense's* capture, see Clarke and McArthur (1807).

60. Captain Rostenne was present on April 23, 1808, as a witness in registering the death of Jean Cazabon, Michel Cazabon's brother: "Sieur Augustine Rostenne marin de profession, demeurant rue du Précipice âgé trente-trois ans, voisin du défunte." 1808 parish register of Saint-Pierre, Mouillage parish. Actes d'état civil, no. 66, view 178, FR ANOM 1DPPC1828, ANOM (anom.archivesnationales.culture.gouv.fr/ark:/61561/ps367cwyw3yd).

61. Michel Cazabon is not found in Martinique parish civil records after 1808. In 1809, the year of the British invasion, the orderly recording of civil acts appears to have been significantly disturbed. Saint-Pierre's Mouillage and Le Fort parish registers were combined and appear to be deficient in recorded births and deaths. Records of the Saint-Pierre military hospital during the British occupation (1809 to 1815) are not available in French records. By 1810, order had been restored by British administrators. Jeanne Rose Cazabon died in September 1810; Michel Cazabon, who had attended all other Cazabon ceremonies, was not listed as a witness. Michel had worked with her husband, Louis Mourot the baker, but after 1808, none of several references to Mourot mentions Michel. We combed Saint-Pierre's and other Martinique parishes without success, concluding that Michel had either died or left Martinique after 1808. We found no trace of Michel Cazabon in US or Canadian census returns. The last identified white Creole Cazabon of that era was Michel's sister, Jeanne Rose, at the time of her death in 1810.

62. See Lémery (1936) for the remarkable text of the 1793 *Adresse des citoyens de couleur de la Martinique à l'Assemblée Coloniale*, signed by Jean Isaac, his brother Joseph Honoré, Édouard Meunier, and over forty other *gens de couleur* of Martinique.

63. On uprisings and short-lived rebellions in Martinique during the Revolution period, see Geggus (1996), Louis (2011), Cormack (2011), Elisabeth (1993), and Kleczewski (1988).

64. See Louis (2011) on restriction of civil rights and privileges of *gens de couleur* in Martinique during the Napoleonic period.

TWO Martinique to Maine

1. Bolster (1998).

2. Daney (1846, 84).

3. See Hayot (1969) on Fort Royal and Saint-Pierre black mariners. On commissionaires, see Tomich (1990).

4. Paul Cuffee's late career almost overlaps with Mitchell's arrival to the United States. In December 1810 Cuffee sailed the ship *Traveller* from Philadelphia to Sierra Leone, Africa, a venture planned with strong British backing to establish an African colony for displaced blacks of the British colonies—not unlike the American Colonization Society settlements in Liberia. Mitchell came to Philadelphia in 1811, a few months after Cuffee's sail to Africa. Cuffee's African colonization interest brought him back to Philadelphia about 1816; there, he had discussions with James Forten, Richard Parrott, and other black leaders who were known to Mitchell. Cuffee died in Westport, Massachusetts, in 1817, aged fifty-eight. It is interesting to consider how Cuffee would have judged Mitchell and what would have been the tenor and content of any conversations they may have had. See Tomek (2012), who recounts Cuffee's involvement in colonization and his encounters with black leaders in Philadelphia.

5. That Mitchell sailed under Prentiss's command is stated in his obituaries in 1872 issues of the *Express and Standard* (Newport, VT) and the *Stanstead Journal*, cited in the previous chapter. The "Outlines" indicate that Mitchell's two voyages under Prentiss were his first at sea, but do not indicate what previous employment or experience he may have had.

6. Nutt and Prentiss (1883).

7. Material on William Prentiss in this and the following paragraphs is from Prentiss (1858), Binney (1883), Nutt and Prentiss (1883), Rowland (1909), and Lombard (1937). George Lewis Prentiss must have written of the recollections of older family members, as by the time of George's birth his father had retired from the sea.

8. Connolly (2001).

9. The US Slave Trade Act of 1794 prohibited Americans from engaging in slave trade commerce. Congress banned the importation of slaves to the United States in 1807, the same year that Britain banned slave trade (but not slavery) throughout its empire.

10. See Rawley and Behrendt (2005, 277–304) for a contemporary review of

New England involvement in slave trade and commerce of the "triangular trade."

11. See appendix 3.

12. In the *Public Ledger and Daily Advertiser* of London it was reported on February 25, 1809, that the British Vice-Admiralty Court had ruled on the case of Prentiss's brig *Triton* and decided that it had been improperly seized and carried by the ship *Alligator* to Antigua. The court ruled that the condemned cargo must be returned to Prentiss.

13. The literature on issues leading to the War of 1812 is extensive, with many studies having been published upon the bicentennial of that conflict. Taylor (2010) was especially useful for this discussion.

14. In 1809, during President's Madison's administration, British envoy David Erskine negotiated an agreement that reopened American shipping to British ports in return for American concessions on trade with France. The apparent agreement collapsed and Britain recalled its minister, claiming he lacked authority. The net effect was the opening of a brief window of trade to the West Indies for Captain Prentiss and many other American merchantmen, between April 25 and August 9, 1809. See Hodge and Nolan (2007, 39).

15. Briggs (1889). The brig *Tropic* 150 tons burden was built by Captain Noah Brooks in the Kent yard of the North River of Plymouth County, south of Boston. The brig's owner, Thomas Motley Jr., originally of Portland, Maine, operated a successful commercial warehouse with his brother, Edward Motley, at India Wharf in Boston, where Prentiss's cargoes where sold.

16. The "Spanish Main" refers to territories, ports, and cities in the vicinity of the South American mainland bordering the Caribbean Sea and Gulf of Mexico, a region once dominated by Spain's New World Empire. The term was commonly used in the Age of Sail.

17. See appendix 3.

18. See appendix 3, trip no. 7.

19. Bolster (1998, 224–25).

20. Mitchell, "Many Minds, Many Men," Dartmouth student essay, n.d., P044_A,2.4, Mitchell family fonds, McCord Museum of Canadian History, Montreal, QC (hereafter, Mitchell family fonds). Throughout this book, lines and passages from Mitchell's writings are reproduced as written, including misspellings and archaic words, unless a correction is needed to clarify meaning.

21. Wilson (2013).

22. Prentiss's seventh voyage (see appendix 3) sold by Thomas and Edward Motley from their warehouse at 34 India Street, Boston.

23. "Marine News," *Federal Republican* (Baltimore), May 21, 1810, 2.

24. Quotes and biographical notes on Abigail Lewis Prentiss from Binney (1883).

25. Although Beman later achieved prominence as a Presbyterian minister and college president, at this stage in his career he was the minister of a Congregational church. Payson became sole pastor of the Second Parish Congregational Church in 1811. In 1820, the small congregation that Beman had served reunited with Payson's church, from which it had split twelve years earlier. The Second Parish Congregational Church building was destroyed in the fire of 1866, but the congregation retained its identity, becoming the Payson Memorial Church. This church, following a merger and other changes, is now an Orthodox Presbyterian church, called the Second Parish Church.

26. Mitchell does not specify where he met and heard Rev. Payson. Histories of early nineteenth-century African American life in Portland note that blacks attended Protestant churches with whites but by 1828 had formed separate, independent congregations. Whether blacks were previously segregated into separate pews—a common practice in antebellum New England—is not stated. See Connolly (2001) and Price and Talbot (2006). Payson was an officer of the Portland Bible Society from the time of its founding in 1809. Its mission included outreach to "soldiers and sailors . . . as well as Africans and aborigines," and it held periodic meetings that may have attracted Mitchell's attention and patronage. See Bible Society of Maine (1809).

27. Peterson (1986, vii).

28. Material on Payson in this and the following paragraph is from Cummings (1830) and Prentiss (1882, chap. 1). Beman's role in mentoring Henry Highland Garnet in preparation for ordination is referenced in several biographies. For example, see *Encyclopedia of African American Religions* (2011), s.v. "Garnet, Henry Highland."

29. Mitchell, "Outlines."

30. Cummings (1830).

31. Naval Office Shipping Lists for Jamaica, 1685–1818, pt. 4. See appendix 3.

32. Lombard (1937).

33. As appendix 3 shows, Prentiss's eight and ninth trips on the brig *George* were actually one long, interrupted voyage, and Mitchell was present only on the first. The voyage began in the fall of 1810 with Mitchell on board. Prentiss first unloaded a substantial cargo of New England products in Jamaica in November 1810. After leaving (with only ballast in the hold) he encountered a storm and, in need of repairs, sought the nearest American port, Wilmington, NC. Mitchell refers to this trip as his "passage home" following a "violent storm." Prentiss had lost two men. At that point, in December 2010, the unnerved Mitchell must have separated from Prentiss, eventually making his way to Philadelphia by early 1811. Prentiss completed the voyage without Mitchell, sailing from Wilmington to "Campeachy" on the Yucatan peninsula of Mexico before returning to Portland in June 1811 with

a cargo of "Campeachy wood." Otherwise known as logwood, this dyewood was once valuable in trade commerce between the Yucatan and American and European ports.

THREE Philadelphia

1. Sources of background information on Philadelphia include Turner (1911), Dubois (1967), Nash (2003), Davies (2008), and Winch (2016).

2. The total black population is generally believed to have been higher than the census figures indicate, in part because fugitives from slavery often evaded census takers. See Dubois (1967) and Bergman (1969). The history of slavery in Pennsylvania to 1833 was discussed by a nineteenth-century resident of Pennsylvania, with comments on censuring methods and the misleading aspects of the census data ("Slavery in Pennsylvania" 1833). That discussion was presented in response to the 1830 Census, which had reported 403 slaves in the state—a figure that that author challenged as having included persons who should not have been considered slaves—and 37,930 free blacks.

3. PBS (n.d.). On the early history of the African American population of Philadelphia, see Dorman (2009).

4. Hopper (1998).

5. On black workers and the jobs they held, see Dubois (1967), Lapansky (1975), Nash (1996), and Clement (1985).

6. Hopper (1998, 1).

7. For studies of Philadelphia's black churches, see Brooks (1922), Hopper (1998), Lapansky (1980), and Ulle (1986). Rev. Absalom Jones's African Episcopal Church of St. Thomas was founded in 1794, the same year as Rev. Richard Allen's Bethel African Methodist Episcopal Church. Rev. John Gloucester's First African Presbyterian Church formed in 1807. Rev. Henry Cunningham's First African Baptist Church of Philadelphia separated from Staughton's original Philadelphia congregation in 1809; Cunningham left Philadelphia well before the formation of the Philadelphia African Bible Society in 1816. The African Zoar Methodist Episcopal church met as a Methodist mission in 1794 before Bethel and St. Thomas and is recognized as the first African American Methodist denomination. Zoar's first settled Pastor, Rev. Perry Tilghman, began in 1834.

8. On the optimistic but cautious attitude of black clergy, see Hopper (1998), who points out that the immediate need to establish functioning, independent religious sanctuaries was paramount: "The early churches did not seek to assert black rights or create movements of social protest" (p. 1).

9. On white antislavery before black activists and the Underground Railroad, see Fisher (1935b) and "Slavery in Pennsylvania" (1833).

10. The organization of black Catholic lives in Philadelphia during the antebel-

lum years is not covered in standard texts. A Catholic Historical Research Center blog post notes that "Black Catholics worshiped at the oldest Catholic churches in Philadelphia, including Old St. Joseph (1733), Old St. Mary (1763), and Holy Trinity (1788), although they worshipped separately from the white congregation. When they did attend mass with whites, blacks often had to sit in certain designated areas which were usually the back of the church or the balcony." Charlton (2011).

11. Minutes of the Sansom Street Church, ABHS Archives.

12. Lynd, Sharp, and Mitchell (1860); Lynd (1834).

13. Mitchell, "Outlines."

14. Cummings (1830).

15. Quoted passage from Brooks (1922, 22). See Lindman (2011, 152–55) on the history of Philadelphia's African Baptist Church and its break from the First Baptist Church.

16. Minutes of the Sansom Street Church, ABHS Archives. On this occasion, the race of these individuals is not mentioned in the minutes.

17. Mitchell, "Outlines." "Exhortations" was a term commonly used at the time for short sermons by lay preachers.

18. See "Bible Associations" (1816) and Lynd (1834, 337) on Staughton's Bible Society work in Philadelphia.

19. Bible Society of Philadelphia (1816, 3). The organization of the Philadelphia African Bible Society with Mitchell as recording secretary is reported in 1816 by the Bible Society of Philadelphia and then carried to newspapers ("Religious Miscellany" 1816). If minutes of the society's meetings were recorded, they have not been preserved. Willson ([1841] 2000) and Winch (2002) give general biographical information on Philadelphia's black leaders of that era; neither mentions Mitchell.

20. In 1818, "E. Mitchell" posted a public meeting notice in Poulson's *American Daily Advertiser*, which reads in part, "The African Bible Society, who have their annual meeting, on Tuesday seventh of April, at half past seven o'clock in the evening in the meeting house of the First African Presbyterian Church, in Seventh below Shippen street" (April 4, 1818, 3).

21. The Bible society movement began in 1804 with the founding of the British and Foreign Bible Society and spread to the United States in 1808. The history is given in Browne (2012). Mitchell would become involved in Bible society work throughout his ministerial career.

22. Bordewich (2005, 436).

23. Smith (1878, 258).

24. Oakes (2007).

25. Oakes (2007, 98).

26. Dubois (1967); Bergman (1969).

27. Quarles (1969); Bacon (2007). According to historian Dorothy Porter (1971),

no minutes or proceedings of these early (1817–20) conventions in Philadelphia and Baltimore are known to exist. Quarles and Bacon compiled information from recollections reported in publications some years later. These early gatherings should not be confused with the "national convention" in Philadelphia in 1830, at which the American Society of Free Persons of Colour was founded. References to material on the 1830 convention may appear, from their titles, to refer to the earlier gatherings of free black Philadelphians.

28. Forten ([1832] 2005, 2). Forten read the resolution at the 1817 Philadelphia; it was republished from the original pamphlet by Garrison in 1832.

29. For a modern account of Dartmouth's founding as school for Native Americans, see Calloway (2010).

30. Saunders (1818a, 8).

31. According to Prof. Raymond Hall (1986), after completing studies at Moor's Charity Indian School, Saunders was rejected for admission to Dartmouth by President John Wheelock. The story has become a tradition in relating the story of black students at Dartmouth, but its source is unknown. There are several published studies of Saunders's remarkable life, notably by Arthur White (1975), which make no such claim.

32. Records of Mitchell's savings account were found in the Philadelphia Savings Society records preserved at the the Hagley Museum in Wilmington, Delaware. Between June 8, 1818, and March 31, 1819, Mitchell made six deposits totaling $56.06 and, with interest earned, he had a balance of $56.72 as of March 31, 1819—after which the society became formally incorporated and further transactions could not be found in its new account books. Mitchell did sign the society's signature book on June 30, 1819, which indicates continued involvement with the savings bank at least until that date. The definitive nineteenth-century history of the savings bank is given by Willcox (1916), with emphasis on its charitable mission, astute management, and consistent profitability to the benefit of its subscribers.

33. Gilman (1919) offers an unusually intimate view of the widely dispersed Gilman family, including Benjamin and Hannah Gilman of Philadelphia, who both knew Edward Mitchell and introduced him to President Brown of Dartmouth.

34. There are two versions of the 1817 directory—Dawes (1817) and J. Robinson (1817, 524)—and only the Dawes publication lists Edward Mitchell on Burd's Row. Robinson lists the same name and address in 1816. During Mitchell's years in Philadelphia, 1811 to 1820, no directories were published for 1812 and 1815. He is listed in the 1816 and 1817 directories. His wife, Legome or Lagune Mitchell, is listed in the 1814 directory. In 1818, Mitchell gave 55 Gaskill Street as his residence in establishing an account with the Philadelphia Savings Fund Society. In the 1820 US Census, the Mitchell family is recorded at a location corresponding to the 55 Gaskill Street

address. He likely lived in this three-story structure in joint tenancy with another family and was not captured by canvassers for the city directories of 1818 to 1820.

35. J. Robinson (1816). The two-and-a-half-story row houses comprising Burd's Row can be found on Philadelphia atlases into the early twentieth century but not after the 1940s. The location sits at the edge of Rittenhouse Square in Center City, Philadelphia. The court and adjacent lanes and alleys carried various names over the years. Although Mitchell is not labeled a "person of color" in the directories, there were no other Edward Mitchells of Philadelphia in that time to confuse his identification in the city's directories. He was identified in the 1820 US Census as a person of color. The fact that his African ancestry was not noted in the informal canvassing performed in compiling street directories suggests that his skin coloration was light enough to confuse casual identification or that he was not physically present and the information was garnered from unreliable sources.

36. The three-block-long Gaskill Street provided one of several convenient samples for a "demographic study" of the social and cultural life in Philadelphia's South Street community (Lapansky 1975). Gaskill Street is two blocks east of the 1890s African American neighborhood examined by Dubois (1967) in his landmark study, *The Philadelphia Negro*. More recently, Nash (2003) offers a critical analysis of the progress and setbacks experienced by Philadelphia's African Americans between 1720 and 1840 and includes another close look at the Gaskill Street neighborhood. For our survey, Gaskill Street residents were identified from the city directories and census records from 1818 to 1820, supplemented by additional research on identified individuals and their families. See appendix 2.

37. Gilman (1919, 259).

38. Dubois (1967) gives examples of the low-wage status and employment discrimination against black porters in nineteenth-century Philadelphia. On wages in the city, see D. R. Adams (1968).

39. That Mitchell had children and a wife is confirmed from Baptist records and in 1820 US Census data for the New Market Ward of Philadelphia. One child's death is documented in Baptist records; his wife and second child died about 1820, but details are unknown. Mitchell's wife, Legome or Lagune, is listed in the 1820 US Census, but her occupancy may have been stated by neighbors or joint tenants—the official enumeration date was August 7, 1820, and recorded occupancy should have referred to that date.

40. The church's records of births, marriages, and deaths among its members were separate from the minutes, having since 1812 been compiled jointly with the records of the other Baptist churches in Philadelphia, and appear to have been lost, perhaps destroyed in a fire like some other early Philadelphia church archives.

41. The US Census of 1820 recorded only heads of household, who in many cases was the respondent and not necessarily the family head. The 1820 Philadel-

phia New Market Ward census return records at Mitchell's residence on Gaskill Street a family of persons of color headed by "Legome Mitchell," which included two adults between the ages of twenty-six and forty-eight and one daughter younger than fourteen. The other occupant of the same or adjacent household, Serrah Sourwalt, was the wife of Anthony Sourwald/Sourwalt, who is listed in the Philadelphia Directory of 1821 as a resident of 55 Gaskill Street.

42. Records of deaths in Philadelphia from 1803 through 1860 have been compiled in readily searchable lists with names, age, cause of death, place of interment, and sometimes other information. Of those listed with the surname Mitchell or with similar names such as Mitchel, Mitchell, Michel, or Michele who died in 1816–1820, data on age or parentage (considered in some cases in combination with data from church records) eliminate all but a few from consideration as having been members of Edward Mitchell's family. We were unable to determine the circumstances under which Mitchell's wife and children died.

43. Although the worst epidemics in Philadelphia during the early nineteenth century were of yellow fever, Mitchell's wife and children probably did not die of that disease, of which only two deaths were reported in that city in 1816. (The compilation was obviously incomplete, but that low figure indicates that there was no major epidemic that year. With so dreaded a disease, the compilers would likely have made a greater effort to record all cases.) Cholera did not appear in Philadelphia until 1832.

44. See Dippel (2015, 7) for a lengthy account of 1816, the year without a summer in Philadelphia.

45. Minutes of the Sansom Street Church, 1816, ABHS Archives.

46. In 1820, about the time that Mitchell left Philadelphia, the Sansom Street Church appointed a committee "to procure a burying ground for the Coloured people" but was still unwilling to provide one for all races.

47. Sansom Street Baptist Church Archives, ABHS Archives.

48. Mitchell's decision to move on after the church officials refused to bury his child is noted in the "Outlines."

49. Staughton discussed these qualifications for the ministry in a "circular letter" written in 1807, entitled "What Are the Qualifications of a Gospel Minister?" This letter was published by Gillette ([1851] 1976, 440–46) and can also be seen online, on the Baptist History Homepage, accessed April 12, 2012, baptisthistoryhomepage.com/1807.cl.phila.html.

50. *Baptist Encyclopaedia* (1881), s.v. "Mitchell, Rev. Edward."

FOUR To Dartmouth College

1. Thelin's (2011) history of American higher-education institutions includes good coverage of the original colonial colleges. See Wilder (2013) for a detailed

analysis of the direct and indirect flow of slave trade profits to American colleges, aiding their expansion and societal influence.

2. On Francis Brown, see Wood (1835) and Smith (1878, chaps. 12 and 13, including material by Rufus Choate and Charles B. Haddock). On events leading to Brown's removal from and restoration to the presidency of Dartmouth, see Bouton (2009) and references cited therein.

3. The account of Daniel Webster's argument is capsulized in many sources but is reproduced in full in Morin (1969, 22).

4. Dartmouth senior student Rufus Choate (1819), quoted in ibid., 32.

5. Gilman (1919, 385).

6. An account by John K. Lord (1913, 189) is inconsistent with Mrs. Brown's journal (see previous note) in several respects. Lord wrote that David L. Nichols, of the class of 1816, "was obliged to leave [the Browns] at Richmond [Virginia] on the return, and was replaced by a young colored boy, named Mitchell, who came home with them and remained an inmate [sic] of the family after Dr. Brown's death." Mrs. Brown's journal states that Nichols left them at Salisbury, North Carolina, while they were still southbound, and that they met and hired Mitchell in Philadelphia on their return. The error with regard to where Nichols left the Browns may be related to his briefly having taught school at Richmond, not long after his trip south with the Browns.

7. "Journal of Elizabeth Gilman Brown (Mrs. Francis Brown), October 12, 1819–June 22, 1820," typewritten transcript, Rauner Special Collections Library, Dartmouth College, Hanover, NH (hereafter, Rauner Library).

8. Gilman (1919, 388–89).

9. Ibid.

10. Ibid, 375–77 (letter from Benjamin Ives Gilman to his son, dated July 26, 1819).

11. "Journal of Elizabeth Gilman Brown."

12. The first major US depression followed the financial panic of 1819 and lasted for three years. Philadelphia's Board of Commissioners informed the public of plans to raise taxes, despite what they deemed to be a "time of general distress." "County Commissioner's Office: A Statement," *Franklin Gazette*, May 5, 1820, 2.

13. Staughton's papers at the George Washington University and his correspondence at the Historical Society of Philadelphia are well catalogued, but no correspondence between Mitchell and Staughton after Mitchell left Philadelphia is known to exist.

14. Warner (1940, 16–17), cites Dr. James McCune Smith, America's first university-trained physician, as presenting to an 1851 Colored Convention, "a long list of disadvantages of urban life, in contrast with the mere chance to organize for trade and education." Life in cities "shortens the Negro's span of years and

surrounds him with moral seductions . . . so that their 'manhood' is, in a measure, demeaned, lowered and kept down." Smith advocated "country living."

15. Lord (1913, 208).

16. Dartmouth College (1924). Although the substantial financial resources brought into the family by Francis Brown's stepmother, née Mary Lunt, had supported Brown's education, the Browns' finances were by this time much diminished. Their trip to the South had been supported by gifts from friends. A Connecticut physician whom the Browns visited on the return segment of their trip commented that those friends must have been insane if they thought so strenuous a journey would do President Brown's health any good.

17. Sarah Parker Parrott to her mother, Hannah Skilling Parker Parrott (Mrs. John Fabyan Parrott), of Portsmouth, NH, June 11, 1828, Rauner Library. Sarah Parrott, then about twenty-nine years old, appears to have been visiting or caring for an ailing relative, probably her younger brother John T. Parrott, in Hanover and was staying at an inn or rooming house at which breakfast was served at 6:00 a.m. Recalling the morning of June 10, she wrote to her mother, "I met such a formidable company of gentlemen yesterday that I thought I would be excluded for the future. Among them was a Mr. Mitchell, nearly black, whom President Brown brought with him from one of the southern states, when he was traveling for his health a short time before his death." Although Sarah Parrott saw Mitchell on that occasion, from the inaccuracy about the "southern states" it seems unlikely that she actually met him (S. P. Parrott to H. S. P. Parrott, June 11, 1828). What she wrote about him to her mother, including his having lost his wife and two children before coming to Hanover, was presumably learned secondhand. The reference to President Brown quoted here, and a comment on the respect in which Mitchell was held by the faculty and his fellow students, obviously did not come from Mitchell himself, but Ms. Parrott did not indicate the source(s) of her information.

18. Dartmouth College (2006).

19. S. G. Brown (1870, 32–33n).

20. In the *History of Dartmouth College* (Lord 1913, 208, citing Worcester [1869] and Samuel G. Brown [1870] as sources), and in an earlier work (Lord 1902, 59), Lord used the wording that Mitchell "accompanied" rather than "had been brought by" President Brown to Hanover.

21. The *Philanthropist*, an abolitionist newspaper edited by Charles Osborn and James G. Birney, was published in Cincinnati, Ohio, from 1836 to 1843.

22. Probably refers to a speech by Rev. Charles Stuart, an English abolitionist, to the New-England Anti-Slavery Convention in Boston in May and June of 1837.

23. "Some Undistinguished Negroes" (1918).

24. Gross (1932). From the citations in her paper it might be inferred that Gross

attributed this information on Mitchell to Woodson (1919), but Woodson did not mention Edward Mitchell in that work. On Haynes, see Saillant (2003).

25. Kendrick (1850, 12).

26. Mitchell, "Outlines."

27. Gitter (2001, 250). Elisabeth Gitter relates the life story of Laura Bridgman (1829–89), daughter of an Etna Baptist Church family and the first deaf and blind child to acquire a formal education. In Gitter's recounting of Bridgman's life, the brief mention of Mitchell—a "Creole 'mulatto' from Martinique" who preached at the Etna church—serves as a sympathetic parallel comparison to her protagonist, both having suffered and overcome seemingly impossible inherited disabilities. Bridgman was born a few months after Mitchell's ordination as an evangelist at the Etna church.

28. During the 1820s and 1830s, some Baptist associations voted to use "Elder" rather than "Reverend" as the honorific for ministers, perceiving the use of "Reverend" to be contrary to the principle of the equality of all members of the Baptist church, although ordination was practiced. Baptist ministers sometimes used "Brother" when referring to fellow members of the Baptist clergy. "Reverend" continued in common use by those outside the denomination when referring to Baptist clergy. "Reverend" also continued to be used by some Baptists, as in some of the church reports quoted in this text, and gradually returned to general usage in the Baptist churches. In more recent times, "elder" has acquired a different usage in the Baptist churches, "elders" being distinguished from both "pastors" and "deacons."

29. Fletcher (1926); Smith, Camp, and Chandler (1881).

30. 150th Anniversary Historical Booklet, American Baptist Churches of New Hampshire 1826–1976, mimeographed copy, Laconia (NH) Public Library. The anonymous, unnumbered entries from the respective congregations are organized alphabetically.

31. Nathan West Jr. (clerk of the "Baptist Church of Christ in Hanover") to "any charitable religious education society," letter of reference, September 21, 1823, P044_A,1.1, Mitchell family fonds.

32. A report that the father of a student from the South had instructed his son to withdraw from Dartmouth if any student of African descent should be admitted is not correctly associated with Mitchell. The *Dartmouth College and the Associated Schools General Catalogue, 1769-1940* (Dartmouth College 1940) lists no student from the South in the classes present at the time of Mitchell's admission. This report may have been based on an event that actually occurred in 1837, the confusion perhaps having resulted from the juxtaposition in the July 28, 1837, issue of the *Philanthropist* of two articles, both of which had originally been published in the *Emancipator*.

33. Worcester (1869); Crosby (1869). Passages in these works are very similar, suggesting that Crosby's role in the preparation of the second (and only extant) edition of Worcester's work may have been considerably more than that of an editor after Worcester's death or, conversely, that some of Crosby's wording might have originated with Worcester.

34. Quint (1922, 125–26).

35. Original petition is ms. 824525, Rauner Library; image included by Tai Antoine (2012) in "Black Greens." The trustees' concern was not altogether unrealistic; in 1832, the admission of Charles Bennett Ray, a student with biracial ancestry, to Wesleyan University was revoked because of protests by the students.

36. Lord (1913); Quint (1922); Worcester (1869).

37. Crosby (1869, 22–23). Dartmouth's next graduates of African descent, after Mitchell, were Samuel Ford McGill, from the medical school in 1839, and Thomas Paul Jr., from the college in 1841.

38. Koren (2010).

39. Hall (1986, 36).

40. Gale (1860); Bouton (2009). Following Brown's death, the Reverend Dr. Daniel Dana had become president of Dartmouth, but the stresses of the office proved too much for his far-from-robust constitution, and he served only six months. Following Dana's resignation, Prof. Ebenezer Adams, who had served as acting president during Brown's illness, was president *pro tempore* for about five months. Tyler was president from 1822 to 1828. He resigned in August of that year, the same month in which the class of 1828 graduated, and was succeeded by the Reverend Dr. Nathan Lord.

41. Niven (1995a, 18).

42. A. D. Smith, quoted in Gale (1860, 46). See also Emerson (1911); Niven (1995a).

43. Richardson (1932, 239–40). See also Chapman (1867); Lord (1913); Worcester (1869).

44. Chapman (1867); Lord (1913); Worcester (1869); S. P. Parrott to H. S. P. Parrott, June 11, 1828; Crosby (1869).

45. Paley (1850, 67) also expressed passionate opposition to slavery, which he called an "abominable tyranny" that rendered any government permitting it "unfit to be trusted with an empire."

46. Dartmouth College Catalogues; Chapman (1867); Emerson (1911).

47. Dartmouth College Catalogues; Crosby (1869). The term "immediate government" was used to refer to the professors and tutors, collectively, until 1828, when it was replaced by the now-familiar term "faculty" (Lord 1913).

48. Dartmouth College Catalogues.

49. There were no grades. The present system of letter or percentage grades

for assignments and examinations, and letter grades for courses, now prevalent in North American colleges and universities, did not come into use at Dartmouth until the 1860s, after decades of appeals from the students for a more satisfactory means of evaluation of their work. Until then, Dartmouth had used a "system of exhibitions, prizes, assignments, etc." (Smith 1878).

50. Howe (2007, 463).

51. Mitchell's view was not far removed from those of the college, which in 1811 proclaimed in a public statement of its mission, "Tragedies, plays, and all irreligious expressions and sentiments are sacredly prohibited." See Smith (1878, 84). This specific expression of college will was not included in the Dartmouth Catalogues of the 1820s.

52. Crosby (1869, 6). Crosby was fifty-eight years old when he wrote these remarks, but it may be relevant to his perceptions of student life that he had been the youngest student at Dartmouth in his time (and perhaps in the history of the college), having been admitted about a month prior to his thirteenth birthday.

53. Richardson (1932, 208). The societies and their libraries were also discussed by C. W. Scott, in Smith (1878, 70–71).

54. Crosby (1869, 86).

55. Lord (1913, 515).

56. Crosby (1869); Lord (1913); Worcester (1869).

57. Chandler (1868).

58. The name of this society at Dartmouth was identical to that of a society founded ten years earlier at Andover (Massachusetts) Theological Seminary, at which some, perhaps a majority, of the members of the Dartmouth Society of Inquiry subsequently became seminarians, but the society at Dartmouth was independent. A series of manuscript notebooks at the Rauner Library, Dartmouth College, contains the Society of Inquiry's successive constitutions and lists of members arranged by graduating class. Some contain minutes of the society's meetings. The extant membership lists were compiled from earlier records; they indicate which members had, by the time of the compilation, become clergymen and occasionally note other professional achievements. These notebooks and a few other documents are filed together as the records of the society. Of greatest significance was the one entitled "Constitution and Historical Sketch, Society of Inquiry, March 15, 1821–July 4, 1831." Society policy called for copies of the exercises presented at meetings to be deposited in the society's archives, but no such items are among the extant records at the Rauner Library.

59. Alexander, Robinson, and Daniell (2006); Ripley (1941).

60. "The History of Phi Beta Kappa," n.d., Penn State Phi Beta Kappa, accessed May 31, 2012, www.clubs.psu.edu/PhiBetaKappa/hist.html; Lord (1913).

61. This house was located at the present site of the Steele Chemistry Building.

It later became known as the Frederic P. Lord House. After several relocations, it is at the time of this writing located on Lyme Road near the intersection with North Park Street (Meacham n.d.).

62. Lord (1913). William and Sarah Chamberlain's children were Francis (born 1824), Mellen (1826), and Sarah (1829).

63. Worcester (1869, 70). Dartmouth's residential facilities were very limited at that time, so the boardinghouses provided by faculty members and townspeople served an important role. The salary of a professor at Dartmouth in the 1820s was seven hundred dollars plus the use of college land, a perquisite valued at around twenty-five dollars. Crosby (1869, 70) considered the faculty members to have been "scantily paid." Providing room and board for students was probably significant both as a source of income for most of the faculty and for meeting the students' need for accommodation.

64. Dartmouth College Catalogues.

65. See previous chapter for references and discussion of Mitchell's obituary.

66. Smith (1878, chap. 23). The transcript of Chamberlain's speech is published in Smith's work.

67. On early Dartmouth and Hanover periodicals, see Edwin D. Sanborn (in Smith 1878, 163–65); Smith (1878); and Chase (1882). Although Chase did not so indicate, both Sanborn and the Dartmouth College library catalog state that the *Dartmouth Gazette* ceased publication in 1820. The *Dartmouth Herald*, presented by its publishers as the successor to the *Gazette*, ceased publication in 1821, after only one year. News of Dartmouth and Hanover constituted only a small proportion of the contents of the *Herald*. Extant issues of the *Herald* at the Rauner Library, Dartmouth College, include articles on the Browns' return from the South, the funeral of President Brown, the recruitment and inauguration of President Dana, and the programs at commencements, but no reference to Mitchell.

68. Dartmouth College Catalogues.

69. Letter from the Baptist Church of Christ of Hanover [Etna], August 29, 1923, P044_A,1.1, Mitchell family fonds.

70. The Massachusetts Baptist Education Society grants to Mitchell covering tuition (but not other student expenses) were reported in the "Annual Account of the Treasurer," *Baptist Missionary Magazine*, vols. 5–8.

71. On scholarship support from the Massachusetts Baptist Education Society, see Lincoln (1825–28). Baldwin had been closely associated with Staughton in Baptist leadership in the United States and in the founding and early work of the General Missionary Convention of the Baptist Denomination in the United States of America for Foreign Missions. He had also served on the executive committee of the Boston-based Education Society for the People of Color. See Adams (1860, 111–12).

72. Student accounts October 1810–August 1829, book 68, ledger F, Treasurer's records, Rauner Library.

73. Lord (1913, 206).

74. Niven (1995a, 18).

75. Crosby (1869, 11).

76. Lord (1889, 293). James Perkins, New London (NH) town archivist, graciously searched for mention of Mitchell in the New London school records, but found nothing more specific.

77. The "Chain of Being," a notion developed during the eighteenth-century Enlightenment, informed Charles Linnaeus's *Systema Naturae*, which classified living organisms and included an ordering of *homo sapiens*, ranking European whites above African blacks. In the nineteenth century, these ideas had infiltrated early scientific teachings in the field of Natural Philosophy, a course taught at Dartmouth. The scientific racism of the nineteenth and twentieth centuries evolved from these early theories.

78. Racial bias and animus has always existed in New England, even in small rural communities that had rare contact with people of color. See Guyette (2010), Clark and Courser (2007), and Fernald (2007) for good examples and discussion. In Hanover, New Hampshire, as late as 1965, a small island in the Connecticut River, a former residential sanctuary for Hanover's small black population of the late eighteenth and nineteenth centuries, continued to be known as "Nigger Island" until renamed Gilman Island by a state legislative act. Before then, a Dartmouth graduate, Edmond B. Frost, wrote in 1933, "At the south end of Main Street, the long hill leading down to Mink Brook was called 'Nigger Hill.' I am not sure how it received its name, but I remember as a very small boy 'Aunt Sophie,' a former slave, who lived in a cottage near the crest of this hill. She was quite a mystery to me, and I was somewhat afraid of her" (p. 13).

79. The letters to Denison are in the Rauner Library, Dartmouth College; those to Sparhawk have been compiled and quoted in full by Schlesinger (1919).

80. Blue (1987, 12).

81. Ibid., 28, 63.

82. Ibid.; Goodwin (2005).

83. Quoted in Blue (1987, 31). Another of Chase's biographers, John Niven, perceives Chase's "conversion" as having been more gradual. According to Niven (1995b, xv), it was not until the late 1830s and early 1840s that Chase "drifted into abolitionist circles through his defense of fugitive slaves" as a lawyer in Cincinnati and still later that he expressed strong feelings on abolition. Chase's "conversion" more or less coincided with a similar phenomenon among many white Americans, in which indifference or passivism was replaced by outspoken and activist opposition to slavery.

84. Obituary of Professor Alpheus Crosby, *Evening Transcript* (Boston), April

18, 1874, 6. Similar or identical obituaries were published in the *New York Times* and other newspapers.

85. Shedd (1922, 26).

86. Grant (2014, 4).

87. As discussed in note 1 of the introduction, Middlebury had unknowingly admitted a student of African descent, Rev. Alexander Twilight, in 1826, a milestone recognized many years later and debated in modern scholarship on the history of early black college students. In 1849, Middlebury graduated Martin Freeman, a black student from Rutland, Vermont, who received honors as salutatorian and emigrated to Liberia afterward. See Grant (2014) for background on Freeman and the epilogue below for more on Twilight.

88. *Boston Recorder*, August 29, 1828, 139.

89. On John Brown Russwurm, Bowdoin 1826, see James (2010), and on Edward Jones, Amherst 1826, see Contee (1973) and Hawkins (1982).

90. Stowe (1834, 303).

91. "An Interesting Fact," *Emancipator* (New York), June 22, 1837, 31.

92. *Vermont Telegraph*, July 26, 174.

93. See Logan and Winston (1982) for brief biographies of John Sykes Fayette and William G. Allen. Also, see "John Sykes Fayette," *Recollections* (blog of Case Western Reserve University Archives), February 17, 2011, blog.case.edu/archives/2011/02/17/john_sykes_fayette. Allen, who graduated in 1844 from the short-lived Oneida Institute, endured a series of racist attacks that forced his exile to England. He gave an anguished account of his trials in *American Prejudice against Color* (1853).

94. Tracy was referring to Charles B. Ray, who was admitted and then asked to leave Wesleyan University, in Middletown, CT, in the face of strong student protest. See Litwack (2009, 117) and the *Liberator*, January 12, 1833.

95. Tracy (1837, 174). Tracy devoted the latter stages of his life to work with the Boston Anti-Slavery Society as secretary, from 1842 until his death in 1874. He was an ardent proponent of the African colonization movement. Nine black Dartmouth graduates were Liberian colonists during Tracy's lifetime. It has been speculated that Dartmouth officers or faculty had connections to the colonization organization in Boston; Rev. Tracy, an 1814 Dartmouth graduate, would have been an obvious (but unproven) intermediary.

96. Wright (1837, 174).

97. Individually and collectively, these episodes of community resistance to educating young black students in the 1830s have received the attention of academic and local historians. See Moss (2009).

98. Paul (1841, 30).

99. Thomas Paul Jr.'s promising career continued to face significant challenges

when he was chosen to head the Abiel Smith School only to encounter a black community controversy over maintaining the school as a *de facto* segregated facility versus agitating for integrated public schools in Boston. Paul Jr. favored the former. See Hancock (1999), Kendrick and Kendrick (2006).

100. Crosby (1872).

101. "Oneida and Oberlin" (1841).

102. Garrison (1845, 186).

103. Crosby (1872).

104. Ibid., 18–19.

105. There are several good accounts of Samuel Ford McGill and his difficult journey to gain a medical education at Dartmouth. See Campbell (1970) and Forbush (1988). McGill was born in the United States, the son of a self-emancipated slave. The family migrated to Liberia, and McGill returned to the United States to obtain a medical education before returning to Liberia. He justifiably can be called not only the first American-trained man of African descent to practice medicine in Africa, but also the first educated in the United States.

106. Draper (1860).

107. There are several good short accounts of Washington's life in Hall (1986) and Dunn, Beyan, and Burrowes (2001). See also "A Durable Memento: Portraits by Augustus Washington, African American Daguerreotypist," National Portrait Gallery, accessed December 4, 2012, www.npg.si.edu/exh/awash/awintro.htm.

108. See Kendrick and Kendrick (2006) for a contemporary look at the school desegregation issues that began during the years when Paul headed Boston's Abiel Smith School.

109. "From the Exeter News-Letter. Commencement at Dartmouth College. Class of 1811, &c.," *Farmers' Cabinet* (Amherst), August 19, 1852. On Gibbs, see Lynch and Whitehead (2012).

110. Joe M. Richardson, "Florida's Only Negro Cabinet Member," *Florida Historical Quarterly* 42, no. 4 (1964): 363–68, quoted in Whitehead (2012, 259–60).

111. See the website *Roudanez: History and Legacy* (roudanez.com/), by Mark Charles Roudané, a living descendant of Roudanez, for a thorough account of his ancestor's remarkable civic and political life in New Orleans.

112. On Humphrey, see Thompson (2008); on Laing, see Nercessian (2004).

113. Bob Vietrogoski, personal communication. See also Vietrogoski (2017).

FIVE Indefatigable Exertions

1. Mitchell, "Outlines."

2. Letter from the Baptist Church of Christ in Hanover [Etna Village], January 20, 1822, P044_A,1.2, Mitchell family fonds.

3. Smith, Camp, and Chandler (1881), chapter 4, n29; Fletcher (1926).

4. Saillant (2003).

5. On Twilight, see Grant (2014) and Ferrin (1877).

6. Lord (1889); Howe (2007).

7. Clark and Courser (2007).

8. Smith, Camp, and Chandler (1881), chapter 4, n29; Fletcher (1926); Worthen (1890).

9. Worthen (1890, 397).

10. Ibid., 393–94.

11. Chapman's (1867) listing of Windsor, Vermont, as Mitchell's next pastorate after Sutton is evidently incorrect. According to a history of the Baptists in Vermont (Crocker 1913), which states that Mitchell served in Grafton, Rev. Leland Howard was minister of the Baptist congregation at Windsor from 1829 to 1833, and Rev. Samuel Lamson was minister of the congregation at West Windsor throughout its existence, from 1802 to 1842. Howard was a highly respected member of the clergy who as a youth had studied in Windsor and who had been minister of that town's Baptist church several years prior to 1829. Other reports do establish that Mitchell spent some time in Windsor, but not as a settled pastor. Reverend Joseph Tracy, an editor of the *Vermont Chronicle* in Windsor from 1829 to 1834 and a member of the Congregational Church of Windsor, recalled in 1837 that "very early in his ministerial life we invited him [Mitchell] to our pulpit and table. He preached for some weeks to the Baptist church where we then resided" (p. 174). Tracy, a Dartmouth College graduate (1814), was the likely source of the misinterpreted information about Mitchell having been a pastor in Windsor. Also, Mitchell penned a poem mourning the death of a friend that concludes with the date and place of authorship, Windsor, Vermont. "To a Friend," February 26, 1831, P044_A,5.1, Mitchell family fonds.

12. Mitchell, "Outlines."

13. Mitchell, "Surveying the Exertions of Christians in the Home Mission Department," n.d. [1827 or 1828], P044_A,9.3, Mitchell family fonds.

14. Bethel (1999, 3). See also Dain (2009) and Rael (2003).

15. "Proceedings of the Seventh Annual Meeting of the Baptist Convention of the State of Vermont, held at Barnet on Wednesday and Thursday, October 23 and 24, 1832," ABHS Archives.

16. Ibid.

17. Scan of item in the *Northern Osiris* graciously provided by Paul Donovan, law librarian, Vermont Department of Libraries, Montpelier. Information transcribed in part by Janice Boyko; see "Northern Osiris Newspaper: 1831–32 deaths, marriage notices: Derby, Orleans County, Vermont," Vermont Northeast Kingdom Genealogy, accessed June 5, 2012, www.nekg-vt.com/news/news-derby-northern

-osiris.php. Most marriages reported in local Derby-area newspapers were recorded at the local clerk's office. In twelve marriages reviewed in a six-month period that included Mitchell's marriage, when the husband was a Canadian resident (two of the twelve marriages), the union was not recorded in Vermont. Mitchell could not become a naturalized US citizen, a privilege granted only to free white persons "of good character" by the 1790 Immigration Act. This fact alone may have precluded civil registration of his marriage.

18. In mixed-race societies that include peoples of African ancestry, the progressive loss of African physical and ethnic attributes following intermarriage with Caucasians is sometimes labeled "whitening," a term that has both formal and informal interpretations in different societies (e.g., in Brazil, the formalized practice is called *branqueamiento*).

19. *National Cyclopaedia of American Biography* (1896), s.v. "Cheney, Moses."

20. Cheney (1867); Pope (1897); Runnels (1881).

21. A series of documents in the Mitchell family fonds relate to Moses Cheney's transfer of his property in Derby to Charles Elliott Durgin of Derby, one of his sons-in-law. Ruth Mitchell evidently held Durgin's mortgage, or entered into a similar arrangement whereby she would receive payments from her brother-in-law, to make the process less bothersome for her father. Although these documents identify the Mitchells as being "of Derby," this was not their actual place of residence, since in fact they were living in Eaton Township, Lower Canada. In 1837, Mitchell's status was that of a missionary from the Vermont Baptist Convention, whose appointment was renewed annually. His status of serving a tour of duty in Canada from a base in Vermont, rather than having emigrated, was probably a requisite for his receiving support from the Vermont and US Baptist church. Also, this was during the Panic of 1837. Baptist missionaries in Lower Canada were dependent in part on financial support from the United States. If that support were to cease they would likely have to return to the United States. With Mitchell being foreign-born and a person of color, the simpler the process of return would be, if it became necessary, the better. Therefore, it might have been advisable to have remained legally "of Derby" so that he could simply "come home" rather than having to immigrate.

22. Cheney (1867, 421).

23. Pope (1897); Runnels (1881); Hughes (1977).

24. From 1791 until 1841, the part of present-day Quebec within the St. Lawrence watershed was called Lower Canada, and the part of present-day Ontario within the Great Lakes–St. Lawrence watershed was called Upper Canada. In 1841 Lower and Upper Canada were combined to form the United Province of Canada, but continued to be distinguished as, respectively, Canada East and Canada West. Prior to July 1, 1867, the name "Canada" was not applied to other parts of what was at that time called British North America. Confederation in 1867 united

Canada East and Canada West—as Quebec and Ontario, respectively—with New Brunswick and Nova Scotia, as "one Dominion under the name of Canada." Other parts of present-day Canada joined or were added later. The abbreviations "L.C." and "C.E.," as found in material quoted or cited this study, stood respectively for "Lower Canada" and "Canada East."

25. The Eastern Townships form a distinctive portion of southern Quebec that borders Vermont, New Hampshire, and Maine on all of its southern and eastern borders, extends about sixty miles northward to the Saint Lawrence River, and lies east of Montreal. With the exception of a few moderate-sized cities, it is a rural region, once covered with dense forests, lakes, rolling hills, and some mountain peaks. Until around 1860, the region had little contact with other provincial territories of Canada but had a thriving interchange with northern New England communities, especially Vermont, with well-developed social and commercial ties maintained across a nearly inconsequential international border.

26. Material in this and the following paragraphs, where not otherwise credited, is largely from the published annual reports of the Baptist Convention of the State of Vermont, minutes of the Danville (VT) Baptist Association, and annual reports of the American Baptist Home Mission Society, especially those for the years 1829–45. These were consulted at the archives of the American Baptist Historical Society, Mercer University, Atlanta, Georgia.

27. Mitchell (1841). The phrase "hopefully converted," as seen here and in the account of the revival at Sawyerville, was commonly used in Baptist writings in the nineteenth century, with "hopefully" in the sense still considered grammatically correct but now seldom seen. It meant that those who previously had been skeptical about or indifferent toward religion had become filled with hope of salvation, with no implication of uncertainty or speculation on the writers' part.

28. Godding (1867, 311). The Union Meeting House in Burke Hollow, built in 1825 and still in existence, was shared by the Baptists, Congregationalists, Methodists, and Universalists. The Baptist congregation at Burke ceased to exist in 1840.

29. May (1869, 153).

30. Fitch (1911); Sawyerville Baptist Church, accessed 13 March 2015, sawyervillebaptist.weebly.com/history.html.

31. Records of the Calvinist Baptist Church at Eaton, L.C., manuscript book, Canadian Baptist Archives, Hamilton, Ontario (hereafter, CBA); Mackintosh (1896); Carter (1980).

32. Mitchell's remuneration was not unusual for a small-town minister in his time. Tyler had begun his pastorate in South Britain, Connecticut, in 1807 with an annual salary of $450. Staughton, an especially renowned minister with a relatively prosperous urban pastoral charge, had received a salary of $1,600 per year in 1819, and the sexton of his church had received $150. The Reverend Henry Shedd, of the

Dartmouth class of 1826 and a graduate of Andover Theological Seminary, averaged $280 per year during his thirty-two years as a minister in Ohio. As a further basis for comparison, the salary of a professor at Dartmouth in the 1820s had, as noted above, been $700 per year, and that of a tutor had been about $350. As late as the 1860s, $400 per year was considered a good salary for a clerk in New York City.

33. Records of the Calvinist Baptist Church at Eaton, L.C.; "Proceedings of the Seventh Annual Meeting of the Baptist Convention of the State of Vermont, held at Eaton, September 21 through October 5, 1836," ABHS Archives; Mitchell (1841); Hubbard and Lawrence ([1874] 1963).

34. "Bread upon the Waters," *Christian Watchman*, November 4, 1836, 2.

35. The five other Baptist ministers employed for varying terms by the Baptist missionary organizations were Jonathan Baldwin, Prosper Powell, Israel Ide, Samuel B. Ryder, and M. Brittain. All but Mitchell, and possibly Rev. Brittain (whose later career has not been determined), returned to the United States.

36. Crocker (1913).

37. Robinson (2012, 38).

38. Ibid., 31.

39. Samuel J. Barrows, quoted in Scott (1993).

40. Records of the Hatley church, from its organization in 1799 to 1844, manuscript book, CBA.

41. American Home Baptist Home Society (signed by Luther Crawford and Spencer Houghton Cone) to Edward Mitchell, letter of appointment, December 20, 1837, original manuscript preserved in a private collection.

42. Mackintosh (1896).

43. The "Gray Map" of the Georgeville area shows the Mitchell dwelling near the Lake Shore (Gray 1863).

44. Information on the mid-nineteenth-century location of the schoolhouse and churches obtained by personal correspondence from John M. Scott of the Georgeville Historical Society. The structures can be seen in an old Georgeville photograph (undated) in the Davidson family fonds, P016, Eastern Townships Research Centre, Bishop's University, Lennoxville, Quebec.

45. From the report of Rev. Henry Wilkes (1842), a Canadian Congregational missionary during a tour of the Eastern Townships. The "neat school house" he refers to can be seen in an iconic painting of Georgeville by William Henry Bartlett (1842), which shows the red-brick schoolhouse and bell tower that could be mistaken for a church steeple.

46. Several items in the local history column "Forests and Clearings" of the *Stanstead Journal* in 1953 reference the Ives schoolhouse: "It is, or was until 1947, right by the cemetery on the Magog-Georgeville road, below the Partington house. I know, as I at one time attended school there more than seventy years ago, as did

my father and his brothers and sisters" (November 12, 1953, 4); and the Sabbath School "established on 'Lord's Day,' April fifteenth [1838] which met at the Ives School with Joseph Merriman as Superintendent and B. H. Ives as Sec'y Treas.' . . . Funding for the Sabbath School Library [was] contributed by Edward Mitchel" (August 13, 1953, 5).

47. In September 1834, he had participated in organizational and ordination services, respectively, at the Baptist churches in Albany and Coventry, Vermont. On the latter occasion he preached the sermon, with Acts 11:24 as his text—on the sending of St. Barnabas, "a good man, and full of the Holy Ghost and of faith," to Antioch. He also gave the charge to the congregation.

48. The trustees initially comprised ten clergymen and twenty-four laymen. The church relinquished control in 1845, and the school, as a private, secular institution, was renamed Derby Academy. It was transferred to the Town of Derby, to become the town's high school, in 1918. "Derby Academy" (1867–91); Hay and Hay ([1967] 1998).

49. H[ouse] (1841, 65–66).

50. "The Eastern Townships, L.C." (1840). Also published as "Eastern Townships, Lower Canada" (1841).

51. Cyrus Thomas's (1866) statement that "the first religious society was formed here [in South Bolton, a community within Bolton Township] in 1826, by Rev. E. Mitchell, a Baptist minister, of Hatley" is obviously incorrect in some respects. Mitchell was still a student at Dartmouth in 1826, and no other Baptist minister with that name served Hatley. Probably "1826" should be "1836," as it is quite likely that the South Bolton church was indeed founded by Mitchell.

52. This quote and related references to the Danville Association are taken from Crocker (1913).

53. Canadian census returns in the years of Mitchell's residence in Lower/Eastern Canada never show more than a few people of African ancestry in the townships and counties where Mitchell lived and worked.

54. See Winks (1997), which covers the history of migrations of slaves and free people of color into the different regions and provinces of Canada.

55. Quotes are taken from Clark (1948, 163–64), who offers important insights into Baptist life in communities of rural, mid-nineteenth century Canada. See also Pitman (1980).

56. In Mitchell's temperance sermon (P044_A,11.14, Mitchell family fonds) he references the "Canadian Civil War" and places himself among those loyal to the British Crown.

57. The 1842 Canadian Census included Lower Canada but did not capture towns in the Georgeville area. Individual sheets in the 1851 Canadian Census relating to Stanstead County (Hatley, Magog, and nearby townships) were lost, but

the statistical summaries survive. The Stanstead County summary tallies one West Indian (probably Mitchell), no "colored," and two "ethnicity not known." In 1861 no "colored" were counted in Stanstead County, although Mitchell is named. In 1871, three natives of Africa were counted; Mitchell was counted as of French origin and not a "métis," a census classification referring to Canadians of mixed First Nations and European settler origin.

58. Fitts (1985, 149).

59. Yeoman (2004) writes of the 1996 controversy in St. Armand, Quebec, that followed a proposal to perform an archaeological dig and designate a slave burial ground as a historical site. This predominantly white francophone and anglophone community is seventy-five miles southwest of Georgeville by roads and just over a mile north of the Canada-Vermont border.

60. See the following note for repositories of copies of the legal documents.

61. These volumes are labeled with Mitchell's name and the year. Several early volumes include handwritten copies of correspondence and documents substantiating Mitchell's status as an ordained Baptist minister in Canada East/Quebec. All volumes contain basic data entered by Mitchell for births, marriages, and burials, usually with an index. In addition to those at the Canadian Baptist Archives, copies exist in the Archives Nationales du Québec.

62. Although it has sometimes been assumed that Mitchell recorded the baptism of his children on this occasion, this was only a registry of their birth. Mitchell remained opposed to pedobaptism.

63. Deed of land in Hatley sold to Edward Mitchell by Russell Rexford, N ½, lot number first, sixteenth range, Hatley Township, January 15, 1845, P044_7.2, McCord Museum.

64. Mae K. Vreedenburg (née Kinsman) of Vallejo, California, who was born in the Ives neighbourhood, reminisced about the late 1870s many years later: "The neighbours around the old Kinsman house were: B. H. Ives, Rice and Russell Rexford, the Olivers, the Wallaces and the Abbots. The other way were the Van Dykes, the Mitchells, the place now owned by Wilfred Brookhouse. Across the road was Ortis Merriman, Wilfred [*sic*; Wolfred] Ives, then the Rickards [*sic*; correct spelling probably Ricard] and the Hollands." Quoted in Maude Gage Pellerin, "Forests and Clearings," column, *Stanstead Journal*, November 12, 1953, 4. The Kinsman house was across the road from the Ives Cemetery and the adjacent Ives School House. Russell Rexford in this context was presumably Russell Sr.

65. Mitchell (1841); anonymous additions to a page on Mitchell copied from Hubbard and Lawrence ([1874] 1963), CBA; Chapman (1867); 150th Anniversary Historical Booklet, American Baptist Churches of New Hampshire 1826–1976; Newton Brookhouse fonds, CA E001 P042, Eastern Townships Resource Centre,

Bishop's University, Lennoxville, Quebec, accessed July 31, 2017, www.townships archives.ca/newton-brookhouse-fonds.

66. Mitchell, Edward, Revd, Magog Stanstead, 100 acres, P Sales, 12 Dec 1857, (North 1/2 of Lot 1, Range 16, 100 acres), and Mitchell, Nathan C, Magog Stanstead, 50 acres, AN Sales, 20 Sep 1866, (W. ½ of S ½ of Lot 1, Range 16), in Quebec [Province] (1891), 1020.

67. John M. Scott, Georgeville Historical Society, personal communication. Scott collated information on the Mitchell farm from the 1871 Canadian agricultural census: Mitchell in that year had 280 [or 283] acres (more than double his 132 acres of 1861), his dwelling house, two barns, one carriage and four wagons, two ploughs, two horses, two colts, four milch cows [milk cows], five other horned cattle, and one swine; he produced wheat, oats, beans, corn, 125 bushels of potatoes, thirty-four tons of hay, five hundred pounds of butter, and fifty pounds of honey from four beehives.

68. John Fountain Jr., a Roman Catholic, listed in the 1861 Census of Canada as a laborer, and Mary E. Merry, from a socially and economically prominent Church of England family in Magog, were married by Mitchell on June 28, 1869. See transcript at www.rootsweb.com/~qceastwn/archives/Sherb_News_bmd_Surname1.html (accessed August 3, 2010).

69. Mitchell, "A Card" [of thanks], *Stanstead Journal*, February 18, 1864, 2.

70. Taylor (2010, 64).

71. Now the city center of Magog, Quebec. Mountain's itinerary did not include Georgeville, and his journal includes no mention of the churches there.

72. This was the Union Church in Magog, built in 1830 to be shared by the Baptists, Anglicans, and Methodists, although pastoral services by the latter two denominations were in abeyance at the time of Mountain's visit. Later, after the other denominations had erected buildings of their own, it housed the Free Evangelical Church. It still exists at the time of this writing. "The United Church of Canada 1925–1975," special issue, *Stanstead Journal*, June 19, 1975.

73. Mountain (1847, 73–75).

74. Wadsworth (1842).

75. Little (2006, 141).

76. Mitchell's handwritten temperance sermon is found in the Mitchell family fonds (P044_A,11.14). It is a fierce, uncompromising view, atypical of the moderate tone of other essays and sermons. The quotation is from Edward Staughton Mitchell obituary, *Stanstead Journal*, January 2, 1879, 2.

77. Mitchell's name is given periodically in reports of the British and Foreign Bible Society as one of the officers of Georgeville's Bible Society. For example, in 1854, the officers were "Rev. E. Mitchell, P[eter]. Merrill, and M[oses]. W. Copp," the latter two prominent merchants of the village. Other society reports with offi-

cer lists were found for 1850 ("Merman, I. Bullock, Mitchell"), 1860 ("J. Merriman, Esq., I. Bullock, Rev. E. Mitchell"), and 1870 ("Rev. E. Mitchell, K. Talbert, J. Merman, D. Austin, Rev. J. Thorneloe").

78. Fortin (1997, 41).

79. Bliss (1853); White (1875); Fortin (1997).

80. Mitchell (1841); Fortin (1997); "When the World" (1998). Miller preached from a window of the schoolhouse while the crowd, which would much have exceeded the building's capacity, was outside.

81. Fortin (1997).

82. Howe (2007, 290).

83. Fortin (1997, 39).

84. Ernest M. Taylor, "Some Sidelights on Eastern Townships History," *Stanstead Journal*, November 10, 1932, 1, 3.

85. Bliss (1853).

86. Manning (1911) (copy in archives of the Georgeville Historical Society, Georgeville, Quebec).

87. *Baptist Encyclopaedia* (1881), s.v. "Mitchell, Rev. Edward."

SIX A Profound Theologian

1. McPherson (1988, 8).

2. Howe (2007, 8).

3. The Baptist historian C. A. Thomas, for example, in an assessment published in 1842, asserted that the Baptists in the United States had been "slow to adopt vigorous and systematic measures for the education of their sons [who were] inclined to the gospel ministry." This he attributed to the perception that "in some leading denominations [there had been] a disposition to lay more stress upon learning than upon piety, and to use coercive measures in sustaining their learned ministry" (p. 188). By 1842, Thomas considered the situation among the Baptists to be much improved. Others have commented that the Baptists and Methodists in the early nineteenth century placed less emphasis on the education of a professional clergy than did some other denominations, especially the Episcopalians. It may be noted, however, that the Baptists founded Brown University in 1765, Waterville (now Colby) College in 1813, Colgate University in 1819, Denison University in 1831, and Wake Forest University in 1833.

4. Payton (2007, 2010); Meehan (2009); and authors cited by Payton and Meehan.

5. Howe (2007, 169).

6. Hoffecker (2001, 1168).

7. Howe (2007, 169).

8. Calvinism and Arminianism, representing the theology of, respectively, John Calvin (1509–64) and Jacob Arminius (1560–1609), are frequently contrasted as

constituting opposing views on the subject of predestined salvation. Arminian theology is defined as rejecting the doctrine of absolute predestination and accepting the possibility of salvation for all, although continuing to accept the doctrine of original sin (Steele and Thomas 1963, appendix). Both Arminianism and Semipelagianism accept the necessity of God's grace for salvation, with Arminianism contending that the first steps of grace are initiated by God, whereas Semipelagianism believes that the first steps are taken by human will, with God's grace subvening later. Taylor, although some characterized his theology as Arminian, had as a stated objective the defense of Calvinism from Arminian attack.

9. Metcalf (1860, 472) quotes the stated positions of Harvey and Tyler in their debate.

10. McPherson (1988).

11. Beecher (1864, 344–45).

12. McPherson (1988, 8).

13. Howe (2007, 180).

14. Ahlstrom (1972, 471).

15. As in other denominations, this trend had developed early—or, perhaps more accurately, never really been absent—among the Baptists in the United States, including those who continued to identify themselves as Calvinist Baptists or Particular Baptists as well as those who identified themselves as Free Will Baptists. For example, in the Philadelphia Baptist Association, with which Staughton would later be affiliated, Rev. Samuel Jones had written a "circular letter" in 1783 entitled "The Freedom of Man's Will," in which he concluded that "man is a free agent." Available online at baptisthistoryhomepage.com/1783.cl.phila.html (accessed April 12, 2012).

16. For example, Mitchell was listed as a "Regular Baptist minister" in the *Canadian Almanac* for 1871. In the edition for 1859–60, he had been listed among the "Baptist ministers," as distinguished from the "Free Will Baptist ministers."

17. See note 8, this chapter.

18. Mitchell (1841, 221–22). This was a report to Baptist colleagues (written in 1840 and published in 1841) on progress in the Stanstead-Hatley Calvinist Baptist Church.

19. "Sermons and notes for sermons," P044_A11.1–14, "The Moral Sense," P044_A4.3, "Christian Eloquence," P044_A3.7, "Homily on John 9:1–41," P044_A4.5, all in Mitchell family fonds.

20. *Montreal Register*, quoted in the *Baptist Magazine* (London, England), no. 38 (1846), 29. Some of these treatises or other works by Mitchell could perhaps be found in a thorough search of the eight-year run of the *Montreal Register*, which was published biweekly, although it was more of a newsletter than a theological journal. At the time of this writing, available microfilms of this paper were ex-

tremely low in contrast, making on-site searches feasible only for items at locations already known, although clearly legible printouts could be made.

CONCLUSION Final Days and Next Generations

1. Minor copying errors in the quotation from Montgomery's hymn and in the printed version of the resolution passed by the Eastern Canada Baptist Convention have been corrected to the original orthography here.

2. Obituary of Rev. Edward Mitchell, *Express and Standard* (Newport, VT), April 2, 1872, 2. Francis Brown commented that upon reading from the New Testament in Greek during his trip to the South, he had been "surprised at the new views [he] obtained from passages the most familiar." Wood (1834, 141).

3. Convention East (1873), minutes of the Fourteenth Annual Meeting, in *Canadian Baptist Register* (Toronto: Canadian Baptist Office), 49–54.

4. *Baptist Encyclopaedia* (1881), s.v. "Mitchell, Rev. Edward." The source of the passage in quotation marks is not stated. William Cathcart, the encyclopedia's editor, may have obtained this assessment secondhand. Although he listed many persons, mostly Baptist clergy, in his acknowledgments, none was a resident of Quebec at the time of the compilation or otherwise appears as the probable source of this quoted material, and only two, Rev. George Armstrong of Bridgetown, Nova Scotia, and Rev. J. D. King of Toronto, were residents of Canada. The original source of the statement may have known Mitchell personally, as he or she mentioned that in his early years Mitchell had "followed the sea" but did not include the myth of his having been "brought from the South."

5. Newton Brookhouse—no relation to the Mitchell, Cheney, or Leavitt families—who had recently come to Canada from England, purchased the farm. Brookhouse is known for his early photographs of Eastern Townships subjects, of which more than three hundred are preserved in the Newton Brookhouse fonds, P042, Eastern Townships Resource Centre (www.townshipsarchives.ca/newton-brookhouse-fonds).

6. Obituary of Ruth Mitchell, *Stanstead Journal*, December 19, 1889, 2.

7. Wilson and Tilton (1993) was a valuable guide to information on members of Mitchell's family.

8. Obituary of Edward Staughton Mitchell, *Stanstead Journal*, January 2, 1879, 2.

9. Obituary of Naomi Clark Mitchell, *Stanstead Journal*, January 2, 1902, 1, and *Laconia (NH) Democrat*, June 6, 1902, 4.

10. "We learn the of the death . . . ," *Stanstead Journal*, July 1, 1909, 5.

11. City directories, Laconia, NH; Runnels (1881); Carter and Holmes (1893); obituary of Nathan Cheney Mitchell, *Laconia Democrat*, June 18, 1909, 4, and a similar obituary in *Laconia News and Critic*; Leavitt Genealogical Database, accessed January 27, 2012, www.leavittfamilies.org/genweb/Leavitt/Leavitt.html. Some

references give Nathan Cheney Mitchell's birthplace as Sanbornton, New Hampshire, but in the 1880 US Census he himself gave his place of birth as "Canada."

12. Commonwealth of Pennsylvania, Department of Health, Vital Statistics, County of Philadelphia, March 13, 1947, certificate of death no. 54092, Edward Mitchell. See also Leavitt Genealogical Database (see previous note).

13. City directories, Laconia, NH; *Wellesley and Needham (MA) Directory 1911–1912*; *Mayflower Descendant*, no. 22 (1920): 130; obituary of Mary Josephine Mitchell, *Laconia Evening Citizen*, September 6, 1965, 3.

14. Records of the South Baptist Church of Laconia, NH; obituary of Naomi C. Mitchell, *Laconia Democrat*, June 6, 1902.

15. How the McCord Museum acquired these papers is not known. The presence of items dating from 1915–25 precludes the possibility of their having been acquired by David Ross McCord himself, as by that time he had been incapacitated by failing health for several years. Although the papers include no material from later than 1925, it seems unlikely that Josephine Mitchell herself donated the papers. Rather than having been sorted, evaluated, and supplemented with explanatory notes, they appear to have been donated in haste, as though by persons who had a great deal to do within a short time. They contain, for example, an instruction card for a carpet sweeper, which would likely not consciously have been chosen for inclusion with Mitchell's papers in a gift to the museum. From the inclusion of such items it appears unlikely that Mitchell's descendants selectively removed items from his papers. Members of the Mitchell family, following the death of Josephine Mitchell in 1965, may have felt that the papers would be of interest to Canadian historians and, having heard of McGill University in Montreal, decided to donate the papers to that school. The McCord Museum staff researched this issue but were unable to document the source or approximate date of the donation.

16. Records of the South Baptist Church of Laconia, NH; obituary of Naomi C. Mitchell, *Laconia Democrat*, June 6, 1902. Information on Flora McDonald Gold Mitchell and Flora R. Mitchell of Takoma Park found in an announcement of the death of Donald Mitchell, infant son of Edward and Flora Mitchell (G. B. Thompson, "Obituaries," *Adventist Review and Sabbath Herald* 92, no. 17 [1915]: 22) and in obituary of Flora McDonald Mitchell (*Evening Star* [Washington, DC], May 2, 1937, 12). On Flora Ruth Mitchell, the daughter of Edward Mitchell and Flora McDonald Gold Mitchell, see E. D. Phillips, "Commencement Exercises of the Washington Sanitarium," *Columbia Union Visitor* 28, no. 43 (1928): 2.

Epilogue

1. In the published version of Samuel G. Brown's 1869 Dartmouth centennial address (Brown 1870), copious footnotes are appended to the main text, including

the comment on Mitchell's graduation in 1824. These added notes were probably not part of the delivered speech.

2. Lord (1913, 208).

3. Wright (2012, 71, 115).

4. John Adams Vinton to Asa Dodge Smith, June 18, 1868, Rauner Library. According to Vinton, a communiqué from a committee organizing a class reunion in 1868 listed Mitchell among the members of the class of 1828 for whom they had no recent address.

5. In 2015, Tailour Garbutt, a Dartmouth undergraduate, requested a librarian's help in accessing the "Mitchell file" to research a planned essay. She wrote an award-winning essay and then a blog post reporting her frustration. Garbutt, n.d., "Individual Invisible," *Speaking Our Truths*, accessed October 15, 2017, sites .dartmouth.edu/speakingourtruths/individual-invisible.

6. Hall (1986).

7. Slater (1994) and personal correspondence.

8. Titcomb (1994/95, 7); *Baptist Encyclopaedia* (1881), s.v. "Mitchell, Rev. Edward."

9. Byas (1943, 261).

10. S. P. Parrott to H. S. P. Parrott, June 11, 1828.

11. Brown (1870); Crosby (1869); Lord (1913); Worcester (1869); Worthen (1890).

12. Aptheker ([1943] 1993) in *American Negro Slave Revolts* published the accounts of the many slave rebellions that occurred in the years leading to Nat Turner's Rebellion of 1831, expanding the list beyond the better known revolts of Denmark Vesey in 1822 (Charleston, SC) and Gabriel Prosser in 1800 (Richmond, VA).

13. Mitchell, "Christian Eloquence," Dartmouth student essay, n.d., P044_A,3.7, Mitchell family fonds.

14. Ernest (2011, 140).

15. Oberlin College, founded in 1833, has a distinguished history of institutional commitment to the education of black men and women. In 1835 its trustees adopted a policy to open doors to black students for pre-college and college studies. In the years before the Civil War, eight black men earned degrees, including the abolitionist, educator, and US congressman John Mercer Langston in 1849. Professor Roland M. Baumann (2014, xv) published a detailed institutional history of the college's commitment to "equal educational access" for African Americans, which, he notes, "was shaped by the cultural ideas coming out of the American Revolution and the Second Great Awakening . . . as well by geography, faith, luck and an openness to new religious viewpoints."

16. See Nercessian (2004) for a comprehensive history of Harvard's graduates.

17. Hopkins (1931, 263).

18. Mitchell (1841, 222).

19. Worthen (1890, 393).

BIBLIOGRAPHY

Archival Sources

American Baptist Historical Society Archives. Mercer University, Atlanta, GA.

Canadian Baptist Archives. McMaster Divinity College, Hamilton, ON.

Dépôt des papiers publics des colonies, Martinique and Guadeloupe. FR ANOM 1DPPC. Archives Nationales d'Outre-Mer, Aix-en-Provence, France.

Mitchell family fonds. 1822–97. P044. McCord Museum of Canadian History, Montreal, QC.

Naval Office Shipping Lists for Jamaica, 1685–1818, pt. 4. 73181-D-04. British Online Archives.

Naval Office Shipping Lists for Martinique, 1809–1814. 73181-E-11. British Online Archives.

"Noyer, Guillaume, habitant de la Martinique, en procès avec Dominique Cazabon, huissier au Conseil supérieur de 'île (1784/1785)," FR ANOM COL E 324, Archives Nationales d'Outre-Mer, Aix-en-Provence, France. anom.archivesnationales.culture.gouv.fr/ark:/61561/up424ysvxwwd.

Philadelphia Saving Fund Society Records. Accession 2062. Vols. 1 (Deposit and General Ledger) and 486 (Depositor Register). Hagley Museum and Library, Wilmington, DE.

Les registres d'individualités et les registres de population esclave de Martinique en ligne. La Banque numérique des patrimoines Martiniquais [Martinique Heritage Database]. www.patrimoines-martinique.org.

Reference Works

The Baptist Encyclopaedia: A Dictionary . . . of the General History of the Baptist Denomination in all Lands. 1881. Edited by William Cathcart. Philadelphia: Louis H. Everts.

Encyclopedia of African American Religions. 2011. Edited by Lane.G. Murphy, J.Gordon Melton, and Gary L. Ward. New York: Taylor & Francis.

The National Cyclopaedia of American Biography. 1896. New York: J. T. White.

Primary and Secondary Sources

Adams, Donald R., Jr. 1968. "Wage Rates in the Early National Period: Philadelphia, 1785–1830." *Journal of Economic History* 28, no. 3: 404–26.

Adams, Seymour Webster. 1860. *Memoirs of Rev. Nathaniel Kendrick, D.D. and Silas N. Kenderick*. Philadelphia: American Baptist Publication Society.

Ahlstrom, Sydney E. 1972. *A Religious History of the American People*. New Haven: Yale University Press.

Alexander, J. Heywood, David T. Robinson, and Jere R. Daniell. 2006. *The Handel Society of Dartmouth College: 1807–2007*. Hanover, NH: Handel Society of Dartmouth College.

Allen, William G. 1853. *American Prejudice against Color: An Authentic Narrative, Showing How Easily the Nation Got into an Uproar*. London: W. & F. G. Cash.

Antoine, Tai. 2012. "Black Greens." Rauner Special Collections Library, Dartmouth College. www.dartmouth.edu/~library/rauner/blackgreens/.

Aptheker, Herbert. (1943) 1993. *American Negro Slave Revolts*. New York: International Publications.

Bacon, Jacqueline. 2007. *Freedom's Journal: The First African-American Newspaper*. Lanham, MD: Lexington.

Bardin, Pierre. 1990. "Religieux aux isles en 1790." *Généalogie et Histoire de la Caraïbe Bulletin*, no. 18 (July–August): 180–82.

Bardin, Pierre. 1998. "Actes de notoriété sur des Antillais à Paris en 1794–1801." *Généalogie et Histoire de la Caraïbe Bulletin*, no. 110 (December): 2370.

Baumann, Roland M. 2014. *Constructing Black Education at Oberlin College: A Documentary History*. Athens: Ohio University Press.

Beecher, Lyman. 1864. *Autobiography, Correspondence, Etc., of Lyman Beecher*. Vol. 1. Edited by Charles Beecher. New York: Harper & Brothers.

Bergman, Peter. 1969. *The Chronological History of the Negro in America*. New York: Harper & Row.

Bethel, Elizabeth Rauh. 1999. *The Roots of African-American Identity: Memory and History in Antebellum Free Communities*. New York: St. Martin's.

"Bible Associations." 1816. *Evangelical Repository* 1 (3):7.

Bible Society of Maine. 1809. "An Address of the Bible Society of Maine, Established in Portland, August 30, 1809, to the Public: To Which Is Subjoined, the Constitution & Regulation of Said Society, and the Names of Its Officers." Portland, MA: Arthur Shirley.

Bible Society of Philadelphia. 1816. *The Eighth Report of the Bible Society of Philadelphia: Read before the Society, May 1st, A.D. 1816*. Philadelphia: printed by William Fry.

Binney, Charles James Fox, ed. 1883. *The History and Genealogy of the Prentice, or*

Prentiss Family, in New England, etc., from 1631 to 1883. Boston: published by the editor.

Bliss, Sylvester. 1853. *Memoirs of William Miller: Generally Known as a Lecturer on the Prophecies and the Second Coming of Christ*. Boston: Joshua V. Himes.

Blue, Frederick J. 1987. *Salmon P. Chase: A Life in Politics*. Kent, OH: Kent State University Press.

Bolster, W. Jeffrey. 1998. *Black Jacks: African American Seamen in the Age of Sail*. Cambridge, MA: Harvard University Press.

Bordewich, Fergus M. 2005. *Bound for Canaan: The Underground Railroad and the War for the Soul of America*. New York: HarperCollins.

Bouton, Jenny. 2009. "The Religious Roots of the Dartmouth College Case." *Dartmouth Apologia* 4, no. 1: 2–5.

Briggs, L. V. 1889. *History of Shipbuilding on North River, Plymouth County, Massachusetts: With Genealogies of the Shipbuilders, and Accounts of the Industries upon Its Tributaries. 1640 to 1872*. Boston: Coburn Brothers.

British and Foreign Bible Society. 1854. *Fiftieth Report of the British and Foreign Bible Society with an Appendix and a List of Subscribers and Benefactors*. London: Richard Clay.

Brooks, Charles H. 1922. *Official History of the First African Baptist Church*. Philadelphia. Published by author.

Brown, Elizabeth Gilman. 1820. *Journal of Elizabeth Gilman Brown (Mrs. Francis Brown), October 12, 1819–June 22, 1820*. Hanover, NH: Dartmouth College.

Brown, Samuel Gilman. 1870. *An Historical Discourse Delivered before the Alumni of Dartmouth College, July 21, 1869, One Hundred Years after the Founding of that Institution*. Hanover, NH: Dartmouth Press.

Browne, George, comp. 2012. *History of the British and Foreign Bible Society*. Vol. 1. London: n.p.

Bruneau-Latouche, Eugène, Chantal Cordiez, and Philippe Cordiez. 2002. *209 anciennes familles subsistantes de la Martinique: Notices généalogiques, acquisitions, ventes*, échanges, alliances et descendances antérieurs à 1901. Aix-en-Provence: E. Bruneau-Latouche.

Byas, Vincent W. 1943. "Ethnologic Aspects of the Martinique Creole." *Journal of Negro History* 28, no. (3): 261–83.

Calloway, Colin G. 2010. *The Indian History of an American Institution: Native Americans and Dartmouth*. Hanover, NH: Dartmouth College Press.

Campbell, Carl. 1980. "The Rise of a Free Coloured Plantocracy in Trinidad 1783–1813." *Boletín de Estudios Latinoamericanos y del Caribe*, no. 29: 33–53.

Campbell, Penelope. 1970. "Medical Education for an African Colonist." *Maryland Historical Magazine* (Summer): 130–37.

Carter, Jane G. (Avery), and Susie P. Holmes. 1893. *Genealogical Record of the*

Dedham Branch of the Avery Family in America. Plymouth, MA: Winslow W. Avery.

Chandler, Charles Henry. 1868. *A History of the Theological Society, of Dartmouth College*. Hanover, NH: published by the Society.

Chapman, George T. 1867. *Sketches of the Alumni of Dartmouth College: From the First Graduation in 1771 to the Present Time, with a Brief History of the Institution*. Cambridge, MA: Riverside.

Charlton, Faith. 2011. "Black Catholics in Philadelphia and the Journal." Catholic Historical Research Center blog, February 24. www.chrc-phila.org/black-catholics-in-philadelphia-and-the-journal.

Chase, Frederick. 1882. "Bibliography of Dartmouth College." *Granite Monthly* 5, no. 10: 321–24.

Chauleau, Liliane. 1993. *Dans les Îles du vent: La Martinique, XVIIe–XIXe siècle*. Paris: L'Harmattan.

Cheney, Simeon P. 1867. "Elder Moses Cheney." *The Vermont Historical Gazetteer: A Magazine Embracing a History of Each Town, Civil, Ecclesiastical, Biographical and Military*, 419–23.

Clark, Lynn, and Rebecca Courser. 2007. "Rural Free Black Settlement in Post-Revolutionary New Hampshire: A Study of Five Towns." *Historical New Hampshire* 61: 48–67.

Clark, Samuel D. 1948. *Church and Sect in Canada*. Toronto: University of Toronto Press.

Clarke, James Stanier, and John McArthur. 1807. *The Naval Chronicle*. Vol. 18, *July–December 1807: Containing a General and Biographical History of the Royal Navy of the United Kingdom with a Variety of Original Papers on Nautical Subjects*. Cambridge: Cambridge University Press.

Clement, Priscilla Ferguson. 1985. *Welfare and the Poor in the Nineteenth-Century City: Philadelphia, 1800–1854*. Rutherford, NJ: Fairleigh Dickinson University Press.

Coke, Thomas. 1808–11. "History of Martinico." In *A History of the West Indies: Containing the Natural, Civil, and Ecclesiastical History of Each Island*, edited by Thomas Coke, 304–31. Liverpool: Nuttall, Fisher, and Dixon.

Connolly, Michael C. 2001. "Black Fades to Green: Irish Labor Replaces African American Labor along a Major New England Waterfront, Portland, Maine, in the Mid-Nineteenth Century." *Colby Quarterly* 37, no. 4: 357–73.

Contee, Clarence. 1973. "History Series: Edward Jones, First Black College Graduate." *Afro-American* (Baltimore), August 7–11.

Cormack, William S. 2011. "Revolution and Free-Colored Equality in the Îles du Vent (Lesser Antilles), 1789–1794." *Proceedings of the Western Society for French History* 39: 155–65.

Cousseau, Vincent. 2009. "Population and Anthroponymy in Martinique from the 17th to the First Half of the 19th century." PhD diss., Université des Antilles et de la Guyane.

Cousseau, Vincent 2011/12. "La famille invisible: Illégitimité des naissances et construction des liens familiaux en Martinique (XVIIe siècle–début du XIXe siècle)." *Annales de Démographie Historique*, no. 122: 41–67.

Crocker, Henry. 1913. *History of the Baptists in Vermont*. Bellows Falls, VT: P. H. Gobie.

Crosby, Alpheus Benning. 1869. *A Memorial of the College Life of the Class of 1827, Dartmouth College: A Centenary Contribution to the History of Their Alma Mater*. Hanover, NH: Dartmouth College.

Crosby, Alpheus Benning. 1872. *A Eulogy Commemorative of the Life and Character of Nathan Lord, D.D., LL. D., President of Dartmouth College Delivered before the Association of the Alumni of Dartmouth College, at the Annual Commencement, June 1872*. Hanover, NH: J. B. Parker.

Cummings, Asa, comp. 1830. *A Memoir of the Rev. Edward Payson, D.D., Late Pastor of the Second Church in Portland*. Portland, ME: Ann L. Payson.

Dain, Bruce R. 2009. *A Hideous Monster of the Mind: American Race Theory in the Early Republic*. Cambridge, MA: Harvard University Press.

Daney, Sidney. 1846. "Histoire de La Martinique depuis la colonisation jusqu'en 1845, vol 5." Fort-Royal: E. Ruelle, Imprimeur du Gouvernement.

Dartmouth College. 1924. *Catalogue of the Officers and Students of Dartmouth College*. Boston: Phelps and Farnham.

Dartmouth College. 1940. *Dartmouth College and the Associated Schools General Catalogue, 1769–1940*. Hanover, NH: Dartmouth College Publications.

Dartmouth College. 2006. "Politics of Memory—A Conference in Honor of James O. Friedman: Welcome and Introduction by President James Wright." News release, October 24. www.dartmouth.edu/~news/releases/2006/10/24b.html.

Davies, John. 2008. "Class, Culture, and Color: Black Saint-Dominguan Refugees and African-American Communities in the Early Republic." PhD diss., University of Delaware.

Dawes, Edward. 1817. *The Philadelphia Directory for 1817: Containing the Names, Trades and Residence of the Inhabitants of the City, Northern Liberties, Southwark and Precincts, with Other Useful Information*. Philadelphia: Whitehall.

"Derby Academy." 1877. *The Vermont Historical Gazetteer: A Magazine Embracing a History of Each Town, Civil, Ecclesiastical, Biographical and Military*, 181–82.

Dippel, John V. H. 2015. *Eighteen Hundred and Froze to Death: The Impact of America's First Climate Crisis*. New York: Algora.

Dorman, Dana. 2009. "Philadelphia's African American Heritage: A Brief Context Statement for the Preservation Alliance's Inventory of African

American Historic Sites." Unpublished paper, Preservation Alliance of Greater Philadelphia. www.preservationalliance/files/HCSAfricanAmericanHeritage .pdf.

Draper, Charlotte G. 1860. "Sacred to the Memory of Edward Garrison Draper." In *For the Presbyterian Female of Color's Enterprising Society in Baltimore: A Free Will Offering*, 78–94. Baltimore: Frederick A. Hanzsche.

Dubois, W. E. B. 1967. *The Philadelphia Negro: A Social Study*. Political Economy and Public Law series, University of Pennsylvania, no. 14. New York: P. Blom.

Dunn, D. Elwood, Amost J. Beyan, and Carl Patrick Burrowes. 2001. "Washington, Augustus (1820–1875)." In *Historical Dictionary of Liberia*, edited by Jon Woronoff, 354–55. Lanham, MD: Scarecrow.

"The Eastern Townships, L.C.: Messrs. Topping and Bosworth's Missionary Tour, during the Months of July and August." 1840. *Canadian Baptist Magazine and Missionary Register* 4: 99–100.

"Eastern Townships, Lower Canada: Some Account of a Missionary Visit to These Parts by Messrs. Topping and Bosworth, Students in the Theological Institution, in the Months of July and August, 1840." 1841. *Baptist Magazine* (London, UK) 32: 529–31.

"Edward Mitchell." 1918. *Journal of Negro History* 3: 90–91.

Elisabeth, Léo. 1989. "Gens de couleur et révolution dans les îles du Vent (1789–janvier 1793)." *Revue Française d'Histoire d'Outre-mer* 76, no. 282: 75–95.

Elisabeth, Léo. 1993. "La République dans les Îles du Vent (déc. 1792–avril 1794)." *Annales Historiques de la Révolution Française* 293, no. 1: 373–408.

Emerson, Charles Franklin. 1911. *General Catalogue of Dartmouth College and the Associated Schools 1769–1910, including a Historical Sketch of the College*. Hanover, NH: Dartmouth College.

Ernest, John. 2011. *A Nation within a Nation: Organizing African-American Communities before the Civil War*. American Ways Series. Summit, PA: Ivan R. Dee.

Fernald, Jody R. 2007. "Slavery in New Hampshire: Profitable Godliness to Racial Consciousness." MA thesis, University of New Hampshire.

Ferrin, Chester E. 1877. "Rev. Alexander L. Twilight." In *The Vermont Historical Gazetteer: A Magazine, Embracing a History of Each Town, Civil, Ecclesiastical, Biographical and Military*, 101–4.

Fisher, Miles M. 1935. "Friends of Humanity: A Quaker Anti-slavery Influence." *Church History* 4: 187–202.

Fitch, Ernest Robert. 1911. *The Baptists of Canada: A History of Their Progress and Achievements*. Toronto: Standard Publishing Company.

Fitts, Leroy. 1985. *A History of Black Baptists*. Nashville: Broadman.

Fletcher, Robert. 1926. "A Brief History Prepared for the Centennial Anniversary

of the Building of the Brick Church in 'Mill Neighborhood' [now Etna, NH]." Mimeograph. Rauner Special Collections Library, Dartmouth College, Hanover, NH.
Forbush, Bliss. 1988. "The Price of Freedom." *Friends Journal* 34, no. 9: 28–9.
Forten, James. (1832) 2005. "Part II: Sentiments of the People of Color: A Voice from Philadelphia." In *Thoughts on African Colonization: Or an Impartial Exhibition of the Doctrines, Principles and Purposes of the African Colonization Society*, edited by William Lloyd Garrison, 9–10. Brighton, MA: Adamant Media.
Fortescue, John William. 1906. *A History of the British Army*. Vol. 4, part 2. London: Macmillan.
Fortin, Denis. 1997. "'The World Turned Upside Down': Millerism in the Eastern Townships, 1835–1845." *Journal of Eastern Townships Studies* 11 (Fall): 39–59.
Froidefond de Boulazac, Alfred de. 1891. *Armorial de la noblesse du Périgord*. Vol. 2. Périgueux: Imprimerie de la Dordogne.
Frost, Edwin Brant. 1933. *An Astronomer's Life*. Boston: Houghton Mifflin.
Gale, Nahum. 1860. *Memoir of Rev. Bennet Tyler, D.D., Late President and Professor of Christian Theology in the Theological Institute of Connecticut*. Boston: J. E. Tilton.
Garrison, William Lloyd. 1845. "[Reply to] Thomas Paine." *Liberator*, November 21, 1845, 186.
Geggus, David. 1996. "The Slaves and Free Coloreds of Martinique during the Age of the French and Haitian Revolutions: Three Moments of Resistance." In *The Lesser Antilles in the Age of European Expansion*, edited by Robert L. Paquette and Stanley L. Engerman, 280–301. Gainesville: University Press of Florida.
Georgetown University. 1873. *A Catalogue of the Officers and Students of Georgetown University*. Baltimore: John Murphy.
Germain, Jean-Cristophe. 1994. "Les frères Michel de la Martinique: Ces cousins méconnus de Belain d'Esnambuc." *Généalogie et Histoire de la Caraïbe Bulletin*, no. 58 (March): 994–99.
Gillette, A. D., ed. (1851) 1976. *Minutes of the Philadelphia Baptist Association, from A.D. 1707, to A.D. 1807; Being the First One Hundred Years of Its Existence*. Otisville, MI: Baptist Book Trust.
Gilman, Emily Hoffman. 1919. *A Family History in Letters and Documents, 1667–1837: Concerning the Forefathers of Winthrop Sargent Gilman, and His Wife Abia Swift Lippincott*. Vol. 2. London: privately printed.
Giraud, Michel. 1980. "Races, classes et colonialisme à la Martinique." *L'Homme et la Société* 55, no. 1: 199–214.
Gitter, Elisabeth. 2001. *The Imprisoned Guest: Samuel Howe and Laura Bridgman, the Original Deaf-Blind Girl*. New York: Farrar, Straus and Giroux.

Godding, Rufus. 1867. *The Vermont Historical Gazetteer: A Magazine Embracing a History of Each Town, Civil, Ecclesiastical, Biographical and Military*, 310–11.

Goodwin, Doris Kearns. 2005. *Team of Rivals: The Political Genius of Abraham Lincoln*. New York: Simon & Schuster.

Grant, Conor. 2014. "Revisiting Middlebury's Racial History." *Middlebury Campus*, March 20, 5.

Gray, O. W. 1863. *Map of the district of St. Francis, Canada East: From Surveys of British and American Boundary Commissioners, British American Land Company Crown Land Department, and Special Surveys and Observations*. N.p.: Putnam and Gray.

Gross, Bella. 1932. "Freedom's Journal and The Rights of Man." *Journal of Negro History* 17: 141–286.

Guyette, Elise A. 2010. *Discovering Black Vermont: African American Farmers in Hinesburgh, 1790–1890*. Burlington: University of Vermont Press.

H[ouse], A. H. 1841. "The Eastern Townships." *Canadian Baptist Magazine and Missionary Register* 5: 65–66.

Hall, Raymond L. 1986. "A Reaffirmation of Mission: The Saga of the Black Experience at Dartmouth." *Dartmouth Alumni Magazine* 79, no. 3: 38.

Hancock, Scott. 1999. "The Elusive Boundaries of Blackness: Identity Formation in Antebellum Boston." *Journal of Negro History* 84, no. 2: 115–29.

Hawkins, Hugh. 1982. "Edward Jones, Marginal Man." In *Black Apostles at Home and Abroad: Afro-Americans and the Christian Mission from the Revolution to Reconstruction*, edited by David W. Wills and Richard Newman, 243–54. Boston: G. K. Hall.

Hay, Cecile B., and Mildred B. Hay. (1967) 1998. *History of Derby*. Salem, MA: Higginson.

Hayot, Emile. 1969. "Les gens de couleur libres du Fort-Royal, 1679–1823, (1re partie)." *Revue Française d'Histoire d'Outre-mer* 56, no. 202: 5–98.

Hodge, Carl C., and Cathal J. Nolan. 2007. *U.S. Presidents and Foreign Policy: From 1789 to the Present*. Santa Barbara, CA: ABC-CLIO.

Hoffecker, W. A. 2001. "Taylor, Nathaniel William (1786–1858)." In *Evangelical Dictionary of Theology*, edited by Walter A. Elwell, 1168. Grand Rapids, MI: Baker Academic.

Hopkins, Ernest M. "The Northern College and the Negro Student." *Crisis*, August 1931.

Hopper, Matthew S. 1998. "From Refuge to Strength: The Rise of the African American Church in Philadelphia, 1787–1949." Unpublished paper, Preservation Alliance for Greater Philadelphia. www.preservationalliance.com/files/aachurches.pdf.

Howard, Martin. 2015. *Death before Glory: The British Soldier in the West Indies in the French Revolutionary and Napoleonic Wars 1793–1815*. South Yorkshire: Pen and Sword.

Howe, Daniel Walker. 2007. *What Hath God Wrought: The Transformation of America, 1815–1848*. Oxford History of the United States series. New York: Oxford University Press.

H.R. Doc. No. 369, 59th Cong., 2d Sess. (1907).

Hubbard, Benjamin F., and John Lawrence. (1874) 1963. *Forests and Clearings: The History of Stanstead County, Province of Quebec, with Sketches of More Than Five Hundred Families*. Sherbrooke, QC: Page-Sangster Printing.

Hughes, Charles W. 1977. "The Cheneys: A Vermont Singing Family." *Vermont History*, n.s., 44: 155–68.

James, Winston. 2010. *The Struggles of John Brown Russwurm: The Life and Writings of a Pan-Africanist Pioneer, 1799–1851*. New York: New York University Press.

Johnson, Kenneth Gregory. 2006. "Louis-Thomas Villaret de Joyeuse: Admiral and Colonial Administrator (1747–1812)." PhD diss., University of Florida.

Kendrick, Ariel. 1850. *Sketches of the Life and Times of Eld. Ariel Kendrick*. 3rd ed. Windsor, VT: P. Merrifield.

Kendrick, Stephen, and Paul Kendrick. 2006. *Sarah's Long Walk: The Free Blacks of Boston and How Their Struggle for Equality Changed America*. Boston: Beacon Press.

Kleczewski, Kieran Russell. 1988. "Martinique and the British Occupation, 1794–1802." PhD diss., Georgetown University.

Knight, Franklin W., and Peggy K. Liss. 1991. *Atlantic Port Cities: Economy, Culture, and Society in the Atlantic World, 1650–1850*. Knoxville: University of Tennessee Press.

Koren, Ore. 2010. "Edward Mitchell and Student Dissidence in the 1820s." *Dartmouth 1820s–1850s*. Accessed December 21, 2012. dartmouth1850s.wordpress.com/student-dissidence-in-the-1820s/.

Lambolez, Charles L. 1905. *Saint-Pierre-Martinique 1635–1902: Annales des Antilles françaises; journal et album de la Martinique; naissance, vie et mort de la cité créole; livre d'or de la charité*. Paris: Berger-Levrault.

Lapansky, Emma Jones. 1975. "South Street Philadelphia, 1762–1854: A Haven for Those Low in the World." PhD diss., University of Pennsylvania.

Lapansky, Emma Jones. 1980. "Since 'They Got Those Separate Churches': Afro-Americans and Racism in Jacksonian Philadelphia." *American Quarterly* 32, no. 1: 54–78.

Laussat, Pierre-Clément de. 1831. *Mémoires sur ma vie, à mon fils, pendant les années 1803 et suivantes, que j'ai rempli des fonctions publiques, savoir: à la Louisianne . . . à la Martinique . . . à la Guyane française*. N.p.: Pau. É. Vignancour.

Lémery, Henry. 1936. *La Révolution française à la Martinique*. Paris: Larose.

L'Étang, Gerry, and Jean-Pierre Arsaye. 2007. *La peinture en Martinique*. Paris: HC Editions.

Lindman, Janet Moore. 2011. *Bodies of Belief: Baptist Community in Early America*. Philadelphia: University of Pennsylvania Press.

Little, J. I. 2006. *The Other Quebec: Microhistorical Essays on Nineteenth-Century Religion and Society*. Toronto: University of Toronto Press.

Litwack, Leon F. 2009. *North of Slavery: The Negro in the Free States, 1790–1860*. Chicago: University of Chicago Press.

Logan, Rayford, and Michael R. Winston. 1982. *Dictionary of American Negro Biography*. New York: Norton.

Lombard, Lucina H. 1937. "William Prentiss, One of Gorham's Early Sea Captains Became Father of Famous Sons." *Lewiston (ME) Evening Journal*, January 30, magazine section, A-1, 9-A.

Lord, John King. 1902. "The Development of the College since the Dartmouth College Case." In *The Proceedings of the Webster Centennial: The Commemoration by Dartmouth College of the Services of Daniel Webster to the College and the State: Held upon the One Hundredth Anniversary of the Graduation of Mr. Webster*, edited by Ernest Martin, 54–80. Hanover, NH: Dartmouth College.

Lord, John King. 1913. *A History of Dartmouth College, 1815–1909, by John King Lord, Being the Second Volume of a History of Dartmouth College and the Town of Hanover, New Hampshire, Begun by Frederick Chase*. Concord, NH: Rumford.

Lord, John King. 1924. "The Diary of Mrs. President Brown on a Journey to the South in 1819." *Dartmouth Alumni Magazine* 17: 111–17.

Lord, Myra Belle. 1889. *A History of the Town of New London, Merrimack County, New Hampshire 1779–1899*. Concord, NH: Rumford.

Louis, Abel Alexis. 2011. "Les libres de couleur en Martinique des origines à 1815." PhD diss., Université des Antilles et de la Guyane.

Lynd, Samuel, Daniel Sharp, and Thomas D. Mitchell. 1860. "William Staughton, D.D. 1793–1829." In *Annals of the American Pulpit: Or, Commemorative Notes of Distinguished Clergymen of Various Denominations. Baptist*, 334–44. New York: Robert Carter & Brothers.

Lynd, Samuel W. 1834. *Memoir of the Rev. William Staughton, D.D.* Boston: Lincoln, Edmands.

Mackintosh, C. H. 1896. *History of Compton County and Sketches of the Eastern Townships, District of St. Francis, and Sherbrooke County*. Cookshire, QC: L. S. Channell.

Mackintosh, Eliane. 2013. "Michel-Jean Cabazon's [*sic*] Bi-centenary Celebration." *Aica Caraïbe du Sud* (blog), July 20, 2013, aica-sc.net/2013/07/20/michel-jean-cabazons-bi-centenary-celebration/.

MacLean, Geoffrey. 1986. *Cazabon: An Illustrated Biography of Trinidad's Nineteenth Century Painter*. Port of Spain, Trinidad: Aquarela Galleries.
Manning, Edwin C. 1911. *Biographical, Historical and Miscellaneous Selections by Edwin Cassander Manning, President Kansas State Historical Society, Winfield, Kansas, March 7, 1838–January 1, 1911*. Cedar Rapids, IA: Torch Press.
May, Samuel J. 1869. *Some Recollections of Our Antislavery Conflict*. Boston: Fields, Osgood.
McCloy, Shelby T. 2015. *The Negro in the French West Indies*. Lexington: University Press of Kentucky.
McPherson, James M. 1988. *The Battle Cry of Freedom: The Civil War Era*. Oxford History of the United States series. New York: Oxford University Press.
Meacham, Scott. n.d. "Notes toward a Catalog of the Buildings and Landscapes of Dartmouth College." Accessed February 16, 2011. www.dartmo.com/buildings/Buildings%20of%20Dartmouth-Meacham.pdf.
Meehan, Chris. 2009. "John Calvin We Hardly Knew Ye." *Banner*, January. Accessed 28 March 2012. thebanner.org/features/2011/01/john-calvin-we-hardly-knew-ye.
Metcalf, David. 1860. *An Inquiry into the Nature, Foundation, and Extent of Moral Obligation: Involving the Nature of Duty, of Holiness, and of Sin*. Boston: Crosby, Nichols, Lee.
Mitchell, Edward. 1829. "Outline of the Religious Experience of Edward Mitchell." Unpublished manuscript. P044_A,6.1, Mitchell family fonds, McCord Museum of Canadian History, Montreal.
Mitchell, Edward. 1841. "The Rise and Progress of the Church in Hatley and Stanstead, L.C.: Letter Dated Georgeville, Nov. 4, 1840." *Canada Baptist Magazine and Missionary Register* 4, no. 9: 221–22.
Moitt, Bernard. 2001. *Women and Slavery in the French Antilles, 1635–1848*. Bloomington: Indiana University Press.
Monnier, Paul. 1828. *Description nautique des côtes de la Martinique, précédé d'un mémoire sur les opérations hydrographiques et géodésiques exécutées dans cette ile en 1824 et 1825*. Paris: Imprimerie Royale.
Moreau de Jonnés, Alexandre. 1822. *Histoire physique des Antilles francaises: Savoir; La Martinique et les iles de la Guadeloupe*. Paris: Impr. de Migneret.
Moss, Hilary J. 2009. *Schooling Citizens: The Struggle for African American Education in Antebellum America*. Chicago: University of Chicago Press.
Mountain, George Jehoshaphat. 1847. *A Journal of a Visitation in a Portion of the Diocese of Quebec, by the Lord Bishop of Montreal, in 1846*. London: Society for the Propagation of the Gospel.
Nash, Gary B. 2003. *Forging Freedom: The Formation of Philadelphia's Black Community, 1720–1840*. Cambridge, MA: Harvard University Press.

Nash, Michael. 1996. "Research Note: Searching for Working-Class Philadelphia in the Records of the Philadelphia Saving Fund Society." *Journal of Social History* 29, no. 3: 663–87.

Nercessian, Nora Nouritza. 2004. *Against All Odds: The Legacy of Students of African Descent at Harvard Medical School before Affirmative Action 1850–1968*. Boston: Harvard Medical School.

Niven, John. 1995a. *Salmon P. Chase: A Biography*. New York: Oxford University Press.

Niven, John, ed. 1995b. *The Salmon P. Chase Papers*. Vol. 2, *Correspondence, 1823–1857*. Kent, OH: Kent State University Press.

Norman, Charles B. 1887. *The Corsairs of France*. London: Sampson Low, Marston, Searle, & Rivington.

Nutt, Seargent Prentiss. 1883. "Genealogy of the Prentiss Family." In *The Life and Times of Seargent Smith Prentiss*, by Joseph D Shields, 441–42. Philadelphia: J. B. Lippincott.

Oakes, James. 2007. *The Radical and the Republican: Frederick Douglass, Abraham Lincoln, and the Triumph of Antislavery Politics*. New York: W. W. Norton.

"Oneida and Oberlin." 1841. *British and Foreign Anti-slavery Society Reporter* 2, no. (10): 112.

Paley, William. 1850. *The Works of William Paley, D. D., Archdeacon of Carlisle*. Philadelphia: Crissy & Markley.

Paul, Thomas, Jr. 1841. "Speech of Thomas Paul; a Colored Student of Dartmouth College; Delivered before the Massachusetts Anti-slavery Society; January 27th; 1841; in the Representatives' Hall; Boston." *Liberator*, February 19, 1841, 30.

Payton, James R., Jr. 2007. "Respecting John Calvin." *Banner*, September. Accessed 28 March 2012. thebanner.org/departments/2011/01/respecting-john-calvin.

Payton, James R., Jr. 2010. "Calvin: Champion of Piety." Lecture (and associated announcement) presented at Redeemer University College, Ancaster, Ontario, January 13.

PBS. n.d. "Philadelphia." *Africans in America*. Part 3, *Brotherly Love, 1791–1831*. Accessed July 27, 2007. www.pbs.org/wgbh/aia/part3/3narr1.html.

Peifer, Douglas Carl. 2013. "Maritime Commerce Warfare: The Coercive Response of the Weak?" *Naval War College Review* 66, no. 2: 83–109.

Pennsylvania Historical and Museum Commission. n.d. *Communities in Common: Black History in Pennsylvania Study*. archive.org/details/CommunitiesInCommonBlackHistoryInPennsylvaniaStudy.

Peterson, Owen. 1986. *A Divine Discontent: The Life of Nathan S. S. Beman*. Macon, GA: Mercer University Press.

Pinckard, George. 1816. *Notes on the West Indies . . . Second edition, with Additional*

Letters from Martinique, Jamaica and St. Domingo. London: printed by S. Gosnell.

Pitman, Walter G. 1980. *The Baptists and Public Affairs in the Province of Canada, 1840–1867*. New York: Arno.

Pope, Charles Henry. 1897. *The Cheney Genealogy*. Boston: published by the author.

Porter, Dorothy Burnett. 1971. Introduction to part 3, "Significant Annual Conferences, 1830–1837." In *Early Negro Writing, 1760–1837*, edited by Dorothy Porter, 167–71. Boston: Beacon Press.

Poyen-Bellisle, Henry de. 1896. *Les guerres des Antilles de 1793 à 1815*. Paris: Berger-Levrault. archive.org/details/GuerresAntilles17931815.

Prentiss, George Lewis. 1858. *A Memoir of S.S. Prentiss*. New York: Charles Scribner.

Prentiss, George Lewis, ed. 1882. *The Life and Letters of Elizabeth Prentiss, Author of Stepping Heavenward*. New York: Anson D. F. Randolph.

Price, Harriet H., and George E. Talbot. 2006. *Maine's Visible Black History: The First Chronicle of Its People*. Gardiner, ME: Tilbury House.

Quarles, Benjamin. 1969. *Black Abolitionists*. New York: Oxford University Press.

Quebec [Province]. 1891. *List of Lands Granted by the Crown in the Province of Quebec, from 1763 to 31st December 1890*. Quebec: C.-F. Langlois.

Quint, Wilder Dwight. 1922. *The Story of Dartmouth*. Boston: Little, Brown.

Rael, Patrick. 2003. *Black Identity and Black Protest in the Antebellum North*. John Hope Franklin Series in African American History and Culture. Chapel Hill: University of North Carolina Press.

Rawley, James A., and Stephen D. Behrendt. 2005. *The Transatlantic Slave Trade: A History*. Rev. ed. Lincoln: University of Nebraska Press.

"Religious Miscellany." 1816. *Boston Recorder*, 3 July 1816.

Remy, Avonelle Pauline. 2015. "Infiltrating the Colonial City through the Imaginaries of Metissage: Saint-Louis (Senegal), Saint-Pierre (Martinique) and Jeremie (Haiti)." PhD diss., University of Iowa.

Rennard, Joseph. 1951. *La Martinique: Historique des paroisses, des origines à la séparation*. Thonon-les-Bains, Haute-Savoie: Société d'édition Savoyarde.

Richardson, Leon B. 1932. *History of Dartmouth College*. Vol. 1. Hanover, NH: Dartmouth College Publications.

Ripley, John Edward. 1941. "A History of the Handel Society of Dartmouth College." Typescript. Rauner Special Collections Library, Dartmouth College, Hanover, NH.

Robinson, James. 1817. *Robinson's Original Annual Directory for 1817: Being an Alphabetical List of More than 22,000 Merchants, Mechanicks, Traders, &c. of Philadelphia and Suburbs, with Useful Information, &c.* Philadelphia: Whitehall.

Robinson, Jody. 2012. "The Loveliest Lake in the New Dominion: Montréal

Villégiateurs on Lake Memphremagog, 1860–1914." MA thesis, Université de Sherbrooke.

Robinson, Robert. 1817. *The History of Baptism*. 2nd ed. Boston: Lincoln & Edmands.

Roget, Jacques Petitjean, and Eugène Bruneau-Latouche. 2000. *Personnes et familles à la Martinique au XVIIe siècle d'après recensements et terrier nominatifs*. Paris: Désormeaux.

Rowland, Dunbar. 1909. "Sergeant [*sic*] Smith Prentiss [1808–1850]." In *Library of Southern Literature*, edited by E. A. Alderman and J. C. Harris, 4209–14. New Orleans: Martin & Hoyt.

Runnels, Moses Thurston. 1881. *History of Sanbornton, New Hampshire*. Boston: A. Mudge & Son.

Saillant, John. 2003. *Black Puritan, Black Republican: The Life and Thought of Lemuel Haynes, 1753–1833*. New York: Oxford University Press.

Salvarelli, Joseph. 1897. *Les administrateurs du département du Var, 1790–1897: Notice biographiques*. Draguignan, Var: Imprimerie Olivier-Joulian. archive.org /details/lesadministrateoosalvgoog.

Saunders, Prince. 1818a. *An Address Delivered at Bethel Church, Philadelphia on the 30th of September, 1818, before the Pennsylvania Augustine Society, for the Education of People of Colour*. Philadelphia: printed by Joseph Bakestraw.

Saunders, Prince. 1818b. *Memoir Presented to the American Convention for Promoting the Abolition of Slavery, and Improving the Condition of the African Race: December 11th, 1818*. Philadelphia: Denis Heartt.

Schlesinger, Arthur Meier. 1919. "Salmon Portland Chase: Undergraduate and Pedagogue." *Ohio Archaeological and Historical Quarterly* 28: 119–81.

Schloss, Rebecca H. 2009. *Sweet Liberty: The Final Days of Slavery in Martinique*. Philadelphia: University of Pennsylvania Press.

Scott, John M. 1993. "Georgeville: Le calme serein dun petit village." *Continuité*, no. 56 (March–May): 20–23.

Sechrest, Larry J. 2003. "Privateering and National Defense: Naval Warfare for Private Profit." In *The Myth of National Defense: Essays on the Theory and History of Security Production*, edited by Hans-Hermann Hoppe, 239–74. Auburn, AL: Ludwig von Mises Institute, Auburn University.

Shedd, Mary L. 1922. *The Measure of a Man: The Life of William Ambrose Shedd, Missionary to Persia*. New York: George H. Doran.

Slater, Robert Bruce. 1994. "The Blacks Who First Entered the World of White Higher Education." *Journal of Blacks in Higher Education*, no. 4 (Summer): 47–56.

"Slavery in Pennsylvania." 1833. *The Abolitionist: Or Record of the New England Anti-Slavery Society* 1: 104–6.

Smith, Baxter Perry. 1878. *The History of Dartmouth College*. Boston: Boston, Houghton, Osgood.

Smith, E. H., David Camp, and Jeremiah Chandler. 1881. "A Brief History of the Baptist Church, Hanover, N.H." Reproduced from a handwritten manuscript. Rauner Special Collections Library, Dartmouth College, Hanover, NH.

"Some Undistinguished Negroes." 1918. *Journal of Negro History* 3, no. 1: 90–91.

Southey, Thomas. 1827. *Chronological History of the West Indies: In Three Volumes*. London: Longman, Rees, Orme, Brown, and Green.

Stowe, Calvin. 1834. "Professor Stowe on Colonization." *African Repository and Colonial Journal* 10, no. 10: 303.

Taylor, Alan. 2010. *The Civil War of 1812: American Citizens, British Subjects, Irish Rebels, and Indian Allies*. New York: Alfred A. Knopf.

Thelin, John R. 2011. *A History of American Higher Education*. Baltimore: Johns Hopkins University Press.

Thomas, C[yrus]. 1866. *Contributions to the History of the Eastern Townships: A Work Containing an Account of the Early Settlement of St. Armand, Dunham, Sutton, Brome, Potton, and Bolton; With a History of the Principal Events That Have Transpired in Each of These Townships up to the Present Time*. Montreal, QC: published by the author.

Thompson, Patricia J. 2008. "Snowden, Isaac Humphrey." In *African American National Biography*, edited by Henry Louis Gates Jr. and Evelyn Brooks Higginbotham. New York.

Titcomb, Caldwell. 1994/95. Letter to the editor. *Journal of Blacks in Higher Education*, no. 6 (Winter): 7.

Tomek, Beverly C. 2012. *Colonization and Its Discontents: Emancipation, Emigration, and Antislavery in Antebellum Pennsylvania*. New York: New York University Press.

Tomich, Dale W. 1990. *Slavery in the Circuit of Sugar: Martinique and the World Economy, 1830–1848*. Baltimore: Johns Hopkins University Press.

Tracy, Joseph. 1837. "Rev. Edward Mitchell—Colored Students and Colored Men." *Vermont Telegraph*, July 26, 174.

Trani, Lionel. 2015. "Le marronnage urbain en Martinique (1802–1809): Une micro histoire." *Page 19—Bulletin des Doctorants et Jeunes Chercheurs* (Centre d'histoire du XIX siècle), no. 3 (Winter): 19–38.

"Trouvailles de David Quénéhervé: Divorces et remariages de Martiniquais déportés à Landerneau en l'an III." 2012. *Généalogie et Histoire de la Caraïbe Bulletin*, n.s., no. 7 (3rd quarter): 2. www.ghcaraibe.org/bul/NS07comp.pdf.

Turner, Edward Raymond. 1911. *The Negro in Pennsylvania . . . : Slavery-Servitude-Freedom, 1639–1861*. Washington, DC: American Historical Association.

Ulle, Robert F. 1986. "A History of St. Thomas' African Episcopal Church, 1794–1865." PhD diss., University of Pennsylvania.

Vietrogoski, Bob. 2017. "Expelled for 'African Blood': The Story of James Parker Barnett." *Newsroom* (Columbia University Medical Center blog), February 24. newsroom.cumc.columbia.edu/blog/2017/02/24/expelled-for-african-blood-the-story-of-james-parker-barnett/.

Wadsworth, R. D. 1842. "Progress of the Cause." *Canada Temperance Advocate* 7, no. 11: 166.

Warner, Robert Austin. 1940. *New Haven Negroes: A Social History*. New Haven: Yale University, Institute of Human Relations.

White, Arthur O. 1975. "Prince Saunders: An Instance of Social Mobility among Antebellum New England Blacks." *Journal of Negro History* 60, no. 4: 526–35.

White, James. 1875. *Sketches of the Christian Life and Public Labors of William Miller, Gathered from His Memoir by the Late Sylvester Bliss, and from Other Sources*. Battle Creek, MI: Seventh-Day Adventist Publishing Association.

Whitehead, Kaye Wise. 2012. "'Rise in the Scale of Being': Jonathan Clarkson Gibbs, Philadelphia Ministry, and Florida Politics." In *Before Obama: A Reappraisal of Black Reconstruction Era Politicians*, edited by Matthew Lynch, 243–63. Santa Barbara, CA: ABC-CLIO.

Wilder, Craig Steven. 2013. *Ebony and Ivy: Race, Slavery, and the Troubled History of America's Universities*. New York: Bloomsbury.

Wilkes, H. 1842. "Journal of a Missionary Tour." *The Harbinger* 1, no. 6: 85–86.

Willcox, James M. 1916. *A History of the Philadelphia Savings Fund Society, 1816–1916*. Philadelphia: J. B. Lippincott.

Williams, Greg H. 2009. *The French Assault on American Shipping, 1793–1813: A History and Comprehensive Record of Merchant Marine Losses*. Jefferson, NC: McFarland.

Willson, Joseph. (1841) 2000. *The Elite of Our People: Joseph Willson's Sketches of Black Upper-Class Life in Antebellum Philadelphia*. Edited by Julie Winch. University Park: Pennsylvania State University Press.

Wilson, Elane, and Jacqueline Tilton, comps. 1993. *Vital Statistics from the Stanstead Journal*. Vol. 2, *1861–1875*; vol. 3, *1876–1890*. Stanstead, QC: Stanstead Historical Society/Société Historique de Stanstead.

Wilson, Victor. 2013. "Saint Barthélemy as a Caribbean Free Port, 1784–1820." Paper presented at Production, Trade, and the Creation of Regional Economies, the 45th Annual Conference of the Association of Caribbean Historians, Belize, May 12–17.

Winch, Julie. 2002. *A Gentleman of Color: The Life of James Forten*. Oxford: Oxford University Press.

Winch, Julie. 2016. *Between Slavery and Freedom: Free People of Color in America*

from Settlement to the Civil War. African American History Series. Lanham, MD: Rowman & Littlefield.
Winks, Robin W. 1997. *The Blacks in Canada: A History*. Montreal: McGill-Queen's University Press.
Wood, Henry. 1834. "Sketch of the Life of President Brown." *American Quarterly Register* 7, no. 2: 133–45.
Woodson, Carter G. 1919. *The Education of the Negro Prior to 1861*. Washington, DC: Associated Publishers.
Worcester, Jonathan Fox. 1869. *A Memorial of the Class of 1827, Dartmouth College*. Edited by Alpheus Crosby. 2nd ed. Hanover, NH: Dartmouth College.
Worthen, Augusta Harvey, comp. 1890. *The History of Sutton, New Hampshire: Consisting of the Historical Collections of Erastus Wadleigh, Esq., and A. H. Worthen*. Sutton, NH: Republican Press Association.
Wright, James. 2012. *Forever New: The Speeches of James Wright, President of Dartmouth College, 1998–2009*. Hanover, NH: Dartmouth College Press.
Wright, Theodore S. 1837. "Rev. Edward Mitchell—Colored Students and Colored Men." *Vermont Telegraph*, July 26, 174.
Yeoman, Elizabeth. 2004. "Je me souviens: About the St. Armand Slave Cemetery, Memory, Counter-Memory and Historic Trauma." *TOPIA: Canadian Journal of Cultural Studies*, no. 12: 9–24.

INDEX

EM stands for Edward Mitchell.